D1104186

Creating
Consciousness

Creating Consciousness is an illuminating work on the problem and potential of human consciousness. As a masterful scholar and Zen teacher, Albert Low draws together, analyzes, and critiques the contributions of many scientific, philosophical, theological, and spiritual thinkers and practitioners. In doing so, Low effectively creates a dialogue between disparate specialists who don't always listen to each other, while adding his own impressive contribution to the dialogue. *Creating Consciousness* deserves a wide readership, especially among those interested in the complex questions and issues underlying the human quest for enlightened being.

~ **Polly Berrien Berends**, author of *Coming to Life, Whole Child/Whole Parent*, and *Gently Lead*

Creating Consciousness

A STUDY OF
CONSCIOUSNESS,
CREATIVITY, EVOLUTION
AND VIOLENCE

ALBERT LOW

WHITE CLOUD PRESS
ASHLAND, OREGON

Inquiries should be addressed to:
White Cloud Press
PO Box 3400
Ashland, Oregon 97520.
Website: www.whitecloudpress.com

Printed in Indonesia

Cover design: David Ruppe, Impact Publications

02 03 04 05 06   · 10 9 8 7 6 5 4 3 2 1

Library of Congress Cataloging-in-Publication Data

Low, Albert.
    Creating consciousness : a study of consciousness, creativity,
    evolution and violence / Albert Low.
        p. cm.
    Includes bibliographical references and index.
    ISBN: 1-883991-39-0
    1. Consciousness. 2. Consciousness--Religious aspects. 1. Title.

B105.C477I.69 2002
126--dc21

                                          2002072236

Contents

To Jean

ACKNOWLEDGMENTS

A number of people have helped in reading and commenting upon the text and I would like to pay tribute to them.

In particular I should like to thank Monique Dumont for her patience and willingness to read the manuscript a number of times and to make many valuable suggestions. I should also like to thank my wife Jean for her editing.

The following have also read the manuscript and made a number of important contributions: Dr. William Byers, Dr. John Kececioglu, Anita Low, Dr. Tony Stern, Dr. Sarah Webb, and Jonathon Harvey. I should like to thank them all.

FOREWORD
by Jonathon Harvey

It is heartening indeed to come across a writer who thinks at the center of things so unremittingly, so courageously, as Albert Low. All of Low's books have teased away at the same fundamental issues, biting at them from different angles like a dog with a bone. Here he brings his understanding to a new clarity and directness — *Creating Consciousness* seems to be a kind of culmination, and it is written with warmth, wit and in so far as it is possible in such a subject, simplicity.

The subject is consciousness itself. But not just consciousness as approached in professional journals and books but as approached by a Zen master who lives, suffers and teaches those suffering consciousness as a matter of life-and-death urgency.

This means confronting ambiguity and its relation to the promised land of unity. As a composer I am consciously or intuitively caught up in this dialectic, or struggle, every day of my creative life. Music, as Albert Low so profoundly points out, is riddled with ambiguity. The more there is, the more most musicians seem to like the piece; the higher they rate the greatness of the art. The more I can set things up and then challenge their identity, crumble their appearance, transform them into everything else, the more I feel a sense of excitement, a sense of recognising a truth, a reality. It is the supreme satisfaction of the creator and seems to herald the glimpse of 'unity' or perhaps even Paradise.

Although, of course using words, Mr. Low is at pains to put words in their place, hence his respect for the non-verbal art of music. But he has much to say also about the function of words as bulwarks which shore us up for the moment against the unbearable tensions of the ambiguous consciousness; therefore his redemption of the word through its own ability to be ambiguous (a simple example is poetry) is also one of the particularly enlightening delights of this book. It itself operates at the level of music.

Creating Consciousness (in its first draft) has been an invaluable influence on my own creative work for several years — clarifying and deepening the mystery of what art is doing, inspiring the emotions of depicting (or rather, being) an impermanent, transitory world in all its beauty and darkness.

My own book on spirituality in music drew heavily on the ideas presented in *Creating Consciousness*. May many others be so inspired by the important statement in these pages!

Part 1

The wounded surgeon plies the steel
That questions the distempered part
T.S.ELIOT [1]

All true good carries with it conditions which are contradictory and as a consequence is impossible. He who keeps
his attention really fixed on this impossibility and acts
will do what is good . . . In the same way all
truth contains a contradiction.
SIMONE WEIL

I think people get it upside down when they say the unambiguous is the reality and the ambiguous merely uncertainty
about what is really unambiguous. Let's turn it around
the other way: the ambiguous is the reality and the
unambiguous is merely a special case of it, where we
finally manage to pin down some very special aspect.
DAVID BOHM [2]

Introduction

When the dominant myths of a culture are being fragmented by contradictions that can no longer be hidden, and when no new myths have fully taken their place, an increasing number of persons become terrifyingly aware of the unstructuredness and naked freedom of human consciousness.
MICHAEL NOVAK

THIS BOOK IS ABOUT CONSCIOUSNESS, about why and how it has evolved. John Hogan, a senior writer at *Scientific American*, said that consciousness is the most elusive and inescapable of all phenomena, adding that this is a problem which so far "seems to have been ducked by most scientists who simply assume that mind is the outcome of complexity. The alternative seems to be an unacceptable dualism in which the mind and matter are two different stuffs and therefore, presumably forever running parallel tracks."[1] The relation of mind and matter will be one of the main problems that we shall be tackling when talking about consciousness and its evolution. However, to do this adequately, we must consider creativity as well because consciousness is a creation, of the same order as the creation of life itself. What we hope to show is that a profound contradiction, a self-inflicted wound, underlies creativity and consciousness. Consciousness acts as a balm and a buffer to this wound and, to act in this way, it evolves by way of continuous creativity. Sometimes the pain from the wound is too great, then creativity fails and violence erupts. Spirituality, all pervasive Unity, is the medium in which this drama is played out.

Such are the main themes of this book. In their development we shall be broaching age-old problems that, until now, have proved intractable: the nature and origin of consciousness, the role that language plays in the inception and subsequent evolution of consciousness, the relation of body, the part played by mind in evolution, the 'life force.' These and their variations will be explored. One contribution our study may well make is to provide a framework within which modern psychology could find a new basis so that it can recognize that spiritual activity has a legitimate place in the ecology of being.

Myth and Science

What kind of book is this? When we meet people for the first time, we often ask them what they do for a living. This helps us to put them into a context, and we can relate more easily to them. Similarly we like to ask of a book, are you a book on philosophy, science, literature, fiction, nonfiction, or what? Alas, in introducing this book to you I am at a loss to know quite how to state its credentials. The book cannot really claim to be neither scientific nor philosophic; it is closer to being a myth, although it is putting forward a theory. But, let me add, I do not mean to apologize in saying it is closer to being a myth. According to Webster's Dictionary myth "serves to unfold part of the world view of a people or to explain a practice, belief, or natural phenomena." Webster admittedly also says that a myth is "an ill-founded belief held uncritically," which has become the more accepted definition. This is because science has taken upon itself the task of dislodging most of the myths on which Western civilization fed in its infancy, even though in its turn, to do so, it is has had to create its own myths. As a myth, our study will make no call for action nor will it put forward any program for action. It has no QED as we had when working with Euclid's geometry. It does, however, provide us with a framework that allows greater intellectual freedom, greater flexibility of thought, than has been possible up till now.

In citing Webster's definition of myth above we left out a part which says that myth is "a traditional story of ostensibly historical events." Darwin, with his myth of the Evolution of the Species, pushed the definition of 'ostensibly historical events' back to include the history not just of mankind but the whole of life on earth. In his famous *The Phenomenon of Man*, the Jesuit priest/scientist Teillard de Chardin pushed back the definition of history even further to include the history of earth itself, just as Stephen Hawkins is trying to push the definition back further yet to include the history of the universe. With this book we have gone back a stage further yet and are looking at the origins of evolution itself.

In many myths the division between origin as time and origin as source is not made. Thus to return to the origin of consciousness, of life, even of existence itself, we do not necessarily have to return in time. If it were necessary then all we could do would be to take the route that theoretical physics is taking at the moment, with its inferences and assumptions that, more and more, have very little hard evidence as support. The original source is not simply in the past, it is also now and, in this case, to understand 'then' we must understand 'now' just as, according to the scientific approach, to understand 'now' we have to understand 'then'. This will mean that meditation no less than mathematics is a way to explore the source.

If we go by way of meditation then we must go by way of *progressive approximation*, that is, instead of knowledge appearing clear and distinct, like a train emerging from the dark tunnel of obscurity carriage after carriage, it is something like a harbor appearing out of the mist as one approaches it by ship in the early morning. In a way it is all there from the first sight, but only gradually do the outlines become clear, only gradually do the distances and relations between the various buildings and equipment become definite and the details obvious. In this book we shall be taking the progressive approximation approach; thus considerable repetition and recycling back to ground already covered will be necessary to show this ground from a newer and more inclusive perspective and so give a firmer basis for the integration of the detail. Unfortunately, this means we cannot always give clear and distinct definitions to all our terms and, now and again, will have to call upon the reader to use his or her own intuition to follow the argument. This may be sometimes trying. Where possible illustrations and examples have been used to make the more difficult points accessible. We have also tried to illustrate the main ideas by calling upon many other writers. So we would urge the reader if some or other part of the book causes them to stumble, to skip that part and just go on. The point will be covered from another perspective later.

The Grain of Consciousness

A phrase that is repeated throughout de Chardin's book, is "first a grain of matter, then a grain of life, then a grain of consciousness." The atom could be looked upon as a grain of matter, and the cell as a grain of life. Just as one could hardly come up with a new theory of matter without at least taking the atomic theory into account, and just as atomic theory makes a whole number of otherwise disparate seeming facts into one whole body of knowledge called physics and chemistry, so I contend one can hardly understand human spirituality, creativity, consciousness, religion, purpose and value, without taking into account the grain of consciousness, and what has led up to its evolution. By taking this grain into account a whole host of otherwise disparate fields are revealed as one coordinated whole. To be able to do this, to be able to take the grain of consciousness into account, we have to reexamine our basic myths of origins and destiny. But neither the theory of the atom, nor the theory of the cell claims to be theories of everything. Similarly, although manifestly we are giving an inclusive theory, we mean by the word 'theory' what it possibly meant originally: a way of looking at the world, a perspective.

An old Zen saying declares "If you want to go North, don't point your cart South." The reason light has not been shed before on the intractable problems that we shall be dealing with is because we have had our cart pointing south, and the light is in the North. We have been looking in the wrong direction. Little of what I have to say is truly original; what I have done mostly is to bring the research and writings of others together within a new perspective. I have written about music, poetry, evolution, creativity, and so on, not to come up with a new theory of music or poetry, but rather to show the value of looking at them within this new perspective. Indeed, there may be some readers who, misunderstanding my intention, might feel that the points I make are sometimes lacking in depth or are incomplete. But all that I want to say is "If you look at these things within this perspective you will find a place for all human endeavor. Nothing need be rejected; nothing is 'wrong,' nothing needs to be thrown away or refuted. As St. Thérèse said, "In my Father's House there is room for everyone."

A New Way of Thinking

A radically new way of thinking is being born. The holographic theory of the brain of Pribram, the notion of the implicate order of Bohm, the morphic fields of Rupert Sheldrake, as well as the logic of simplicity of Lamouche, and the logic of the inclusive middle of Lupascu, chaos theory and the theory of complexity, to a greater or lesser degree, come out of this new way of thinking. An old order is dying, and a new one is taking its place. This new

way of thinking is being fed and watered also by the teachings and practices of Buddhism, Taoism, Sufism, and Hinduism, all of which are enabling
us to see the limitations and shortcomings of the old linear and reduction-
ist way of thinking.

The old view was based upon clear and distinct ideas and was ushered
in by Descartes, among other thinkers. It gave birth to the belief that concepts could be clearly and uniformly defined, that the world could be considered a closed system and understood in the same way that a machine could
be understood. Underlying this old view was a single, unified point of view;
a viewpoint originally attributed to God but subsequently adopted as the
objective eye of science.

The new view, on the other hand, will be based upon ambiguity, upon
alternate realities, as well as upon multiple points of view of observers who
cannot be abstracted from what they are observing. We are at a crossroads. In
the way we think and in what we do during the next few decades we shall
set a course for human nature from which there will be no possible retreat.
The old view gave us science, technology, industry, and commerce based
upon new kinds of motive power: steam, gas, and electricity. It gave urban
dwelling, massive cities and large economic units. In its early years, during
what we call the Renaissance, art and culture flourished as well as a new
found freedom in which the human being was the judge and controller of
his fate.

The new view is already giving us a radically new technology based new
information, and we are yet to determine what we are to do with this
newfound possibility. Chaos theory, theories of complex systems, computer
simulation are newcomers to the field of human experience and offer completely new ways of looking at the world. We are entering a world in which
it will be possible, in addition to changing, fashioning, and adapting reality to
our needs, to create reality. This means not simply to create new forms of life
or new materials, but whole universes, new global and integrated experiences
from sensations artificially created. In this lies a dreadful danger, because a
human being is not simply an observer of the world. A human being is also
a participant. Being both observer and a participant is a curse but it is also
the gateway to heaven. With the new technology more people, for longer
periods of time, will simply be observers of virtual reality.

Because we are at a crossroads, we are faced not only by danger but also
by wonderful possibilities. One of the consequences of the old point of view

was that the soul was banished along with its accompaniment of consciousness, purpose, creativity and values, none of which can be reduced to clear and distinct ideas and all of which imply involvement and participation. The trend towards 'virtual reality' and all the danger that it implies is simply a continuation of the view that it is possible to reduce a human being to being simply an observer. However underlying the new viewpoint is the acceptance of ambiguity. This acceptance will allow us to rediscover consciousness, purpose, value, and meaning as necessary and integrated aspects of an understanding of the world. It will be possible for us to see that we are not simply passive observers of the cosmos but immediately and directly involved in it. This will allow us to see spirituality and science as two aspects of one seamless whole.

The Insight into the Grain of Consciousness

What is the grain of consciousness? The answer to this question cannot be given in precise, clear, and distinct terms. It might help to begin by saying how insight into the grain of consciousness, with its correlate of the importance of ambiguity, came about, because (as will be obvious later) this insight does not have a logical root. The pivotal point of the book (and to some extent of my life) came while my wife and I were living on a ranch in the Northern Transvaal in 1957. We had gone there, with our two-year-old daughter, so I could embark upon an intensive period of study in philosophy and psychology. At least that was the overt reason. The other, unspoken reason was that I had reached a point in my life when nothing was making sense anymore and I desperately needed time to think things through.

The ranch was a vast, sprawling, and inhospitable range of land on which grass barely survived. It was was dotted with stunted trees, gnarled and tortured by a scorching sun and lack of rain. The main life forms supported by this land were snakes, some of which were poisonous, and white ants, millions and millions of white ants who constructed their termiteries up the trunks of those poor, starved trees using their wood as a form of sustenance. The trees would eventually die and so innumerable anthills ranged across the landscape looking like the pillars of some blasted temple in a wasteland.

Our nearest neighbor (not counting the family of baboons who lived across the valley) was a farmer six miles away whom we saw once during the whole year we were there. We had no electric light, no telephone, no car and no kitchen — my wife cooked on an open fire in the open air. The nearest village, a small one, was 12 miles away. We got our food supplies by putting money, and a shopping list, under a stone at the gate of the ranch. A bus driver would pick these up once a week. Two days later he would drive by with the supplies.

But it was heaven. The silence was alive; it was vibrant like no other silence I have ever known. This isolation and silence made for the perfect conditions for deep meditation. Even in this region of death, the silence was never hostile and as far as I can remember I was never afraid of it nor of the velvet blackness that was the night. Even the laughter of the hyenas who were attracted by the dead cows (blackwater fever would regularly take at least one per day) did not seem fearful, nor did the vultures who came hovering during the day.

What is Reality?

I spent the day mainly in study and among the texts was Kant's *Critique of Pure Reason*. One of the problems that Kant addressed in this critique was the problem of what we could know of the outside world and how we could know it. This was a problem that had haunted me ever since I started asking questions seriously, and as this problem forms an essential basis to this book, we must dwell on it for a few moments.

What do we mean when we say the world is real and how do we know it is real? If one removes sense data, that is what we can learn about an object through our senses, what is left? For example, we see a green leaf. But, we are told, it is not the leaf that is green but the light which has not been absorbed by the leaf, and so has been reflected by it. Green is what the leaf is not. Similar arguments can be made about the other senses. A car does not make a noise; noise comes from the vibrations of air striking the eardrum. The smell is not of the rose but of molecules in the air surrounding the rose. So what is a leaf when stripped of all that the senses tell us about it? The modern physicist, who asks about quantum reality, is now posing this same problem. I have put their conclusions in Appendix A, and if you are not familiar with them you might want to look them over. Some of them are quite surprising.

The problem is often summed up in the question: "If a tree falls in the forest and there is no-one there to hear it, does it make a noise?" The same question was posed by the Buddha when he asked, "Does the ear go to the sound or does the sound go to the ear?" What, or how much, is contributed by the physical world and how much by the mental world?

A limerick puts it all in a nutshell:

> There once was a man who said "God
> Must think it exceedingly odd
> If he finds that this tree
> Continues to be
> When there's no one about in the Quad"

One answer that was given to this was:

> Dear Sir, Your astonishment's odd
> I am always about in the Quad
> And that's why the tree
> Will continue to be,
> Signed, yours faithfully, God.

This view says that 'everything is in the mind,' the mind of God. The other view, more favored by the scientists, is that there is no God, no mind, no perception just movements of matter in space and time. This means that two principal responses to the question, what is left if you take away sense data, are possible. Nothing is left, as everything is ultimately a creation of the mind: this is idealism or in the extreme solipsism; everything will still be the same, because everything is just what you see. This is naive realism. But Kant came up with a third view, the view that 'something' is left but we cannot know what it is, and he called this the noumenon.

How Can We Know We Do Not Know?

Kant's solution set up a puzzle in my mind that became more and more troubling. How could we know anything about something we could not know, not even that it exists? This puzzle became refined to "How could we even know that we do not know?" It was, in its way, the ultimate Zen Koan. I struggled with it, completely dumbfounded for some time and then, out of the blue, came the resolution: We are both at the center and at the periphery of the world simultaneously. How that is an answer to the question is one of the things I have had to find a way of explaining, while trying, at the same time, to explain what this answer means. For months afterwards I felt as though a tremendous burden had been lifted from my mind, and I seemed to exist in a new medium. The value of this insight into what I am calling the grain of consciousness has increased for me over the years.

Over the years I have accumulated a small library of books each of which, in its own way, makes perfect sense of the insight and each of which in its turn is given a deeper meaning in the light of the insight. This accumulation was neither intentional nor systematic. On the contrary, books have come my way from secondhand bookshops, catalogues, recommendations and browsing among recent releases. So in this way, what I have called a myth, has taken form of its own over the years. This book therefore is the result of years of meditation on this insight, trying to make it accessible to others.

Through the years I have tried to write about it in different ways. First, in a book on management called *Zen and Creative Management,* which I wrote in 1970, I wanted to show that the basis of management, and also of the mind, is not solving problems, as one is often led to believe by seminars on 'scientific' management, but making decisions. Furthermore, we have to make decisions because of dilemmas, not problems, and these arise out of the basic ambiguity of being 'inside' and 'outside,' participant and observer, centre and periphery, simultaneously. In another book called *The Iron Cow of Zen* (the 'iron cow' being the grain of consciousness) I tried to show the value of this insight in understanding the human predicament, and how the koans of Zen Buddhism were an expression of this basic ambiguity. Then later in another book called *The Butterfly's Dream* I tried to show how this same ambiguity lay at the basis of all spiritual work, and how it made this work both necessary and possible.

The Wounded Surgeon

Each of us is an individual: that which cannot be divided. But each of us is at the center and periphery simultaneously. Each of us is divided. The whole book is about this 'impossible' situation, this ambiguity. All that I can do at the moment is very briefly sketch in the broadest implications.

Because we are at the center and periphery simultaneously, yet by our very nature indivisible, a fundamental conflict, schism or wound, a blessed wound it has been called, yawns in the heart of each of us, the source of our pain, as well as of our ecstasy and joy. Because it is in the depths, indeed at the source, of our being we have great difficulty in talking and even thinking about it. To see what is meant by this schism we have to go up upstream of experience, upstream of logic, because logic and experience themselves arise as ways of trying to deal with it. We do not experience conflict; conflict is at the very root of experience. The word 'experience' has its etymology in a

Latin word *periculum* meaning both 'attempt' and 'peril,' and I cannot help wondering whether experience was not originally an attempt to escape the peril of this schism. In any case, this etymology will underlie the use that I make of the word experience in the succeeding pages. We would do anything, anything rather than fall into the hell of this schism. Psychosis now seems to me to be the state wherein someone is incapable, for one reason or another, of finding a stable point of reference, or what I have called a center, by which to avoid the vicious circle that comes out of the divided state of being at the center and periphery simultaneously. The feeling of 'I' is precisely that stable center. The extreme inflation and paranoia that strike some psychotics are a way by which they try to hold on desperately to some lifebuoy in a sea of madness. On the other hand, without this wound, creativity, spirituality, even evolution would not be possible.

During my life I had been prey to bouts of horror, moments when I felt as though I were being swallowed by a nothingness. These feelings started early in childhood and sometimes were more than I could bear. They took on a focus when I was about 17 and saw, at the movies, some films taken of the concentration camps. Someone, I think it was Winston Churchill, had decided to let us know what the war had been about, and had chosen this way, which was as effective as it was brutal. After the feature film, its title, plot, characters all now obliterated from my memory by what followed, another film was shown. It was made up of footage of Belsen, Buchenwald, Auschwitz, footage taken by the allied armies as they stumbled across these testaments of our shame.

Shown, as they were, to an audience half hypnotized into docile receptivity by Hollywood glitter and tinsel they went home to the marrow. Going out of the cinema later, into the vast summer twilight, one could do little more than blink in a vacant way. Not blink back tears of shame, rage or regret: those would come later, some of them much later. No, just blink in a stupid way, wondering somewhere in the groggy depths: what do we do now, what is one supposed to do after that?

Later I realized that what made it all the more horrible was that I could not be sure that had the occasion been just so, had I been in one situation rather than another, I would not have been an SS man also. The horror was not Germans were dehumanizing Jews, but human beings were doing this to human beings, and I was a human being. Later this fear was made more reasonable still when, seeing into our wounded being, I was convinced that we do these most terrible things to one another because behind us yawns the chasm, the horror of being swallowed by our own mind.

I cannot say that this film of the concentration camps remained a constant, conscious problem. Like everyone else I just forgot about it. But, at a deeper, subconscious level, what happened on that summer's afternoon has never left me and has undoubtedly been a spur to my trying to understand others and myself. When, on the ranch in the Transvaal, I saw into this schism it was then I could see how horror came from the loop that the schism created in the very center of my being. I am at the center, but that of which I am central to is me, also at the center. This means I am peripheral to me, but I cannot be peripheral to me because that very same me is at the center. Later in the book I shall show that only one center is possible and so this schism threatens to be a war of complete annihilation in the very depths of our own being.

The upshot has been this: in order to come to terms with suffering whose root I had clearly seen, for thirty years I have followed (as best as my inertia and cluttered mind would allow) the path of Zen Buddhism. During this time I have had one fairly deep awakening, or 'satori,' and two others of less intensity. The consequence of the first was to realize immediately and not simply as a theory or belief, that there is no thing-in-itself. No thing has an independent existence; as a Zen Master put it, "from the beginning not a thing is." At the same time I realized there is no permanent ego or person, the word 'I' does not refer to any entity either subtle or gross. Of the two lesser awakenings one is of particular relevance to this book. It came during an intensive seven-day retreat several years after the initial awakening. I saw clearly into the meaning of the expression 'All is One,' and it became quite clear how everything is the One. This awakening is the awakening to equality and is well known by others who have practiced Zen or some other spiritual tradition over a fairly long period of time. It was quite apparent to me from reading the *Enneads* that Plotinus was inspired in part by this same awakening. That everything is the one included the realization that each person too is the One. We are not part of some greater whole. Each is the whole. Each is what the philosopher Leibnitz calls the Monad, or, as the great Zen master Hakuin Zenji said, "From the beginning all beings are Buddha."

There is a Latin tag which says something to the effect that life is short, but art is long, and now that I am entering my seventy-first year I feel all too poignantly the truth of this. This book comes out of these years of travail and triumph, anxiety and joy. With all its limitations and shortcomings I write it in the hope that it will contribute, in some small measure, towards bringing us together as human beings. We do have to find a new way of thinking, a thinking which includes but is not limited by the opposites, a thinking which is also a thanking,[2] a thanking or gratitude which comes from seeing that we are truly sons and daughters of God that we all, all sentient beings, are Buddha, that our true home is in wholeness or Oneness.

Notes

1. Editorial: *Scientific American* (Special issue, Sept. 1992).
2. The etymological roots of thinking and thanking are the same.

Chapter 1

Ambiguity
The Wound in the Heart

Every Persian fairy tale . . . opens with
this contradictory formula,
Yeki bud, yeki mabud:
There was one, there was not one.

A FUNDAMENTAL AMBIGUITY, a kind of primordial double bind, lies
at the origin of consciousness, of life, perhaps even of matter itself?
A Zen master held up a stick to his assembly of monks saying, "If you call
this a stick I'll give you thirty blows; if you say it is not a stick I'll give you
thirty blows. What is it?" This Zen koan was used by Gregory Bateson to
introduce the notion of a *double bind*, the principle feature of which is this:
No matter what we do, we cannot win. Ambiguity is the primary double
bind from which consciousness and life have evolved. The philosophical
'problems' that we have created about the origin of life from matter, of
mind from the brain, of value from fact, are attempts to break open this
ambiguity and make it accessible to the intellect.

In the introduction we spoke about me-as center/me-as-periphery
which is like the *uroboros* of the ancients, the snake which swallows its own
tail, but who knows which 'me' is the head and which the tail? After all,
there can only be one me. Evolution and creativity emerge from the endeavor to escape from the pain that this primary double bind causes, the

pain that brings about not only our own personal conflicts and antagonisms, but the wars of the world as well.

This century has been full of war, civil war, death and destruction. At
one time we came near to destroying the whole planet, and even now this
threat still rumbles and grumbles in the background. That we could even
conceive of this total destruction seems not so much frightening as incomprehensible. Seeing on TV or at the movies the kind of destruction a modern war could bring, we are, without doubt, anxious and fearful; but over-
riding the anxiety and fear is the question, how is it possible? How was
Verdun possible, or the Somme in World War I, or the battle of Stalingrad
in World War II, when whole armies were locked in orgies of destruction?
How can we can do such things to one another? What is this terrible force
of violence, conflict, and destruction at work in us?

I hope to show that this force can be understood, and in a way that is
completely new. Not only this, but also that this *same force* is the force of
creativity and the force behind evolution, human evolution as well as the
evolution of all life. In human beings it is also the source of spirituality. We
shall talk about evolution, creativity, spirituality and violence, but not as
separate processes but as the outcome of a single force to which we give
different names.

The Origin of Conflict

The question of what causes violence is by no means new; humankind has
always wondered about it. Unfortunately, the usual way it has been accounted
for has simply made things worse. This is so, not because the understanding
is wrong, but because it is incomplete, so our diagnosis is something like a
doctor who confuses the symptoms with the disease and in treating the
symptoms simply makes the disease worse. In order to understand what I
mean by this, let us take a look at the way conflict is currently viewed. In
doing so, we will see several things: that conflict is not learned; that it is not
in itself experienced, but is the basis of experience; and that conflict is also
the basis of creativity—and therefore, that some violence is failed creativity.

During the cold war a cartoon appeared in a Montreal newspaper. Two
dinosaurs were fighting, using their huge tails as weapons. One of them
towered above New York, the other above Moscow; the first had the face
of the American president, the second, the face of the Russian leader. Each
will destroy his own city if he swings his massive tail. This cartoon says
many things about the force of conflict at war within us; so let us use it as
a way to uncover the way we typically think about conflict.

Others Are To Blame

What catches the eye first are the heads and faces of the two world leaders. The cartoon implies the two men are fighting to satisfy their lust for power, regardless of the havoc they might wreak upon their own people. Many of us feel our leaders are the cause of national and international tensions; we believe that, if only they would let go of their search for power, the world could become a peaceful place. Such an attitude underlay most of the peace demonstrations of the 1960s. Somehow, we feel, *they* must be made to change their ways; *they* must be made to sit down and talk and so work things out. Those advocating this view encourage us to write to our politicians, or to the newspapers, to bring concentrated pressure to bear, which in time, the advocates believe, will reform *them*.

We often feel the same way about problems and troubles in our own personal life. If only our boss, our spouse, our friends would be more understanding, tolerant, sensitive, they would not cause us so much grief. Psychoanalysis has reinforced this notion by attributing our suffering to the way we were brought up. We tend to feel that our mother, or father, or teachers were the cause of our troubles: if only they had brought us up differently we should not be so anxious, so hesitant, so lacking in this or that way, that we would not suffer.

In a way this view is an optimistic one: we have a problem, have identified its cause, and can now tackle and resolve it. If our leaders are the cause we can apply the full democratic process to it and resolve it. If it is others that are causing us our problems, we can try to change them, change our jobs, our friends, our spouses and in this way get rid of the trouble they have caused.

A Conspiracy of Oppression

But this view is haunted by a profound pessimism as well, arising from a fear that perhaps the two figures are nothing but figureheads or masks for other faceless ones who pursue their lust for power in a social twilight, pulling strings and manipulating regardless of the consequences: the CIA, the KGB, the Pentagon, the gnomes of Nuremberg, the military/industrial complex—sinister forces beyond the reach of reason and democracy, intent solely upon expanding their own gain regardless of the costs. In our personal lives we see ourselves as victims: women victims of men, blacks victims of whites, citizens victims of government, students victims of teachers.

But underlying the pessimism is the same belief that underlies the optimism: conflict, created consciously and deliberately by specific people or groups, cause our troubles. Through erroneous perception and behavior, or inherent evil, these people bring the rest of us into conflict with each other, and with ourselves. We are suppressed, held down by others. Conflict, and the unhappiness it causes, can be resolved by correcting the perception, changing the behavior or eradicating the evil.

It is Only Natural

The cartoon also showed two *animals* fighting, and as animals they are not pursuing conscious, albeit misguided or evil aims, but are simply giving vent to a natural instinct for aggression. This instinct, some say, is present in humankind as well, and therefore it is 'only natural' for human beings to fight. They are only animals, it is said, and they share in the common pool of instincts and drives of all animals. All animals fight for territory, for mates, for supremacy, so why should we be surprised to find fighting and conflict among humans or feel we can do something to prevent it? Men are violent because of testosterone, or dammed libido, or thwarted aggression. After all, life forms have evolved through conflict and the weak and unfit have thereby been eradicated. Viewed this way, conflict, far from being a curse, is a biological blessing because it ensures only the best survive. This is the optimistic side of the evolutionist argument, but the evolutionists, too, have their pessimists.

A Tragic Mistake

These pessimistic evolutionists believe nature took a wrong turning somewhere, and the human being is the result: a tragic mistake doomed by its very brain structure to self-annihilation. According to this view, the human being is an evolutionary sport of no real consequence. Arthur Koestler, in his extremity, proposes that the only way out was a 'happy pill.' "When one contemplates the streak of insanity running through human history," Koestler observers, "it appears highly probable that *homo sapiens* is a biological freak, the result of some remarkable mistake in the evolutionary process."[3] The development of a happy pill is possible, he contends: "It is not utopian to believe that it can and will be done. Our present tranquilizers, barbiturates, stimulants, anti-depressants and combinations thereof, are merely a first step towards a more sophisticated range of aids to promote a coordinated, harmonious state of mind." Koestler is serious about this pill, adding, "We must search for a cure for the schizo-physiology inherent in man's nature, and the resulting split in our minds, which led to the situation in which we find ourselves." If we do not, he threatens, "The old paranoid streak in man, combined with his new powers of destruction, must sooner or later lead to genosuicide."

This view is implied by the cartoon, as well: dinosaurs are extinct because they were a failure in the rigorous competition of the school of life; why, then, should mankind not fail? Viewed from this vantage point, the cartoon depicts a tragedy: no matter how hard we strive, the impersonal forces of selection will destroy us; indeed, our very struggles, and the destruction they entail, are simply blind forces working out our destiny.

Meditating on this cartoon, we penetrate deeper and deeper levels of cause. First, the surface layer: two intractable and selfish men are caught in a squabble and, unable to lose face, bring down the world as a consequence. From this personal, psychological layer we penetrate to the social, political layer of groups seeking power and manipulating social forces. Moving deeper, we reach the biological layer of instincts and territory, aggression and reproduction; and then the evolutionary layer, where a cosmic force works out its inherent potential through trial and error, fits and starts.

The Triumph of Good Over Evil

But, we can go deeper yet. The fighting figures are made up of human *and* animal elements: the head is human rationality and reason; the body instinct and passion. The head is high in the sky among the gods; the body rooted to earth. Is this, then, the cause of conflict? Is the outer conflict simply the projection of an inner one? Are we at war with ourselves through the collision of incompatible forces, such as reason and instinct, the angelic and demonic? Do we seek relief from the ensuing tension by dramatizing the conflict onto a more accessible stage, by projecting it onto others? With this question we have penetrated another stratum—the religious one. The problem is no longer 'his' problem, or 'its' problem but *my* problem, a problem concerning me and what 'me' means. A deep intuition of unity is violated, split in two incompatible halves—a mind half and a body half—each with its own demands. I am an individual and yet divided: part of me soars to the heavens, the other grovels in the mud. The holy and the diabolic cannot live in the same house, so each tries to destroy the other, blind creatures fighting and thus destroying what they hold dear. This is the view held by many Christians, Buddhists, and Jews, and it is implicit in the psychoanalytic movement as well. The human being is torn between the conscious, rational realm and the instinctual, unconscious realm, split between the forces of good and evil.

From this point of view the resolution of our conflict is seen as the triumph of the conscious over the unconscious, taming the instinctual by the rational, or the defeat of Evil and the victory of the Good. Conflict to end conflict, war to end war. Good is the end of conflict; evil is the cause.

But all the above leaves unresolved why there should be conflict in the first place. It tells us how conflict makes itself known, the way it is expressed, the elements involved, but it does not tell us about the origin of conflict. We experience pain, aggression, anger, and so on, but these are the *outcomes* of conflict, not conflict itself. Conflict is at the root of experiencing, *it is not itself an experience.* We cannot *learn* conflict because learning itself is an outcome of experience given back to us through memory. We cannot account for conflict either by evoking an 'instinct of conflict' or an 'instinct of aggression.' This simply substitutes one unknown—the cause of the conflict—by another unknown—instinct. *Any* situation has conflict underlying it. This intuition permeates the whole of Buddhist teaching. The most fundamental axiom of Buddhism, or as it is more commonly known, the first noble truth is that life is founded on suffering. If this is the case, we cannot understand ourselves or the world we live in unless we understand conflict.

Conflict is Inherent in Any Situation

Conflict is inherent in any situation, and cannot be resolved in the way a resolution is normally sought; that is, by the elimination of one side over the other, the triumph of one side, or the merging of two into one harmonious, loving, and utopian whole. According to the scenario in which good and evil are at war, conflict comes from a horizontal split in experience, in which the higher level wants to raise the lower up, while the lower wants to drag the higher down.

But wars are not simply wars of good against evil. Each side in a war sees it as just war, a holy war; each side fights for what it conceives of as the good. Germans wore 'Gott mittens' on their buckles of their belts in war. But the English and French were certain that God was on their side. Any war, therefore, is the good against the good. From this point of view, each of the two parties to a conflict has an equal right to be, although each would deny the other that right. This means that with the alternative view that we are now offering, the split is not horizontal but vertical: What is good for me is bad for him, what is bad for me is good for him. If we adopt this point of view, we must surrender the belief in an absolute good, an absolute right and superior with their corollaries of absolute wrong and inferior.

The Elements of Conflict
Duality

In the cartoon *two* sides are opposed; that it takes two to make an argument is obvious. The basic axiom of Buddhism—all is suffering—bears this out. The Sanskrit word used in Buddhism for suffering is *dukkha,* which means twoness, duality. The double bind of Bateson referred to at the beginning of this chapter is based upon two opposing commands given to a person each of which *must* be obeyed, under pain of punishment, but only one of which *can* be obeyed. According to Bateson, two people must be involved in establishing a double bind: the victim and the person giving the conflicting commands. However, this is not necessarily so because we can give ourselves opposing commands. "I promised my wife that I would get home early tonight so I must leave now. I promised the boss that I would get this job wound up tonight so I cannot leave now."

However, duality alone does not cause conflict. Polarity, complementarity, even ambiguity, as it is normally understood, are examples of duality in which no conflict occurs. Kenneth Boulding, an American economist who made a study of conflict and competition, has written, "Conflict may be defined as a situation of competition in which parties are aware of the incompatibility of potential and future positions and in which each party wishes to occupy a position which is *incompatible* with the wishes of the other."[1] I have emphasized incompatible because, reduced to its simplest, one could sum up what Boulding is saying thus: Conflict arises in the presence of two viewpoints *only one of which* can prevail.

Unity

In thinking about conflict and competition, we often forget that they require (indeed, are based upon) *co-operation.* An *agreement* more fundamental than conflict makes conflict possible. This cooperation comes from an underlying 'sameness.' In the days of dueling, a 'gentleman' (which originally meant 'of the same clan') would only duel with another gentleman; it would have been unthinkable for him to duel with a commoner.

Those who share the most in common suffer the greatest tension among themselves. Two members of the same business firm are more likely to hate each other than are two strangers. Two stamp collectors, two tennis players, two suitors are more likely to have antagonisms than, say, a stamp collector and a tennis player, or a suitor and a stamp collector. 'Sharing in common' is often expressed through adherence to rules and a common purpose. When two nations fight, they must agree on something to fight about. For two boxers to fight, they must agree on the rules and both must want to win: that is, be the One. Without that agreement no fight can take place. Underlying the duality of conflict, indeed causing conflict, is Unity.

A Zen story illustrates what I am saying: One night some brigands burst into a Zen temple. With drawn swords they seized the temple priest and threatened to kill him. The priest said, "Before you kill me I should like just one thing."

"What is that?" cried one of the robbers.

"A glass of wine," replied the priest.

Astonished the man let go his grip on the priest, who quietly and without haste went to a cupboard, opened the door, and took down a glass and a bottle of wine. He carefully covered the table with a white cloth, polished the glass and set it and the bottle of wine in the middle of the table. He then drew up his chair, opened the bottle of wine and poured out a precise measure. After corking up the bottle and returning it to its place in the center of the table, he took a sip of wine. When he looked around, he found the robbers had left.

A similar story tells of an event said to have happened in the trenches during World War I. It was breakfast time, and in a British trench the soldiers were preparing breakfast; inevitably, some were brewing tea. A German patrol leapt into the trenches with fixed bayonets. A British soldier, terrified, automatically and without thinking held out a cup of tea to the German who was about to stab him. The German turned and fled.

Conflict and Creativity

For most people conflict is at worst an evil, at best undesirable; it is the gateway to violence and destructiveness that one day may well wipe out the whole earth; it is the way to damnation and death. In a particular individual, according to Bateson, the double bind could, in the extreme, bring about schizophrenia. But Bateson also noted that the double bind is also common to humor, poetry, and art. In other words, conflict also can be seen as the gateway to salvation, life, creativity, and love; and, as the koan of the Zen master shows, an awakening to spirituality.

Duality and Unity are the two basic ingredients for creativity as well as for the conflict of violence. In his book *The Act of Creation*, Arthur Koestler says creativity arises when a single situation or idea is perceived in "two self-consistent but habitually incompatible frames of reference."[2] Creativity therefore involves a *twoness* (the two self-consistent frames of reference) and *oneness* (the single situation or idea). Koestler goes on to say that the situation "vibrates simultaneously on two different wavelengths," and he coins a word *bisociation* to refer to this way of perceiving. The two mutually incompatible frames of reference, or, what we called earlier, the two viewpoints of the single idea, generate a tension that explodes at the moment of creation. In talking about this creative tension Koestler uses words such as 'clash,' 'explosion,' 'collision,' 'confrontation'; words that can just as well, indeed often do, describe conflict. This definition of Koestler's is strikingly similar to a definition of humor made by an English poet of the eighteenth century James Beatty.[3] He said that laughter arose "from the view of two or more inconsistent, unsuitable, or incongruous parts or circumstances, considered as united in one complex object or assemblage." The close tie with creativity is underlined by the fact that, according to one Hermetic source, the world was created by laughter.[4]

Koestler's definition of creativity is also very similar to Boulding's definition of conflict: duality, the 'incompatibility of the position of the two parties' and *unity*, 'the single position to which each is aspiring'. 'Creativity is duality, two (the incompatibility of two frames of reference) and unity' (the single situation or idea.) Creativity and destructiveness, love and hate, cooperation and competition, come from a common source. Creativity is not on this side with conflict on the other, love on this side and hostility on the other; they are the outcome of the fact that *'this side'* and *'that side'* are mutually exclusive and yet, insofar as each is the manifestation of unity, are mutually dependent. Therefore for one side to prevail it must destroy the other. But if it does so then it destroys that upon which it is dependent and so destroys itself. It is like a cosmic catch-22. Conflict lies at the heart of creativity, while unity lies in the heart of conflict. Conflict and creativity both have the peculiar property of *arising out of* which is at the same time *a duality;* out of a duality seen simultaneously as Unity. This ambiguity is known in Zen Buddhism as *not one not two*. The Sufi refers to and duality as a *unus-ambo*.[5]

We do not need to invoke an instinct of aggression to explain conflict in the world. Although others are invariably an essential element in our times of aggression, hostility, and struggle, we cannot blame them for our suffering. We suffer because we are human, because we are alive. To see conflict as a necessary part of the situation allows us to review all the so-called instincts: creative instinct, aggressive instinct, reproductive instinct, and so on. Furthermore, and this will make it unpalatable to many people, it will do away with the notion of any fundamental or lasting peace. Life is hazardous, always at the crumbling edge. Every resolution, whether through creation or destruction, sets the stage for more conflict, thereby calling for more creativity or more destruction. But while this point of view does away with the hope for everlasting peace, it also does away with death, as we normally understand it. Everlasting, absolute peace has its counterpart in the notion of everlasting, absolute death.

In this book we will explore as fully as possible the implications of saying we cannot experience conflict, that it arises out of two that is one, the Not One Not Two. We will explore *unus-ambo* as unity divided against itself.[6] Ambiguity as we use the term is not simply a passive, vague, confused view, but the structure of a struggle to restore Unity by an act of love, Unity which gives rise to and sustains both the universe *and each of us as the universe*. We will explore this *unus-ambo* as 'Me,' a self which, although One and indivisible, is at the center yet, at the same time at the periphery of all; a self which is wounded in its heart. A blessed wound. To clarify what we mean by 'one being divided against itself' and why we say conflict cannot be experienced requires a lot more elaboration; the rest of Part 1 will be devoted to this. First let us be clear about what we mean by Unity.

Notes

1.   Kenneth E. Boulding, *Conflict and Defense* (New York: Harper & Row, 1962), p. 5.
2.   Arthur Koestler, *The Act of Creation*, (London: Pan Books, 1964), p. 35.
3.   Barry Sanders, *A is for Ox* (New York: Vintage Books, 1995), p. 89.
4.   Brian P. Copenhaver, *Hermetica* (Cambridge, UK: Cambridge University Press, 1992).
5.   Unus = one; ambo = two.
6.   Henry Corbin, *The Man of Light in Iranian Sufism* (Boulder, CO: Shambhala, 1978), p. 7: "Perfect Nature can only reveal itself 'in person' to one whose nature is perfect ... their relation is this unus-ambo in which each of the two simultaneously assumes the position of the I and the self-image and mirror: my image looks at me with my own look; I look at it with its own look."

Chapter 2

All is One?

It is by the One that all beings are beings. (If) not a one, a thing is not. No army, no choir, no flock exists except that it be one. No house, even, or ship exists except as the one.

PLOTINUS

A LL IS ONE." This is the fundamental theme of the book. Everything I want to say is dependent upon it. Yet how are we to understand this statement, all is one'? And what would be the value of this understanding? On the face of it, it seems too dense to penetrate, too opaque for the light of understanding to shine through. *All*—is this not the most general of words, encompassing not less than everything? And *one*—is this not in its turn the most abstract and least substantial of words? Is not one what is left after all other qualities have been stripped away? It seems the most general meets the most abstract in "all is one," a meeting of ghosts at midday.

The *Rig Veda*, a collection of the oldest religious hymns of India, has a verse, that reads as follows:

There was neither death nor immortality then. No signs were there of night or day. The One was breathing by its own power in infinite peace. Only the One was: there was nothing beyond. Darkness was hidden in darkness. Then all was fluid and formless. There in the void by the fire of fervor arose the One.

The One was breathing by its own power. What power does One have? *By the fire of fervor arose the One.* What is the fire of fervor that arouses the One?

The One was and is the origin of all; the origin not only in time but also in order. The One not only was the first but also *is* the first. From the One comes all: trees, houses, cars, you, and me, the 'all' that is the world. Yet even so, the One is the goal, the last—that which, by 'the fire of fervor,' is sought after, longed for. The One is Alpha and Omega.

Human beings have called it God, Brahma, Jehovah, Allah, Buddha, and many other names. It cannot be known by the intellect or through any intermediary, any sign symbol or idol. To know God truly (truly as opposed to simply knowing *about* God) is to *be* God and to be God is to transcend every kind of form or distance, every kind of abstraction or definition. In Buddhism this One is seen as 'empty,' without restriction or limitation, without inside or outside. Buddha said:

> There is that sphere wherein is neither earth nor water, fire nor air: it is not the infinity of space, nor the infinity of perception; it is not nothingness, nor is it neither idea nor non-idea; it is neither this world nor the next, nor is it both; it is neither the sun nor the moon.
>
> It neither comes nor goes, it neither abides nor passes away; it is not caused, established, begun, supported; it is the end of suffering.

Animals, we are told, have an *environment*, while human beings have a *world*. Whether animals do or do not have a world, the distinction between a 'world' and an 'environment' is interesting. By an 'environment' is meant disconnected happenings and things, a confused appearing and disappearing of shapes, colors and noises. By world we mean an integrated totality, a whole. William James said the experience of a baby is a buzzing, blooming *confusion*. Research suggests this may not be so, but there is the same sharp difference between buzzing, blooming confusion and a world that is ordered and whole, wherein each part is organically related to, even interdependent with, each other part and with the whole. Out of interdependence comes a pattern, a structure in which sameness and difference are woven together in space and time by purpose and design in a single tapestry called 'my life,' or 'my world.' A limited use of the word world means the earth, but we would like to use it in a more inclusive way. The origin of the word world is 'the life of man.'

We have no doubt that our world is one coherent whole. Our need for meaning and value comes out of this intuition of wholeness. Each of us expresses this coherence in our own *weltenschauung*. A *weltenschauung*, or worldview, is a global grasp, a comprehension in which each part finds its place and by which we assimilate new experience. If an experience cannot be assimilated within this worldview, it is rejected, denied, or the source of the experience destroyed. The theories of Galileo, for example, so threatened the worldview of the time they could only be dealt with by suppression and destruction.

So another name for the One is Truth. Humankind has always contemplated the world and wondered about its coherence and has looked for the One truth of coherence. More recently this has given rise to the search for a general field theory, a theory of everything. But Truth is neither something added to the One, nor is it a property of the One to be discovered and known: Truth *is* the One. Philosophers for centuries have looked for a formulation in a metaphysics, which would show the grand unity underlying God, the human soul, and the world. We like to believe in progress, that we are privy to a truth higher than the one our more primitive ancestors knew. But truth does not evolve; its expression may be sophisticated or crude, but it is always the same all-pervading Oneness at issue, whether with Archimedes or Einstein, Plato, or Bradley.

Turning Towards the One

Plotinus said, "It is by the One that all beings are beings. (If) not a one, a thing is not. No army, no choir, no flock exists except that it be one. No house, even, or ship exists except as the one." Thus, the One is not simply the whole, the all, what we call the world; everything is one: an army, a flock of sheep, a house, a chair a desk. What ever you see is one. This is taken for granted but that should not obscure it truth. One is the all and all is one. One informs everything, not simply as a concept of the one but as an organism or a thing

The world is a 'universe,'—a word that, etymologically, means *turning towards the one*. What, then, is the One toward which we turn? Earlier thinkers looked for one substance: air, fire, water, earth or ether, from which all has been made. Later thinkers have substituted *relations* for substance and have tried to formulate these relations in a single theory, one unified field theory, one grasp of the essence as relationship. Einstein's faith in Oneness led him to say that the theories of science are constant throughout the Universe. It also led him to reject the quantum theory as a final statement, because it implied a basic contradiction or split wherein something as basic as light would have to be perceived now as a wave and now as a particle.

We should not be surprised to find science and philosophy clashing with religion because the former seek a Unity called truth, the latter seek the same Unity but calls it God. Nor is it surprising such a clash should have brought about wars and revolutions. Just as the Crusades were an attempt to have he One as God prevail over the One as Allah, so the Reformation could be seen as the attempt of the secular One to prevail over the religious One.

The Will to Power

The struggle to determine the form in which the One should manifest— as truth or as God, as God or as the state, as God or as Allah—is often considered by the cynic to be simply a disguised form of the struggle for power. The cynic says humankind is dominated not by the will to truth or the will to the holy but by the will to power. But this will to power is itself yet another variation in the struggle for Oneness to prevail. The craving for power is the craving to *be* the One, the center and source of all initiative. We cannot easily separate power, oneness, and religion. Eric Hoffer, for example, points out, that the religious nature of the Bolshevik as well as the Nazi regimes is generally recognized.[1] The hammer and sickle and the swastikas served the same purpose for many of the devotees that the cross serves for the Christian. The ceremonial parades had all the characteristics of a religious procession.

In the late 1950s, Americans were stunned when they heard a simple sound: beep-beep, beep-beep. As Sputnik circled the earth, the American dream of being Number One was crushed. But the dream of being Number One is not only an American dream. It is a British, French, German, Japanese dream. Indeed, it is the dream of all tribes, groups, and nations. To be number One is to be the One, unique, without compare, superior beyond all. The dream of power and of fame is the dream that this unique-ness can be finally made to prevail— that at last it will become evident to all that I am the One.

However different the holy causes for which people die, they basically die for the same thing. According to Hoffer, this one thing underlying all mass movements is Unity. All wars are holy wars. Seeing the One as power gives us a preliminary and brief insight into the 'dynamic' quality of the One. The quotation we gave at the beginning of this part of the book says, "One is the means by which the whole exists and towards it the whole tends." One goes toward the One. This will be the basic theme of this book, and we hope to be able to show it to be a profoundly meaningful statement. We affirm Oneness to be dynamic and compelling, and to help open up this point of view, in the following chapter we will look at oneness from a slightly different angle—that of the *simple*.

Notes

1.   Eric Hoffer, *The True Believer* (New York: Harper and Row), p. 27.

Chapter 3

Unity as the Simple

At the basis of universal order there is not just simply a principle of unity, but rather a principle of simplicity which is itself, at the same time, a principle of economy and a principle of harmony.
ANDRÉ LAMOUCHE

One and Simple

PLOTINUS SAID, "The word 'one' is useful to the extent it designates absolute simplicity; but even then this designation must be promptly eliminated."[1]

"Words," said the English philosopher, Hobbes, "are money for fools, but counters of the wise."

'One' has no currency really and, some might believe, to say it designates 'absolute simplicity' adds insult to injury to those who have adopted the counterfeit. This is why Plotinus said the designation must be 'promptly eliminated.' However, some words, including words used to talk about the One, can be likened to the stain used to examine slides under a microscope. Sometimes the specimens on these slides are sliced so thinly they are quite transparent and when examined with the aid of bright light and a power lens, if left in their natural state, their secret would be missed. But with a touch of stain, the specimen becomes available for inspection. Similarly, some words can stain the bright radiance of the One and with their help we may detect some of its secrets. With this in mind let us ask ourselves about the 'simple' of Plotinus, bearing in mind that the word 'simple'—as well as the word 'same' —comes from a Latin root word *sem* which means 'One.'

The Simple

When a dancer practices her art she simplifies her movements, eliminating the extraneous, retaining only the essential. These essential moves she refines and integrates, each movement flowing into the other, following a continuous and subtle shift of a center of gravity. All great art is like this: even if it is highly complex with regard to the material used, it finds simplicity in being integrated around a dynamic center which gives unity and flow. Unity, harmony, and radiance (Lamouche would add economy) are the requirements of a great work of art.

To understand what is meant by 'simplicity integrated around a dynamic center,' one only has to consider a person learning to skate and compare him with an expert. Those learning to ice skate flail their arms trying to keep their balance; to do so they crouch over, trying desperately to preserve a stable center of gravity. Periodically they lose this center of gravity and, with whirling arms and thrashing feet, crash to the ice. How different the professional hockey player who progresses in a series of falls-averted by a constant shift of center around which is maintained perfect balance through an economy of movement in a smooth display of simplicity in action.

Of course, we must not confuse the simple with the easy. To skate like a tyro is easy, but only constant practice and hard work can make a professional. When we look at a dancer, a painter, or a musician, we see the same two requirements: Eliminate what is not essential and integrate what remains into a harmonious whole around a dynamic center.

Two meanings of 'Simple'
Quantitative and Qualitative

Eliminating what is unnecessary leads to simplicity. What has fewest parts is the simplest: The fewer the independent actions, the simpler the movement; the fewer the moving parts, the simpler the machine; the fewer the lines, the simpler the drawing. The more parts of which something is composed, the less simple it is. Therefore, 'one,' would be the simplest of all, and simple would mean *'not-composed.'* The ultimate in not-composed is the one, a quantitative or numerical one.

This however is not the full story of simplicity. In addition to a *quantitative* aspect of the simple, and complementary to it, is a *qualitative* aspect. This makes possible another understanding of simplicity: the simplicity of the *not-complex*. We said the skater eliminates what is not essential and integrates what remains into a harmonious whole around a dynamic center. Not-complex simplicity comes from integration or order among the parts; the more integrated something is, the simpler it is. A modern automobile engine is considerably less simple, in the number of independent parts it has, than earlier models. A great deal more goes on under the hood, and the car has many more components. On the other hand, the operation of the car is much simpler because the various functions of starting, choking, acceleration, stopping, changing gears, wiping the windshield, signaling, etc., are more integrated.

A cardinal principle known as Occam's razor rules philosophy and science. According to this principle one must not multiply assumptions and unknowns unnecessarily. Other things being equal, the theory with the fewest assumptions and unknowns is preferred. However, a theory cannot only be judged on the number of assumptions, it must also be complete. For centuries people believed the earth was like a still, flat plate with a domed sky, across which a parade of heavenly bodies traveled. Each of these bodies had its own source of power and particular deity as guide. Some of these travelers would weave a drunken route lurching forward and staggering back. A very complex mathematics was necessary to account for these movements. A simpler view was adopted which saw the sun rather than the earth as the center around which the heavenly bodies moved according to a single law based upon the law of gravity. A host of assumptions about the gods, progression, and retrogression could then be dispensed with. Not only this but the movements of the heavenly bodies were found to follow the same law as the terrestrial bodies. This opened up a new and elegant view of things. Thus a great deal of what otherwise was complex and unrelated experience could be integrated into a simple, not-complex whole.

For many people, though, the theory seemed more complex because to understand it meant readjusting (reintegrating) a lot of ideas based upon the notion the earth was flat. Not the least among these was the belief humankind was at the spatial center of the universe; it was believed heaven was up and hell down and, because of the central position of earth, God was primarily, if not exclusively, concerned with the events on earth. In that the new theory called for at least a readjustment of these views, if not a complete rejection of some of them, many people, unable or unwilling to make the adjustment, found the new theories too complex and rejected them. This is often the fate of new theories, because they so often call for a readjustment of existing beliefs, a readjustment that sometimes is too great for some people to make. Even today we still say the sun has risen or set because it is simpler than saying the earth has turned sufficiently to allow the appearance of the sun over the eastern horizon. Also—and perhaps this is more important—to talk in this way is more satisfying psychologically.

Another example, that of work simplification, will help clarify not-complex simplicity. In one of the better-known forms of work simplification, an aim is to reduce the number of people, parts and movements involved in getting work done. In other words, it goes towards 'not-composed' simplicity. But another equally important form of work simplification is to ensure everyone knows what part they play in some task, as well as knowing where and when their contribution should be made. Job descriptions, organization charts, pert charts, and so on, are all essential for simplifying the work by ensuring the *relationship* between all the elements of a productive system are *made known*. This implies that *to make relations known* is essential to not-complex simplicity.

Think about starting a new job. For some time the geography of the building can be quite confusing. Furthermore, the relationships between people—not only the formal, organizational relationships, but also the informal ones—are confusing. How one's job fits into the whole and relates to other jobs cannot always be known right away. For the first few days or even weeks one has to painfully find one's way around the physical and social terrain. But little by little the relationships are identified and *made known,* and gradually a whole picture begins to emerge. With this whole picture comes a lot less wasted time and a lot less stress.

Going back to the example of the skater for a moment, we have said it takes constant hard work for the skater to become skillful. Such hard work implies *attention* to detail, which allows unnecessary moves to be eliminated (not-composed simplicity). But, at the same time, attention is also necessary to ensure the parts retained are harmonious, and the relation between these parts is 'known.' Attention is closely allied to '*intention*—each implies oneness in action. Action painters to the contrary, a good work of art comes out of long hours of practice. It does not just happen. The long hours of practice are made possible because of an intention. Another word related to both attention and intention is intuition. Not complex 'simple' is based on knowing. When we look for simplicity through understanding, we use intuition; when we seek it in action, we use intention. In each case attention is first necessary. Thus by knowing we do not necessarily mean *conscious* knowing. We shall clarify what we mean by this later, but it is important to mention it at this point.

Intuition is certain because it grasps unity through the simple; nevertheless, intuition is fallible because so often what was thought to be simple turns out to be complex. One is mistaken because some of the relations between the entities or between other relations remain unknown. Science does not progress in a straight line but meanders like a river veering east, towards quantitative not composed simplicity, or west, towards qualitative not complex simplicity. What was formerly thought of as simple (e.g., the atom) is shown to be highly complex. What was formerly thought to be complex (e.g., the relation between electricity and magnetism) is shown to be simple.

The two forms of simplicity, let us repeat, are *quantitative* (not-composed) simplicity in which the number of elements, that is items, parts, terms, entities, or elements is minimized; and *qualitative* (not-complex) simplicity in which the number of *unknown relations*, are minimized. A whole, which has a multiplicity of parts, *can only be simple because it is known to be simple*. Knowing converts the buzzing, blooming confusion into a *world*. People blind from birth who have undergone an operation to give them sight often find the first experience of sight painful and confusing. They do not see *things* but just a tormenting confusion. Painfully they must integrate this complexity into a whole, sorting out triangles and squares, spheres and cubes, colors and shapes, while at the same time maintaining an awareness of the whole. Identifying the part and clarifying the relationship between all the parts into a simple elegant whole does this. This is similar to the work of an artist who takes a number of separate and disparate things: fruit, a bottle of wine, a pipe and so on, and composes a still life picture from them, in such a way as to bring out the inherent unity.

A Need for Oneness

So far we have considered the simple from the point of view of understanding and human action only. Lamouche, the former director general of naval construction in the French Naval Ministry to whom we are indebted for the distinction between quantitative and qualitative simplicity, argued in his three-volume study on simplicity that it was not just a logic that was in question, but also a *principle of nature*.[2] In other words, *nature itself is going towards the simple,* quantitative as well as qualitative. Simlicity, is a force, then, a drive; and evolution, we suggest, is its outcome.

Throughout this book we shall be drawing attention to the pervasive influence of unity, the drive towards unity in all humankind's endeavors, which grow out of the truth, 'all is one.' In particular, we shall show the part this drive to the One, the drive of simpliciy, plays in the evolution of consciousness. To help with this, we shall call on various authors' writings and illustrate this influence in music, in the visual arts, in poetry, in modern theoretical physics. We hope to show how differences in religious belief can be reconciled in this understanding and how the theory of evolution can be enriched by it. We shall also investigate the influence of unity in creativity and spirituality, as well as in violence. We will explore, as thoroughly as possible, the nature of Oneness: What seems so obvious and straight forward is not so; what people take so much for granted is full of mystery. Oneness is not static and dead, nor is it simply a state or condition of being; rather it is dynamic with a tendency towards the simple. *All is One* is not simply ghosts meeting at mid-day. On the contrary, it is a phrase which 'stains' a dynamic and vibrant mystery, a mystery with which we are always at one level or another trying to come to terms.

Notes

1. Elmer O'Brien (trans), *The Essential Plotinus* (New York: New American Library, 1964), p. 75
2. Andre Lamouche, *Le Principe de Simplicité dans les mathématiques et dans les sciences physiques* (Paris: Gauthier-Villiers, 1955).

Chapter 4

The Lion's Roar as Oneness

A mighty fortress is our God.
CHRISTIAN HYMN

The Roar of Oneness

To HEAR THE ROAR OF A LION in the wild, in the African veldt —
the power, courage, invincibility—means one can never again stand to
see a caged lion in a zoo. I remember once hearing this roar while traveling
through the Kruger National Park, in South Africa. Our camp was on a rise
leading down to a wide river. The sun was going down quite fast, as it does
near the tropics at sunset; it was dusk and a keen sense of urgency hung in
the air. Herds of zebra, wildebeest, springbok were drinking at the river. One
after another, a zebra or springbok would throw up its head listening, ex-
pecting, waiting. The air was charged with an unseen power. Then, just as
night was falling, came the roar; almost before the echo had started, the roar
came again. Through the tall grass the pride of lions moved in procession
down to the river whose banks were now empty.

The lions' roar. Zen Buddhists use it as a way of talking about awakening, the revelation of wholeness. 'Revelation' is not quite the right expression, but then no expression can be the right one. How can one talk of that
wholeness which gives the power and ability to talk, and not only the power
to talk, but also the power to be, to exist? And so we talk of the lion's roar.
Naked, powerful, untamed: Dynamic unity.

The One That Cannot Be Counted

In *The Butterfly's Dream*, I told this story: There were ten people who had to cross a river swollen by floods. The crossing was very precarious. When they had crossed they decided to count their number to confirm all had made it across. One of them stepped forward and counted: 1-2-3-4-5-6-7-8-9. There were only nine! Another stepped forward counted . . . there were only nine. They were all bewailing the loss of one of their group when a stranger came along and asked what the problem was. They said, "There were ten of us on the other side of the river and now, after a difficult crossing, there are only nine. We have lost one of our friends." The stranger said, "Let me count." So he counted: 1-2-3-4-5-6-7-8-9-10. They were so relieved they went on their way rejoicing.

However, the stranger too was wrong. Can you see why? If you think he should have counted eleven and not ten, you too will be mistaken.

We always overlook the one who counts. To know this one is to know 'the lion's roar.' It might well be asked how could we overlook something so obvious as wholeness which holds us all in its sway. The answer is that, for something to exist for the conscious mind, it must have some distinguishing characteristic, something by which it can be distinguished and remembered. The tenth person, the One who counts, is beyond all form, all limitations definitions and characteristics. This lion's roar, a mighty fortress of the Christians, is the One the Jews called Jehovah, the jealous god, the One who said, "You may not look on my face and live."[1] This One that is overlooked, is the God of war,[2] of reality. It is also the God of formal logic, the God who says it is either one or it is not one and it cannot both be one and two at the same time.

Pain as the Voice of the Impossible

Unity can be grasped only by unity; only the One can contain the One. A Zen master said, "My body is so big there is nowhere to put it." For there to be other than One, unity must be divided against itself—and yet *this is impossible*—it just cannot happen. This impossibility, the one that is two, as we have already pointed out, is the subject of this book. By impossible I mean what is contrary to logic, reason, and experience and for which no explanation can be found. This impossibility, that which 'simply cannot happen,' we experience as agony and as ecstasy. When we look into the heart of pain, we know the impossible. It is said, with good reason, suffering has no voice. People ask, "Why do we suffer?" "Where does suffering fit in the world?" But there is no reason; suffering does not fit into the world. We have tried many ruses to make it fit: "suffering is good for the soul." "Suffering is just retribution for past sins." "Suffering is the outcome of past environmental mishandling." "Suffering is just bad luck." Suffering does not fit into the world because the world itself is an attempt to make sense of the impossible, the impossibility of the One being divided against itself. All reasons, all justifications, all judgments, come out of suffering; they are struggles to resolve the impossibility whose voice is a scream of pain. The power in the atom, the immense gravitational forces in galaxies and in galaxies of galaxies, even the force, beyond all imaginings, of the Big Bang, all are manifestations of the impossibility of an irresistible force, the One, contained by an immovable impasse which is the same One; a force arising out of One being divided against itself.

For the Christian there is the ever-unresolvable contradiction: the origin of evil in a world made by an omnipotent God who is good. If God is good, he seeks the welfare of all; if he is omnipotent, he will ensure the welfare of all. Then why do we suffer? A celebrated Japanese Zen Master of the 12th Century asked a similar question, "If it is true, as Buddhism teaches, that we are whole and complete, that we lack nothing for a life of felicity and well being, why do we have to work so hard to realize this?" The theoretical physicist, too, has his contradiction: What set off the Big Bang? Before the Big Bang there is just wholeness and symmetry. How does symmetry become asymmetrical? Can wholeness be divided against itself?

To anticipate our conclusions: we shall endeavor to show that Oneness in conflict with Oneness creates an intolerable situation. All creativity, all evolution, comes out of the endeavor to overcome this intolerable situation. Furthermore, because evolution goes towards the rediscovery of unity, it therefore has *a direction and purpose*. But this rediscovery can never be fully accomplished; with each advance towards unity comes a corresponding retreat from it.

To understand this we have to go to the origins of our everyday consciousness, and to do this we must go upstream of experience, which means, among other things, upstream of traditional logic. But what lies beyond consciousness, experience and existence? The supernatural? Cosmic consciousness? Heaven, or some fairy land? What can be found beyond logic that is not simply nonsense? Beyond consciousness, and out of which consciousness appears, lies ambiguity and we must now say what precisely we mean by this.

The Fundamental Ambiguity

Ambiguity, or contradiction, is generally considered to be evidence of shoddy thinking. If we encounter it in a scientific or philosophic argument we usually conclude a thinker has failed to follow through sufficiently with his thinking. For examp. ⸤llowing comes from a popular book on thinking and logic:

> To tolerate contradiction [or ambiguity] is to be indifferent to truth. For the person who, whether directly or by implication, knowingly both asserts and denies one and the same proposition, shows by that behavior that he does not care whether he asserts what is false and not true, or whether he denies what is true and not false . . . for whenever and wherever I tolerate self-contradiction, then and there I make it evident, either that I do not care at all about truth, or that at any rate I do care about something else more.[3]

The word 'ambiguity' can mean vague and hazy, but we shall not be using it in this way at all. We shall use it to assert and deny one and the same proposition. The word has its origins in *ambi*, meaning two. Thus *ambidextrous* means two hands, *ambivalent* means two directions, *ambivert* means introvert and extrovert and so on. *Ambiguous* means two faces. Here is a well-known illustration of ambiguity:

FIG.1:

If we study this illustration for a moment we shall see two faces: one the face of a young woman, the other the face of an old woman. But note that *we can only perceive one face at a time.* If we see the old woman, we do not see the young woman, and vice versa. Each of these two faces is a valid representation of the black- and white field; each is the One. But, because of the other, each of these two faces is not the One. Thus the two faces are mutually exclusive, or to use the expression of Koestler and Boulding, they are incompatible.

Each of the two faces is *dependent* upon the other: because of the young lady there is the old lady and vice versa. They are also *mutually dependent* (the outline is the same for the young lady and the old lady).

However, we shall be talking about the fundamental ambiguity, an ambiguity which itself is ambiguous. With the fundamental ambiguity one face is ambiguous while the other is not.[4] In our illustration, as we have already pointed out, the young woman and the old woman are both valid representations of the black-and-white field. These make up the face that is ambiguous. However, we can also ask ourselves, is the illustration just a black-and-white field, or is it a young/old lady? The black-and-white field contains no ambiguity. The original face of no ambiguity proclaims all is *One* and, because this is so, there can be no ambiguity, no two faces. This unambiguous face is the lion's roar, the face of fundamental Unity.

Suppose now we were to ask, Which is "the right" face? Suppose that one man, or one nation, said that it was the old woman, another man, or another nation, said it was a young woman. We might suppose, somewhat wildly that the old woman stands for democracy and the young woman for communism. By the "right face," we mean the One face. Is it not possible that this could lead to a war in which the world could be destroyed?

Let me repeat, if there is unity there cannot be two. If there are two, then where is unity. Yet our deepest intuition affirms Unity; one which is undivided. Everyday experience says that there are two. Are there not you and me? Are there not me and the world? Are there not good and bad, right and wrong, here and there? In each case we encounter duality, two.

Hence the formulation of the basic ambiguity reads thius way: an ambiguity, one face of which (unity) says there is no ambiguity, while the other face (duality) says there is ambiguity. So that we can readily keep in mind the notion of ambiguity, we shall use the mark (/) to mean ambiguity. Simply stated, the fundamental ambiguity is One/(yes/no).

Notes

1. Exodus 20:5.
2. Exodus 15.
3. Andrew Flew, *Thinking about Thinking* (Glasgow: Fontana, 1975).
4. See also Albert Low, *The Iron Cow of Zen* (Boston: Charles E. Tuttle, 1992); Albert Low, *The Butterfly's Dream* (Boston: Charles E. Tuttle, 1993).

Chapter 5

The Theology of Science
Accident vs. Creativity

What can be the attraction of getting to know . . .
a tiny section of nature thoroughly, while one leaves everything
subtler and more complex shyly and timidly alone?
Does the product of such a modest effort deserve to
be called by the proud name of a theory of the universe?
ALBERT EINSTEIN[1]

WE WANT TO SHOW THE ROLE of unity, a unity which is also a duality, in the evolution of consciousness; and we want to show how both creativity and violence come out of this same uno–ambus. Scientists have always held to the intuition of unity as a guiding beacon in their research. In his book *On the Thematic Origins of Scientific Thought*, science writer Gerald Holton affirms this:

> Underlying research has been the conviction of a unity and singularity of natural knowledge. The paths to an understanding of nature may be infinite as the successes of even the most specialized interests indicate, and each of these paths is expected to have difficult, even insurmountable barriers. But all paths have been vaguely thought to lead to a goal, an understanding of one nature, a delimited though no doubt complex rational corpus, which some day a person's mind would be able to make

one's own (as the layman today says, somewhat nervously, 'one great formula' that tells everything there is to know about nature).[2]

In the third book of his *Principia,* Newton endorsed the importance of unity as well as the possibility of this one great formula with his four rules, the first of which said, "Nature is essentially simple; therefore we should not introduce more hypotheses than are sufficient and necessary for the explanation of observed facts." We must take careful note that he says that *nature* is essentially simple. Is it possible that scientists could ever come to any understanding at all if it were not so? If nature is simple, then simplicity must not only be a *principle* of simplicity, but it must be a *drive* towards simplicity also.

It was Darwin's tour de force to see the steady unfolding of a harmonious unity in evolution rather than a series of discrete and unrelated creations. This insight gave a great impetus to the rediscovery by Western society of a unity that was lost when the mediaeval paradigm broke down. The analogy that comes irresistibly with Darwin's theory is the idea of a tree: life is one, a single growing organism, an organism impelled and organized by unity. With Darwin's theory of evolution the intuitive need that we have for grasping the whole in a dynamic and integrated way was satisfied.

With the coming of Darwin's theory the belief in an independent creator gradually faded, until, for many people, the idea of creation itself became redundant. Darwin, for example, said:

We can no longer argue that, for instance, the beautiful hinge of a bivalve shell must have been made by an intelligent being, like the hinge of a door by man. There seems to be no more design in the variability of organic beings and in the action of natural selection than in the course which the wind blows."[3]

By saying this Darwin set the stage for accident, fragmentation, and blind chance to be reintroduced, not only in the production of individual creatures, but at the very heart of creativity itself. With time creativity became dethroned completely, its place usurped by accident and blind chance; awe and mystery became shrouded in esoteric formulae; and unity became an empty phrase.

Modern science, which owes so much to men like Kepler, Galileo, and Newton, began with feelings of awe and reverence. It is said that when Kepler contemplated the heliocentric cosmos, he was thrilled by realizing that "in a truly heliocentric system God can be brought back into the solar system itself, so to speak, enthroned as the fixed and common reference object which coincides with the source of light and with the origin of the physical forces holding the system together."[4] Unfortunately, this awe and reverence have been lost in the mad scramble for grants and recognition, and their place taken by a misplaced toughness mistaken for objectivity.

As could be expected, a strong reaction rose up against the accident theory, a reaction generated by those who found it difficult to assimilate this new and, within the context of the nineteenth-century world view, simpler idea. This reaction was the beginning of a creationist versus evolutionist argument that has flared up again and again. Unfortunately, the religious revolt brought about its own counter-revolution. Most of the scientists who had anything to do with the development of the theories about evolution went to extremes to enthrone their own dogma in opposition to what they considered to be the dogma of the opposition. The success of the analytical method of reductionism has entrenched this dogma to such an extent that for many of our leading scientists it cannot even be questioned. Yet it is not necessary to retain a particular world idea in order for God to find a place in the world if we consider God to be Unity, wholeness manifesting as love and intelligence.

Creation as an Accident

Jacques Monod, a French professor and scientist, is an example of this newer scientist. He once said, "Man has to understand he is a mere accident. Not only is man not the center of creation; he is not even heir to a sort of predetermined evolution that would have produced either man or something very like him in any case."[5] In other words, the whole of evolution is just a series of accidents, without purpose or goal. Monod made this statement shortly after Crick and Watson discovered the molecular structure of DNA. Life, Monod added, is a tale told by an idiot. Full of sound and fury, it signifies nothing.

Monod's assertion, of course, comes from a belief—indeed, from a religious belief—held with passion and conviction, as is shown by his tone when he says, "man *has* to understand." Although the emphasis has been added, it is nevertheless implied by what Monod says. His tone is the tone of dogma. When he says this he steps out of the role of scientist into the role of priest or prophet. To continue the quote, Monod says, "Man has to understand he is a mere accident." One wonders why he says a "mere" accident. When he says this and follows it up by saying, "Not only are we not the center of creation, we are not even heir to a sort of predestined evolution," he is preaching an anti-theology, because, after all, he has no scientific basis for what he says. Although he was an esteemed scientist, his opinion about the place of human beings in the scheme of things is, at best equal to, but of no more value than that of a peasant woman who makes offerings to the Virgin Mary. Alas, it may even be of less value, as he admits he only has the tenuous thread of logic with which to anchor his opinions: "I have to stick to a linear, logical thread. Otherwise I am lost."[6] But, for all that, his lifeline of logic still ends with his leap into theology. That the world is an accident is not a logical conclusion from scientific research, but a leap of faith.

Creation as Intention

To the layman, one of the more interesting things about the discovery of DNA's structure—the discovery which inspired Monod into his prophetic flight—is the account given of *the process of discovery* itself by Watson, in his book *The Double Helix*. Anyone who reads this account must forever lose any notion that science is a logical, systematic, and reasonable enterprise. Leaving aside the clash of personalities, the intrigues, politics, and competitiveness among the chief characters of the drama, the very process of discovery itself is shown to be neither reasonable nor logical. For example, Watson says, "The idea of the genes being immortal *smelled* right" (emphasis added).[7] On another occasion he says, "The instant I saw the picture (of an X-ray of DNA) my mouth fell open and my pulse began to race."[8] Later he adds, "Not until the middle of the next week, however, did a non-trivial idea emerge. It came while I was drawing the fused rings of adenine on paper . . . suddenly I realized . . . despite the messy backbone my pulse began to race."[9]

Einstein once said, "Science as an existing, finished [corpus of knowledge] is the most objective, most impersonal [thing] human beings know, but science as something coming into being, as aim, is just as subjective and psychologically conditioned as any other of man's efforts."[10] Excitement, despair, triumph, stress, these are essential ingredients of the scientific endeavor. Discovery is not only uncovering by cool, objective logic and reason a structure lying dormant, but also a vital, exciting creation of relationships that enable this structure to emerge into consciousness. It requires deep commitment, intention and a sense of purpose.

But how do creativity, commitment, and purpose appear in a world governed only by accident? It is true that accident plays a part, perhaps even a major part, in creativity. A chance remark of a colleague, a book, a visit to the cinema, anything can act as a jolt, a source for a new line of thought. But as we see in Watson's account, what is much more significant is the *relentless* drive that governs creativity; there is a sense of constantly hovering about the center of things, a sense of significance. This does not mean that the creative urge is infallible, quite the contrary. More often than not one is wrong and the line followed leads nowhere; the feeling of significance and purpose evaporates and one is left with despair in the place of hope, dejection in the place of boundless energy, dullness in the place of scintillating wit. The dynamic drive of commitment is lost. Nevertheless, hope, energy, and scintillating wit return again and again. How is this possible in a world of accident?

The theory of accident is widespread. What is worse, many people feel this theology has a "scientific" (that is, incontrovertible) basis because they believe that science is a solid, rational, coherent, and incontrovertible body of truth that has the right to act as final arbiter on the destiny of mankind. The very title of the book from which we have taken the quotations from Monod, *The Eighth Day of Creation*, has a biblical ring about it. Monod himself obviously believed that science has the inside track, that it can be the final arbiter of the destiny of the human being. The authoritative way he speaks comes from his certainty that in his role of scientist he has the authority to speak and declaim in this way. "Anything can be reduced to simple, obvious, mechanical interactions," he says. "The cell is a machine; the animal is a machine; man is a machine."[11] But are they *only* machines?

The Underlying Unity of Accident and Creativity

But do we really have to make a sharp dichotomy between accident and creativity? If we look at these two more closely we may find that they are not opposed at all; that what is an accident when seen from one point of view, may be creativity when seen from another. Both occur abruptly, suddenly; both are unpredictable. Although one can say there are general conditions surrounding both of these—conditions which decree that an accident, or creativity, is likely to occur—none of them allows us to make a positive prediction about which one will. For example, a parent may say to a child, "If you go on riding your bicycle like that you will have an accident." But this is not a prediction. In a similar way one can say that by looking at a situation within two different contexts (for example, looking at "structure" as it appears in music and as it appears in a business situation) creative ideas may emerge. But this is not a prediction, either.

Although accident and creation are both unpredictable both are also crystallizations, or the outcomes, of forces in a field of activity, and so for neither is it necessary to designate a creator. The 'I' one might believe to be the creator is itself part of the creation, no less than the observer is part of the situation under observation. In a similar way we do not necessarily have to postulate a God as creator. Finally, neither in the case of accident nor in the case of creativity is it necessary even to postulate any kind of reflective thought. Both accident and creativity are sudden, both are spontaneous, both arise out of a situation, both are "pre-" or "un-" conscious.

We must understand creativity and realize the importance of purpose because, unless we do so, we cannot understand consciousness and therefore we fail to understand what makes us essentially human. If we are truly to come to grips with the problems that beset our civilization, we have to let go of our prejudices and our dogmas. In his book *The Way Things Are*, Nobel Prize winner P. W. Bridgman, called for *integrity*, and said that the most pressing intellectual need is simple integrity.[12] He added,

> For me integrity in the individual implies 'intellectual honesty,' but it is more than this. It is a frame of mind. Integrity demands that I *want to* know what the facts are and that I want to analyze and understand my mental tools and know what happens when I apply these tools to the facts...if I have a new vision of something which I did not appreciate before, I may not try to put the vision back and pretend that I did not have it and refuse to admit that there may be consequences.[13]

On the difficulty of talking about 'value,' 'purpose' 'consciousness' and so on Bridgman had this to say:

> [Language is unable] to deal with reflexive situations as we would like.

Language has to be handled with great circumspection if we are to avoid paradox, as is well known with regard to some of the situations in elementary logic. A special case of self-reflexive situations is afforded by introspection. It is very difficult to get into words what I mean by the 'quality' of my sensation of red.[14]

Any theory has a creative element, and integrity demands that we recognize this, not only as a psychological fact, but as a cosmological one also. The human being does not stand apart from nature. The human being is nature in action. Let us suppose for the moment that the "facts" (whatever that word means) on which a theory is based *may* be discovered; even so *the interpretation* of these facts is not discovered. One does not *discover* an interpretation—one *makes* or (more idiomatic) one *gives* an interpretation. If this is the case, then the interpretation of facts must include determining what is and what is not a fact. For example, within the scheme propounded by Monod, ESP could find no place, it has no status as a 'fact,' not by reason of the evidence, but by reason of its incompatibility with the existing scientific world view. Raw phenomena are converted or made into fact by interpretation. The word fact comes from the French word *faire* which means to "make." In French a fact is *un fait*: that which is made. Put into other words, a fact has status only within a whole or gestalt, within which that fact can be integrated. We call that whole a theory, a word that originally meant a way of seeing. It had its origins in the Greek *theoros*, which means "spectator" (probably *thea*, a viewing + *oros*, seeing.)

Advanced theoretical physicists are now aware of the dynamic and inseparable interplay between the scientist and his field of research: the very act of observing *changes,* some even want to say creates,[15] that which is under observation. The very fact of choosing an area for research, of setting the apparatus up one way rather than another, of choosing one method rather than another method to record the data, all, at the very least, modify what is under observation. Furthermore, a wider array of facts is presented to a good researcher than is presented to a poor researcher. The good researcher *sees* things that the poor researcher is liable to overlook. This in turn means that research is not determined by what is "there" but by what is *seen* to be there. Moreover, a scientist cannot discard at will his beliefs and claim that he has access to a disinfected world uncontaminated by them; these beliefs, most of which he takes completely for granted, include the very beliefs he holds about the efficacy of the scientific method, and even about what constitutes valid science.

This will mean that a scientist is not a neutral blank on which the world impinges. The belief that life began as an accident is a belief coming from, and feeding back into a *weltenschauung*[16] or world idea. Monod, like all of us, is at home with others who share his world idea; he seeks their approval, is influenced by their judgments while being indifferent or even scornful of others whose world idea is different. He is constrained by his world idea to see life as the result of an accident in the same way that another world idea constrains, say, a peasant woman, to see life as being lived in the benevolent care of the Virgin Mary. Not based on facts, rarely subject to profound criticism or alteration, operating in a 'preconscious' way, this world idea gives structure to all conscious activity. To change a world idea is often much more difficult, painful, and time-consuming than ignoring what does not conform to it. Facts are facts because they conform to, and in conforming confirm, the world idea from which they emerge. This feed back creates a steady state and eventually an inertia that is difficult and painful to overcome.

Nevertheless, the world idea is not static, like a filing cabinet or a window. When Monod sets up his experiments, works with his mathematics, tests and asserts, assesses and denies, clarifying observation with theory and theory with observation, he does so from a world idea. This idea is not static, inert, passive like a window is inert and passive with respect to all that passes through it, but from a world idea which is intensely active, purposeful and dynamic. Instead of being simply a passive window, the world idea is more like a field of forces under tension; a field in dynamic equilibrium, fluid but within limits, but a fluidity that is elastic; a dynamism that can arouse, as we saw with Watson, intense energy, excitement, and stress. In Chapter 16 we shall return again to the notion of idea as a field under stress and elaborate upon it.

We all know the excitement of creativity. Any creative work, and this might be just redecorating the bathroom, brings with it excitement, energy and stress; it enlivens and enriches, as well as focusing the mind with intensity and a sense of purpose, sometimes over long periods of time. Someone asked Newton how he managed to discover the laws of gravity, and he replied, "I never thought of anything else."

Now it is evident that human beings are creative and inventive, and, as they are part of what we call the universe, then that universe must be, to a greater or lesser degree, a creative universe having purpose and intention as ingredients. We shall endeavor to show that this kind of purpose is inherent in the evolution of the universe and in the evolution of consciousness. This purpose, as we shall show, comes from dynamic unity. Furthermore, we hope to show that human beings do indeed have a special place: a special place and a special responsibility. This is said not because one is afraid to face up to an implacable and austere truth, but because it would be simply lacking in integrity not to say it. Before going on, let it be said the aim of this book is not to reintroduce a creationist viewpoint in some new guise. God, as Laplace has said, is an unnecessary postulate, if we mean by God a transcendent creator apart from the world, a being who created it out of his own thought and imagination once and for all. Accident is an essential element in the world, and evolution is an ongoing and never ending process. As the Big Bang theory demonstrates, the whole universe is evolving and we must consider the implications of this because the world as well as consciousness, and all that consciousness implies, evolves out of the mystery of Unity, the One that is two.

Notes

1. Albert Einstein, *Ideas and Opinions* (New York: Crown, 1954).
2. Gerald Holton, *On the Thematic Origins of Scientific Thought* (Cambridge, MA: Harvard University Press, 1988), p. 19.
3. Robert Augros, and George Stanciuu, *The New Biology* (Boston: Shambhala, 1987), pp. 228–229.
4. Holton (1988, 6).
5. Horace Freeland Judson, *The Eighth Day of Creation* (New York: Simon & Schuster, 1979), p. 217.
6. Judson (1979, 353).
7. James Watson, *The Double Helix* (New York: Signet, 1968), p. 98.
8. Watson (1968, 107).
9. Watson (1968, 118).
10. Holton (1988, 6).
11. Judson (1979, 21).
12. P. W. Bridgman, *The Way Things Are* (New York: Viking Press, 1959).
13. Bridgman (1959, 319).
14. Bridgman (1959, 320).
15. See Appendix 1.
16. *Weltenschauung* can be translated as both world view and world idea.

Chapter 6

De Chardin and Unity
An Alternative World Idea

*There is less difference than people
would think between research and adoration.*
TEILHARD DE CHARDIN[1]

I N THE LAST CHAPTER we said the scientist cannot be separated from
the problem he is researching and the claimed "objectivity" of the scientist is but one of the myths of science. A French writer, Teilhard de
Chardin said:

> [Scientists] are beginning to realize that even the most objective of their
> observations are steeped in the conventions they adopted at the outset
> and by forms or habits of thought developed in the course of the growth
> of research; so that when they reach the end of their analyses they can-
> not tell with any certainty whether the structure they have reached is
> the essence of the matter they are studying or the reflection of their own
> thought.[2]

Teilhard de Chardin was a Catholic priest and a scientist. He was born
in 1881, and at the age of eighteen began his training to become a Jesuit.
Later he went to the University of Paris and obtained a doctorate in the
natural sciences. He took part in a number of scientific expeditions and

did a considerable amount of original research. The bibliography of his technical contributions covers forty compact pages. He conducted his research in three distinct areas: geology, mammal paleontology, and human paleontology; his main contribution in this latter field being the discovery, along with three other paleontologists, of Peking man, an important find in the field of human paleontology.

But undoubtedly his most important work, and the one to which his whole life was devoted, was the book *The Phenomenon of Man*. The conclusions that de Chardin comes to in this book go as far in the opposite direction to those of Jacques Monod as it is possible to go. The subject of the book is evolution, evolution not only of life but of the Universe, and not only in terms of the past but in terms of future evolution as well. For de Chardin evolution is more than a theory, system or hypothesis, "it is a general condition to which all theories, all hypotheses all systems must bow and which they must satisfy henceforth if they are to be thinkable and true."[3]

Just as we saw the obvious biases of Monod, so, within a few pages of his book, it is obvious that de Chardin also has a clear bias. Indeed, for a Jesuit priest this is not surprising. Whereas Monod would have wanted at all costs to keep God, Christ, and religion out of the arena, for de Chardin these are important ingredients in his whole program. He was tormented by a constant struggle to find some way by which the two divergent viewpoints, the religious and the scientific, could be brought together.

Consciousness and Unity

The Phenomenon of Man begins with de Chardin proclaiming that the whole of life lies in the verb "to see." He says the history of the world can be summarized as "fuller being through closer union."[4] And union is increased, he says, through consciousness. Indeed, for de Chardin the whole purpose of evolution was the perfection of consciousness around an ultimate center called the Omega point. In other words, evolution is not pushed by changes in the past, but drawn by purpose to the future.

He also says, and this is relevant to what we have said about Oneness and wholeness. "Around us as far as the eye can see the universe holds together and only one way of considering it is possible, that is to take it as a *whole, in one piece*."[5] He adds, the "stuff of the Universe, woven in one single piece according to one and the same system but never repeating itself from one point to another, represents a single figure. Structurally it forms a whole."[6] And for him the human being is "a wholeness that unfolds."[7] Human kind, the universe, is evolving as a unity, towards unity or union around the Omega point.

The central role of consciousness in evolution is emphasized when he says, "To think the world, as physics is beginning to realize, is not merely to register it but to *confer upon it* a form of unity it would otherwise be without."[8] This statement echoes our point in the last chapter, that without creativity, without the creative idea, the world would not only be different, but, indeed would not even exist. This is not to say the universe is "nothing but" an idea, but the form the universe has for us would not be possible without the idea that brings this form into being.

Although the intuition of unity underlies all de Chardin says, nevertheless his unity, like simplicity, is not simple. On the one hand he says that, in its most imperfect form, unity reveals itself in the astonishing similarity of elements met with. It is almost as though the stuff of which the universe is made were reducible to some simple and unique kind of substance, which we have called quantitative simplicity. On the other hand he speaks of a collective unity: "*Something holds together in one whole* the innumerable foci which share a given volume of matter. Far from being an inert receptacle the space filled by their multitude operates upon it like an active center of direction and transmission in which the plurality is organized."[9] This we have called qualitative simplicity. In other words, wholeness is not a passive container but a dynamic, centering process, oneness; it holds together all in one whole.

Unity, Plurality, and Energy

De Chardin elaborates by saying unity, plurality and energy are the three faces of matter. By plurality he means "the profoundly atomic" nature of the universe. He explains, "Bewildering in its multiplicity and minuteness, the substratum of the tangible universe is in an unending state of disintegration." But even so he says, "the more we split and pulverize matter artificially the more persistently it proclaims its unity."[10] He is referring to quantitative simplicity. But he goes onto say:

> Furthermore, whatever space we suppose it to be in, each cosmic element radiates in it and fills it. However narrow the heart of an atom may

be circumscribed its realm is co-extensive with that of every other atom. We shall come across this again even in the human molecule. The innumerable foci which share a given volume of matter are not therefore independent of each other.[11]

This is qualitative simplicity.

Wholeness, de Chardin stresses later, is not simply an empty, monolithic whole. On the contrary, there are spheres or levels of different kinds in the unity of nature, each of them distinguishable by the dominance of certain factors, which are imperceptible or negligible in an adjacent level. These spheres or levels of different kinds in the unity of nature are the result of evolution, which he describes vividly in the following way:

> To begin with at the bottom of matter there is still unresolved simplicity, luminous in nature and not to be defined in figures. Then suddenly came a swarming of elementary particles through the long series of the atomic scale. Then comes the immense variety of compound bodies in which the molecular weight go on increasing up to a certain critical value above which, as we shall see, we pass onto life. *There is not one term in this long series but must be regarded, from sound experimental proofs, as being compounded of nuclei and electrons.* This fundamental discovery that *all bodies owe their origin to arrangements of a single initial corpuscular type* is the beacon that lights the history of the universe to our eyes.[12]

He simplifies all of this by saying, *"after the grain of matter, the grain of life, then the grain of thought."*[13] Later still he says, "The fundamental problem of all thought is how to give to each and every element its final value by grouping them together in the unity of an organized whole."[14]

The Grain of Thought

The grain of thought is what we called, in the introduction, the grain of consciousness, and for de Chardin, evolution is an ascent towards greater consciousness. De Chardin says logically, therefore, it should culminate in a supreme consciousness. This supreme consciousness in turn should contain in the highest degree the perfection of our consciousness, which is unity and diversity.

Wholeness is the very stuff of de Chardin's universe, and as we have stressed this is not simply a dead, static unity but dynamic and above all purposeful: purpose is of the very essence. *Unity as wholeness is striving towards Unity as Omega point, the dynamic center of a Universal consciousness.* Another word for striving is *evolution,* in which accident and randomness have their part to play. The cynic might well smile at the naiveté of de Chardin's enthusiasm. He has an almost school boyish charm in the way he writes, and one might in particular want to smile at the legerdemain by which he pulls Christ out of the cosmic hat as the center of it all. But the smile would be ill-placed as de Chardin raised issues which are becoming ever more important: his insistence that "seeing" is basic, that consciousness is endemic to the world and is as primary as matter; that what is implied in consciousness, transcends consciousness, and this is the Omega point; that the human being is indeed a measure of all things. Furthermore, his passionate call for a science for which wholeness would be the dynamism as well as the fundamental structure of the world, his insistence on the Universe as purposeful, and perhaps above all, the recognition that we are in the presence of a mystery that is both wonderful and awful, much of this, many years after the publication of his book, is now becoming a matter for serious thought among more advanced scientists. All of it is the subject of this book.

We have quoted at length from de Chardin to show the influence that Unity or Oneness had on his thinking. He was drenched in it. Nevertheless, this wholeness is converging towards a new unity, a unity of consciousness converging on and integrated around a central point. This unity converging upon unity and ultimately transcending it was for him the origin of meaning and purpose in the universe, a theme we have already introduced. Meaning is not something added to the universe, nor is it a property of the universe, but is the very dynamism of the Universe itself.

Purpose, de Chardin says at the outset, can be summed up in the verb "to see." In this de Chardin echoes what we shall be exploring later, that creativity and evolution are at bottom the same and are both the unfolding of idea (we must remember that for de Chardin the human being is a wholeness that unfolds). We shall want to establish clearly that the idea that unfolds is a field, which has a central point as focus. De Chardin calls this central focus the Omega point. "All bodies owe their origin to arrangements of a single initial corpuscular type." Moreover, not only bodies, but consciousness also is of this corpuscular type. He says, when talking about the first step into consciousness, the "living element, which heretofore has been spread out and divided over a diffuse circle of perceptions and activities, was constituted for the first time as a center in the form of a point at which all the impressions and experiences knit themselves together and fuse into a unity that is conscious of its own unity."[15] The ancients saw this clearly and made ⊙ the symbol for consciousness, the sun and for gold. The sun, for them, was the emissary of the life force. This same symbol is the symbol for the grain of consciousness.

Summing up

To truly grasp what we are referring to as Oneness one must see it as a power, or rather *the* power which is irresistible and by which the whole universe is carried forward. Turned back on itself, Unity is both a creative as well as a destructive power. One which is two, unus–ambo, is inconceivable except as ambiguity.

We have tried to show Unity as a force within human affairs by reference to simplicity: not-composed and not-complex simplicity. André Lamouche in his monumental work on simplicity has shown it to be a force in the physical, biological, and psychological realms. Out of unity turned back on itself come both the particle and the universe, each being what de Chardin calls of a "corpuscular type" consisting of a center and a halo. The center for the universe is, for de Chardin, the Omega point around which all is clustering in an ever-increasingly conscious way. According to de Chardin, then, development of consciousness is the purpose of the Universe.

Notes

1. Teilhard de Chardin, *The Phenomenon of Man* (London: Fount Paperbacks, 1959), p. 275,
2. de Chardin (1959, 36).
3. de Chardin (1959, 241).
4. de Chardin (1959, 59, 35).
5. de Chardin (1959, 48).
6. de Chardin (1959, 49).

7. de Chardin (1959, 39).
8. My emphasis.
9. de Chardin (1959, 46).
10. de Chardin (1959, 45).
11. de Chardin (1959, 45-46).
12. de Chardin (1959, 52); my emphasis.
13. de Chardin (1959, 192).
14. de Chardin (1959, 275).
15. de Chardin (1959, 183).

Chapter 7

The Interaction
of Body and Mind

Ever the same the moon among the clouds;
Different from each other, the mountain and the valley.
Wonderful, wonderful, wonderful. Is this one, or two?
MUMONKAN

God makes us to know him, and his knowing is his being.
MEISTER ECKHART

LET US RETURN NOW to ambiguity, or rather the ambiguity of ambiguity. Our deepest intuition says Unity is fundamental; One which is one and cannot be divided. Intuition also tells us that two is also fundamental: you and me, me and the world, good and bad, right and wrong, here and there? Everywhere we look we find duality. Is it one or two? As far as possible we must maintain the tautness of mind this invokes while reading this book. We have said that to embrace this ambiguity we must find a logic more fundamental than classical logic, which is based upon the law of identity, the law which insists that unity alone is basic. This more fundamental logic we are calling the logic of ambiguity.

The Relationship of Body and Mind

To see the dilemma that we are dealing with more clearly, consider one of the most intractable of all problems: the relationship of body and mind. This, according to Nobel Prize winner Francis Crick and his co-author Christof Koch, is the "overwhelming question in neuro-biology today."[1] In an article titled "On The Problem Of Consciousness," they said that "radically new" concepts may be needed to resolve the body/mind problem. They cited the new modifications of scientific thinking, forced on us by quantum mechanics, as an instance of science having to yield to a new way of thinking. It is worth noting that quantum mechanics has ambiguity as its foundation, and therefore the logic of ambiguity may well be just the new concept they are calling for.

Body and mind: Are these two, or are they one? Is mind dependent upon the brain; is it simply an epiphenomenon? If so, then our intuition of unity is satisfied. We are dealing with one "substance," a physical substance, in the form of the brain. The brain is governed by all the known laws of physics and, according to this point of view, our research into the mind would simply be an application of these laws. It is surprising to what an extent this point of view permeates our society. For example in a recent special edition on this very problem, *American Scientist* published twelve papers, only one of which addressed the mind in itself. The others took it for granted that the mind and brain were synonymous terms. The same bias is to be found in articles in a recent issue of *Time* magazine, as well as in *Maclean's* magazine.

If this point of view is the correct, it means that all our loves and hates, all that we treasure and value, our dearest hopes and fondest dreams are but movements of molecules, or the interactions of neurons. "Most neuroscientists," according to *American Scientist*, "now believe that all aspects of mind, including its most puzzling attribute — consciousness or awareness — are likely to be explainable in a more materialistic way as the behavior of large sets of interacting neurons."

However, in their article Crick and Koch are quite frank when they say:

> Until quite recently most cognitive scientists ignored consciousness, as did all neuro-scientists. The problem was felt to be either purely 'philosophical' or too elusive to study experimentally. It would not have been easy for a neuroscientist to get a grant just to study consciousness.[2]

It is true that science, by and large, has ignored consciousness. But another, opposing point of view says that it is not the mind that is the epiphenomenon of the brain but the brain (indeed all form) is an epiphenomenon, or creation, of the mind. This point of view is called *idealism*, and is held by some modern theoretical physicists (see Appendix 1). The idealist point of view, like that of the materialist given earlier, has the merit of satisfying our deep intuition of unity: There is only one substance, a *mind* substance.

Nevertheless it appears to be both given and irrefutable that "a world" exists which "I" encounter. We accept this implicitly, even though it also implies that the world is one kind of substance and I am another. The world is solid and real, but I seem to be something ephemeral, almost ghostlike. Descartes had doubts about the status of "I," but he resolved them in a very reasonable way. He simply said that even though I may doubt my own existence, the very fact of doubting proves my existence. "I think therefore I am." The result of his musings has become to be known as the Cartesian split because, according to him, the world was divided into two substances: a thinking substance and a physical substance, a *res cogitans* and a *res extensa*.

It should be pointed out that, although Descartes crystallized out a dual world view for the West, this view is not simply an historic accident. On the contrary it is implicit in the very root of our culture, which is based upon the Indo-European language. For example, one school of Buddhist thought says, "there are two, and only two sources of knowledge, the senses and the understanding, and . . . . they are utterly heterogeneous, so as to be the one the negation of the other."[3] A more recent Buddhist scholar affirms, "We . . . have a double world, in India just as in Europe, a sensible one and an intelligible one a *mundus sensibilis* and a *mundus intelligibilis* . . "

Is mind a product of matter, is matter a product of mind, or do mind and matter have equal status so neither is dependent upon the other? Are we dealing with one substance or with two, or with one substance that is two, a unus-ambo? Before going on, I want to change the wording of the question to: "Is *knowing* a product of *being* or is being a product of knowing?" Mind and matter are both loaded terms. Mind has many psychological overtones, and in recent years, matter has been seen to dissolve into particles and these particles into quanta of energy. For our purposes, the word "being" will refer to all that is not knowing; the word "knowing" will refer to all that is not being.

We must remember here that most neuroscientists are of the opinion that all aspects of mind, "including its most puzzling attribute — consciousness or awareness," can probably be reduced to material causes. This is where the integrity that Bridgman called for becomes important. Recall that Bridgman said, "Integrity demands that I *want* to know what the facts are and that I want to analyze and understand my mental tools and know what happens when I apply these tools to the facts."[4] He also said, "It is very difficult to get into words what I mean by the 'quality' of my sensation of red."[5] We know that a color can be analyzed in terms of wave length. But we also know that no quantitative analysis of color will tell us what the color red is. All that a physicist knows about color can be taught to a blind person. But one cannot teach a blind person what the color red means. An unbridgeable abyss lies between what the physicist and neurologist know about the color red and what you know about the color red when you see a red apple. A hiatus, which no amount of analysis can overcome, lies between knowing and being. To admit this strikes a mortal blow at classical logic. This blow has already been struck by the discovery of quantum reality, with the recognition that a photon is both a particle and a wave. The most elementary introspection will demonstrate the truth of what I am saying, and what was said by Descartes before me: knowing and being have equal status, they are irreducible to one another; the one is not the outcome of the other. Again we must return to the question: is it one, is it two? The impulse that drives the scientist to reject mind and to claim that all mental phenomena are physical phenomena in disguise, is not cussedness, but comes from the deep intuition of unity.

Mind and Matter: One Whole

One of the main themes developed by de Chardin, and important to what we are saying here, is that consciousness, or what we have called knowing, is inherent in the universe. It is not something that arrived in the world after a certain degree of complexity of matter had been attained. Although, as de Chardin pointed out, knowing is completely evident only in the human being, we should not therefore be tempted to believe it to be simply an isolated instance and of no special interest to a science of cosmology:

It is impossible to deny that, deep within ourselves, an interior appears at the heart of being, as it were seen through a rent.... Since the stuff of the universe has an inner aspect at one point of itself, there is necessarily a double aspect to its structure... co-extensive with the without there is a within to things.[6]

In his book, *Wholeness and the Implicate Order,* well-known scientist David Bohm says something similar:

Relativity and quantum theory agree, in that they both imply the need to look on the universe as an undivided whole, in which all parts of the universe, including the observer and his instruments, merge and unite in one totality . . . Mind and matter are not separate substances. Rather, they are different aspects of one whole and unbroken movement.[7]

Consider this analogy: A cup has an inside and an outside. These are obviously quite different, and we can scarcely confuse one with the other. But neither can we one reduce one to the other and say it is a derivative or is dependent upon the other. Yet it is one cup, not just an inside and an outside, but one seamless whole. Using this analogy, it might be said that mind is the inside of matter; matter the outside of mind; but, even so, there is one seamless whole. Just as we cannot confuse the inside with the outside, so we cannot confuse mind and matter, nor can we say that one is primary and the other secondary, nor that one is dependent upon the other.

Rollo May, a well-known psychologist, once wrote that "the human dilemma is that which arises out of a man's capacity to experience himself as both subject and object at the same time."[8] He went further and said that a colleague of his had remarked that, as a therapist, he alternated, "as in a tennis game, between seeing the patient as object — when he thinks of patterns, dynamics, reality testing, and other aspects of general principles to which the patient's behavior refers — and as subject, when he empathizes with the patient's suffering and sees the world through the patient's eyes."

This same ambiguity was pointed out, from a slightly different angle, by R. D. Laing who said,

even the same thing, seen from different points of view, gives rise to two entirely different descriptions, and the descriptions give rise to two entirely different theories, and the theories result in two entirely different sets of action.[9]

Later he says, "There is no dualism in the sense of the coexistence of two different essences or substances there in the object, psyche and soma: there are two different experiential Gestalts: person and organism.[10]

In a similar way we can view the color red from two different points of view: the physicist sees red as a quantity; when he puts away his instruments, however, he sees it as a quality.

The young/old women illustration in Chapter 5 represents, before we see it as a picture, *one* field of phenomena. This one field appears in two radically different ways: as a young woman on the one hand (which we can say represents knowing,) an old woman on the other (which we can say represents being). As Laing concluded, we are not talking about a dualism of two different substances: a mind substance and a material substance. Bohm said mind and matter are not separate substances. "Rather, they are different aspects of one whole and unbroken movement." One whole and unbroken movement is what we are calling dynamic unity. But even so, knowing is knowing and being is being.

Knowing and being are the dual aspect of Unity; as Eckhart says in the epigraph to this chapter "God's knowing is his being." Oneness/(knowing/being) should be seen as one seamless whole, not as three separate ingredients brought together. You cannot have Oneness without knowing/being, neither can you have knowing/being without Oneness. Nevertheless, a clear distinction must be made between knowing and being. Being can be studied by physics; knowing cannot. The aim of physics is to reveal and formulate relations between phenomena, but these relationships are revealed by knowing. Knowing itself, therefore, is not a phenomenon and has no parts between which relationships can be found. This means we should not try—as so much research into the mind, memory, and the brain is doing nowadays—to transform knowing into a complex, even a fantastically complex, set of relationships. Likewise, we must beware of trying to transform knowing into a subtle energy coterminous, so to say, with being and subject to the laws of physics. David Bohm, on another occasion, suggested this solution in a conversation with Renée Weber. "Consciousness," he suggested, "is possibly a more subtle form of matter and movement."[11]

All of this puts us into a quandary: is oneness homogenous? If so, how can it be knowing/being, which, if knowing and being are distinct, would imply it is two? Is it then two? If so, how can it be One? Laing said that there is no dualism in the sense of the coexistence of two different essences or substances there in the object, psyche and soma: there are two different experiential Gestalts: person and organism. But two different gestalts of what, and what is it that experiences the two different gestalts? If we say it is "the subject," we are simply driven back again into the ambiguity: is the subject soma or psyche, mind or matter? Logically, oneness is oneness: as such, it would have to be either knowing or being, and could not be both. This is confirmed by our illustration in Fig. 1: we cannot see the old woman when we see the young woman.

We seem to be at a complete impasse, caught up in an ultimate double bind something like that proposed by the Zen master who, holding up a stick said, "Do not say this is a stick; do not say this is not a stick. What is it?" Are we at an impasse because what we are talking about cannot be explained by normal logic, which has, as a basic axiom, A is either A or not-A (that is to say, A is either one or not one, two or not two, knowing or being)? As we have seen, a similar problem has been encountered in physics in the notion of the quantum field, and this prompted a French philosopher and mathematician, Lupasco, to develop a logic that bears some considerable resemblance (although there are also considerable differences) to the logic we are proposing.

In an article entitled "The Logic Of Conflict And Complementary Opposites," Marc Beigbeder wrote of Lupasco's logic:

> according to Lupasco one is always made up of two, more or less at the same moment. . . . The law of identity happens to be twinned at each moment and in all circumstances by its contrary principle, which is ignored by the law of identity. It co-exists, more or less everywhere with it. As for the second law of classical logic, the law of non-contradiction, it is no longer Manichaean, because the reality is the opposite of this law: A and not A are both true, real simultaneously; or rather they both share in the true, the real, because the true, the real, is what holds them together.
>
> As for the third law of classical logic, the logic of the excluded middle, A cannot both be A and Not A, it has its twin: the law of the included middle; these two laws also always go hand in hand, antagonistic and complementary, one with the other.[12]

In the same article, Beigbeder continued:

> Moreover Lupasco's logic is quite different from Hegel's or the implicit logic of Marx. Both these, it is true, have the force of contradiction in the dialectic; but in the first place, the dynamics of contradiction is found in succession rather than in coexistence. Antithesis arises after thesis and then causes synthesis. But, more than this, Hegel's logic suppresses the conflict by a non-conflicting fusion, the synthesis. In Lupasco's dialectic this fusion is not possible.[13]

Although Lupasco does not have an extensive following in America, mainly because his books have not been translated into English, nevertheless he is treated with considerable respect in France. In order for us to understand consciousness, creativity, evolution, and violence, then, it will be necessary for us to have recourse to a logic other than classical logic: the logic of ambiguity. This logic will include Lupasco's "logic of conflict and complementary opposites" but goes beyond it. The logic of ambiguity also includes classical logic. It must do so; one face of the ambiguity says there is no ambiguity, indeed there cannot be ambiguity: one is one; A=A. In the next chapter, we will explore this further.

Notes

1. Francis Crick and Christof Koch, "The Problem of Consciousness," *Scientific American* (Special issue, Sept. 1992).
2. Crick and Koch (1992, p. 153).
3. T. Stcherbatsky, *Buddhist Logic*, Vol. 1 (New York: Dover Publications, 1930), p. 74.
4. P. W. Bridgman, *The Way Things Are* (New York: Viking Press, 1959), 319.
5. Bridgman (1959).
6. de Chardin (1959, 61).
7. David Bohm, *Wholeness and the Implicate Order* (London: Routledge & Kegan Paul, 1980), p. 11.
8. Rollo May, *Psychology and the Human Dilemma* (New York: Van Nostrand, 1967), p. 8.
9. R. D. Laing, *The Divided Self* (London: Pelican, 1965), p. 20.
10. Laing (1965, 21).
11. Renée Weber, *Dialogues with Scientists and Sages* (London: Arkana, 1986).
12. See Marc Beigbeder, "The Logic of Conflict and Complementary Opposites," *Nouvelle Acropole* (Paris: juin-juillet-août, 1982), pp. 66-67.
13. Beigbeder (1982).

Part 2

Chapter 8

Evolution and the Basic Ambiguity

I am convinced that the two points of view, the materialist and the idealist, will 'unite in a generalized physics in which is the internal as well as the external.
TEILHARD DE CHARDIN

THE UNIVERSE IS SELF-GENERATING having no need for an exterior agency to initiate it or control it. Self generation is for some "evolution," for others "metamorphosis," and for others still, "emergence." Whatever we call it, self-generation is not the result of blind chance working in the dark with no purpose or meaning. Awareness, light, and meaning are fundamental to the universe, and therefore are intrinsic to evolution.

Artificial Intelligence

Recently a number of different scientists have created computer programs to simulate evolution. Their intention has been to show how, within a few parameters built into a program, forms or structures evolve, compete with other, mate, and procreate. The success of the programs has led these scientists to claim they have thereby proven that no *deus ex machina*, no *élan vital*, no purpose or intention is necessary for an understanding of the evolution of life forms. Evolution "just happens" once the preliminary and simple limits have been imposed.

The irony, however, is that these programs demonstrate quite the opposite.

For example, the claim that evolution does not need a *deus ex machina* is refuted by the presence of the scientist himself. He is the *deus ex machina* and chooses among a vast variety of highly sophisticated mathematical formulae in order to find the appropriate one to establish the necessary parameters. He is, moreover, likely to choose it initially on the basis of a hunch, a *feel* for its appropriateness.

The claim that intention or purpose is not necessary is refuted by the scientist's own purpose, which is to simulate a purposeless evolution. Whitehead points out the irony of this when he says, "Scientists animated by the purpose of proving they are purposeless, constitute an interesting subject for study."[1] If a particular formula for proving that evolution is possible without purpose does not give the desired result, it is refined, improved upon, or rejected, and another is sought. Thus, built into the program, is the scientist's intention. By "built in" I do not mean that one finds it in the binary logic of the program, but that the sequence and pattern of this program embody the scientist's intention.

The claim that *élan vital* is not necessary in the simulated evolution of species is refuted by the fact that, if a power failure occurs, the evolution stops; and, unless an automatic "save" has been installed into the program, all evolution would be lost. In other words, the electric current flowing from positive to negative gives the thrust to the simulated evolution. Another way of putting this is that time, or *durée*, or a dynamic unity is given by the current, which makes evolution possible.

Finally, the simulated evolution of the species does not proceed *ex nihilo*. On the contrary, the computer itself simulates a highly sophisticated cosmic gel or cosmic soup in which the new "life forms" crystallize. One only has to touch the innards of a computer inadvertently, and again evolution crashes to halt. This inadvertent touch is perhaps a metaphor for a slight change in the environment within which life forms arise and within which they can be destroyed.

Thus far from proving what he sets out to prove—that the evolution of life forms is a purely materialistic, purposeless, and valueless affair—the scientist, with his ingenious programs, might well prove just the opposite. Furthermore, the forms generated are not material forms at all, but purely symbolic forms, animated mathematical formulae with interesting graphics.

Just as chess playing programs do not *understand*, in an intuitive way, the strategies they use as a chess master does, so, within the working of these evolutionary programs, no creativity is involved. Perhaps evolution does not require creativity, and perhaps the chess master does not need to understand the moves he makes in an intuitive way, but these programs can do nothing to resolve the question, all that they can do is to pose it in a newer and more interesting way. Indeed, from what I have been saying it would seem that a kind of Godel's law could be proposed: One cannot consciously and intentionally prove the nonexistence of consciousness and intention.

Idealism Is Not an Answer

However, while we cannot reduce things down to mindless, purposeless movements of matter, idealism also is not a way to resolve the dilemma. Reality, standing apart from knowing, is not the product of knowing, and this is evident in the very "shock of encounter" and the way we respond to it. An English philosopher, on hearing of an idealist's argument that the world was simply an idea, struck the table in front of him and declared, "Thus do I refute him!" Just as integrity demands that we accept knowing, so we must accept being in the ecology of existence. And yet this shock of encounter, this opposition between *knowing* and *being,* also can be understood in the self-generation of the universe. It is just this opposition that provides the impetus and purpose for self-generation. The purpose is to restore harmony and unity, which is lost when knowing and being are separated through opposition. The force of Oneness provides the impetus, *"that there can be no 'other.'"* Harmony is restored, not by a retreat to an original unity but by constant creativity, a constant self-generation.

It could equally be said that self-generation comes from the need to resolve conflict. Sometimes the resolution of conflict fails, or is incomplete, and destruction takes the place of construction. Destruction, therefore, is also fundamental. Inner conflict comes from the basic ambiguity: there is an ambiguity, one face of which says there is *no ambiguity* while the other face says there *is ambiguity.* This is the simplest formulation possible of the logic underlying self-generation.

The Struggle: Duality Within Unity

Evolution comes from a struggle, and the struggle is a yearning, what the Sufi's call the sigh of God—a sigh that is expressed in the words, "I was a hidden treasure and I yearned to be known, then I created creatures in order to be known by them."[2] "Yearning to be known" is unity yearning to reveal itself, and to know itself, expressed mystically as, "through the One to see in One with the eye of One."[3] Giving to the universe emotions such as yearning, talking about striving to resolve the basic ambiguity, may give the impression I am reverting back to animism or even to an anthropomorphism gone mad. However, I am following the time honored formula of "As above so below." The idea that the microcosm is *isomorphic* with the macrocosm is an idea as ancient as reason. It is echoed today in the mathematics of fractals, in holography, and in the notion of harmonics;[4] it is also basic to the understanding of the monad. The notion of isomorphism is embedded in the very notion of "reason" and the "rational,"[5] words which have the same origin as "ratio." It was this insight into the isomorphism of the microcosm and the macrocosm that inspired de Chardin to say, "That all bodies owe their origin to arrangements of a single initial corpuscular type is the beacon that lights the history of the universe to our eyes."

In the introduction, we said that each person is not part of the whole but, instead, is the whole. The traditional way of speaking about this was to see each individual as a microcosm. However, the word *monad*, which is Greek for *One* suits our purposes better because it refers both to the macrocosm as well as to the microcosm.

The Differentiation with the Monad

A pearl grows within an oyster because a particle of sand is deposited within its shell. This particle causes an irritation and, in its endeavor to free itself from this irritation, the oyster produces a pearl. This could be looked upon as an analogy for evolution; evolution occurs because of a deposit within the monad itself. The analogy must not be pushed too far because the particle of sand comes from outside the oyster, whereas the deposit, from which evolution unfolds, has its origin *within* the monad.[6]

What I am proposing and will shortly demonstrate is that the monad, which I have also called One/being/knowing, through the dynamism inherent in the basic ambiguity, will evolve through the many stages of matter and life into an individual human being with consciousness. What I am going to suggest further is that the purpose of evolution comes from the need to reabsorb what I shall be calling the *null point*, just like the pearl comes from the need the oyster has to assimilate the particle of sand.

The Null Point

Earlier I quoted de Chardin, saying that the whole purpose of evolution was the perfection of consciousness around an ultimate center called the Omega point. Unity as wholeness is striving towards Unity as Omega point, the dynamic center of a universal consciousness. As we shall see, de Chardin's Omega point and what I mean by "null point' are quite similar. Let us explore the implications of this.

Because oneness is not simply an abstract principle or an empty box wherein everything finds its place, it can be regarded as an imperative—a cosmic, categorical imperative. "Let there be One!" In terms of knowing/being, one alternative of this imperative would command: "Know or Be!" Using the young/old woman as analogy again the command would be "Young or old woman!'

The Opposition of Knowing Being

That the world *is*, is (except to some philosophers drowning in words) incontestably the case. In fact, many people like to emphasize this *isness* by saying not simply "it is" but "it is *real*." But what do we mean when we say this? How do we know that the world (for example, this page) *is* or is real? Some people would respond, "Because I see it, feel it, touch it." But is the page real because we see it, or can it be seen because it is real? If the former, then the reality of the page [being] is dependent upon being seen (knowing), a point that the idealists latch on to for their argument; if the latter, then being is independent of knowing. The idealist would support his argument by saying that while we dream, what we dream is real, while under the influence of hallucinatory drugs, the hallucinations are real. We are mistaken if we confuse dreams or hallucinations with the everyday world, but we are not mistaken when we say each of these is real. Dreams, delusions, and hallucinations as well as seeing hearing feeling are all forms of knowing/being. But I maintain that this argument simply proves that knowing and being cannot be separated, not that being is dependent upon knowing. Consider a mirror and its reflection: A mirror is not its reflection, neither is the reflection the mirror. But they cannot be separated.

Some people may want to say the so-called waking world is more real than the dream world, because it has a greater impact. But then many people who have had what are called "spiritual experiences" say that these experiences are much *more* real than what is encountered in the waking state. Impact, therefore, cannot be a criterion, but neither can certainty. Uncertainty and anxiety are unquestionably real to the people who suffer them, although what they are anxious about may not be real for another. What I want to say, therefore, is that, although things are real, this reality is *given* to them, or to our experience of them, or to our feelings about them; it is not found "in" them, nor is it known "through" them.

Reality, furthermore, is not agreement. A pain I have is real, whatever its source, while to another my pain has no reality at all. Reality is reality and, because irreducible to knowing, it is not dependent upon knowing. Knowing and reality—or, as I have preferred to call them, knowing and being—are therefore two and of equal status. The conclusion we must come to is that the only criterion we can use to determine whether something is (is real) is the criterion of reality itself. To judge that something *is*, we use the criterion of isness itself. What I am saying, therefore, is that we cannot know being; to know being would be to make it subservient to knowing. On the other hand, however, without being there would be nothing to know. This means that the command "knowing *or* being!"—coming from the imperative "Let there be one!"—cannot be obeyed. For knowing and being to be reduced to one, either knowing would have to be derived from being, or being would have to be derived from knowing. Yet neither knowing nor being can give way to the other.

But the imperative cannot be denied either.

The Evolution of Basic Ambiguity

Let us trace the evolution of the basic ambiguity inherent within One/ knowing/being remembering that it can never be resolved, but at each new level it simply shows another of its faces. Remember, this evolution occurs within the monad and that "the natural changes of monads come from an internal principle." To trace this evolution, we will start at the very beginning, at the generation of the null point, which emerges out of the clash of opposites of knowing and being. This means that the null point emerges out of the attempt to find unity. When I write of wanting to re-absorb the null point, I mean just that: wanting to restore unity. This is the archetypal creative act, and a creative act, as Koestler pointed out earlier, comes from the unity of "two self-consistent but incompatible frames of reference."

The injunction "Oneness: knowing or being!" and the impossibility of obeying it brings about what I call a confrontation between knowing and being. As a very rough analogy, which must not be pushed too far, we could think of two tomcats staring at each other. This contest is between two incarnations of the One. The imperative, "Let there be One!" is im-placable, but neither can give way to the other because each is the One. Often cats do just back off, look away, and, after a while, turn and leave the scene. But sometimes neither will back off, tension mounts, and a field of force is generated. This confrontation could well end in a battle: a will to destroy the other's will, to force the other to submit and so recant its claim to be the One.[7]

This battle will only occur if the two are so evenly matched that neither can give way to the other. A field of force is generated within the field of awareness of each cat. Each cat is both the one staring *and* the one stared at, both center and periphery. Each cat is unity, that which enables it to retain its integrity, to remain whole. If it gives way, the cat will have to tear this wholeness in two, to separate itself from itself. Sooner or later, undoubtedly one or the other cat would have to give way because of the implacable Oneness in the guise of the other cat. The break down of the cat's resolve comes from its losing the center and so it becomes power-less and must flee the scene. After it has fled, with the accompaniment of humiliation and pain, a healing process will be possible and the center restored.

But in the "confrontation" of knowing/being, *neither can flee, nor can one vanquish the other.* They are like two perfectly matched, equally invin-cible cats. Their polarization creates a field of force much in the same way that the north and south poles of a magnet create a field of force. But this confrontation does not occur between a center and an outside periphery. It occurs within the monad, within a center, which is also at the periph-ery of itself as center. Because of the imperative of Oneness, such a con-frontation cannot go on indefinitely; after a while a resolution has to be found—a resolution through *oscillation.* It is as though the cats simultaneously take to chasing each other in a circle, each chasing but at the same time being chased. Oscillation could be given a variety of names such as alternation, cyclicity, and spin, but it too can only last for so long—that is, it can only last until, through the force of the imperative, oscillation reaches the maximum possible speed.

When maximum speed is attained a hiatus or *null interval* will emerge in the oscillating field of knowing/being, a null interval which is *neither knowing nor being* but which instead is pure unity, an interval without content or quality. The null point will emerge out of the null interval.

To illustrate this we must leave the analogy of the cats and refer back to the picture of the young and old lady that we have used as the paradigm of ambiguity.

I ask you to do a simple exercise to help demonstrate what this null interval means. First see the old lady; then see the young lady. You might like to do this once or twice to get the feel of it. What is important to notice is that, in order to see the old lady and *then* to see the young lady, you must momentarily let go of both. In other words, a leap must be made, a leap across a null interval. *Now* one sees the old lady, *now* one sees the young lady. Although the "now" is continuous, the "seeing" is not. No bridge spans the two "seeings," no transitional step marks the way. Between seeing the young lady and seeing the old

Fig.2:

lady is a point which is neither the one nor the other. The point where neither young nor old lady can be perceived is what I have called the null interval.

If now, instead of talking about the old lady and the young lady, we refer to knowing/being, we see that the null interval is *neither knowing nor being*. What this means is that, because of this hiatus in the knowing/being field, an interval of negation, negation as negation of knowing and negation of being simultaneously emerges. This negation we may refer to as "not-knowing" on the one hand, or "nothing" on the other.

The struggle, nevertheless, continues. Because neither side can yield to the other, and yet one must triumph over the other, the rate of oscillation between knowing and being increases. This increase corresponds to a diminution in the duration of knowing   on the one hand and of being on the other. The rate of oscillation will increase until it reaches a given level where the duration of the null interval will be as long as the duration of either   knowing or being. *This will cause the field to freeze as negation,* and a null point emerges having independent existence.[8] If this freezing did not take place then both knowing and being would be swallowed in a vortex of annihilation. The null point prevents this swallowing.

An etching of Escher's illustrates this hiatus well. It shows a man looking at a picture in a gallery. The picture that he is viewing is that of a man, himself, looking at a picture in a gallery. The man is both an *observer* of the picture and a *participant* in that same picture. Thus Escher's picture is an illustration of a center which is also at the periphery of itself as center. He has painted a white circle that covers the point of hiatus that arises as one switches viewpoint from observer to participant. This white circle is there because he cannot depict this point of transition in the picture because this point *is a negation,* so to say a kind of black hole.

One can experience this impossibility for oneself in another way. Imagine, for the moment, that you are on a stage as an actor [a participant] in a play. Now imagine that you are in the audience [as an observer] of the same play. Now be both at once! One obviously cannot do this, but if one tries an oscillation occurs and a moment of transition arrives when one is nowhere—neither audience nor actor, neither knowing nor being.

The null point is negation, which arises out of a basic oscillation, an oscillation that perhaps gives rise to all energy vibrations. Interestingly enough, the idea of an oscillating universe is to be found in the Buddhist and Sufi traditions and has also recently reappeared in the writings of a modern scientist, David Peat. I have included what they have to say in Appendix 2.

The null point is a cosmic irritant that brings about evolution. Again let me draw upon de Chardin's intuition that the thrust of evolution is towards the Omega point: "Man is not the center of the universe as was once thought in our simplicity but something much more wonderful—the arrow pointing the way to the final unification of the world in terms of life."[9] The arrow toward final unification of the world in terms of life is the thrust towards reabsorbing the null point. On another occasion de

Chardin says, "the evolution of the cosmos has to be seen as a movement oriented upon a cosmic central point." This cosmic point could well be the null point. When talking about the world he says, "The noosphere (and more generally the world) represent a whole that is not only closed but also *centered.*" The whole that is not only closed but is centered is what I have referred to as the monad.

A fundamental difference between what de Chardin is saying and what I am saying, however, is that in my view the impetus to evolution is not to *arrive* at the center but to *reabsorb* the null point. This attempt to reabsorb the null point comes from the thrust towards unity, an attempt that is doomed to failure and which makes the universe a perpetual motion machine. The attempt as it persists will bring forth different guises for the center, first the original monad, then the atom, then the cell, then the grain of consciousness, then, according to de Chardin, the Omega point. But why should it stop there?

Before leaving this place, I need to make an adjustment to the definition of fundamental ambiguity. I said before that there is an ambiguity one face of which says there is no ambiguity while the other face says there is ambiguity. Now I must qualify the definition further by saying "the face that says there is no ambiguity is not unambiguous being both the Inclusive and the exclusive One."[10] The new definition therefore reads there is an ambiguity one face of which says there is no ambiguity, but this face itself is not unambiguous.

Notes

1. Alfred North Whitehead, *The Function of Reason* (Princeton, NJ: Princeton University Press, 1929).

2. Henri Corbin, *Creative Imagination in the Sufism of Ibn 'Arabi* (Princeton: Bollingen Series, 1969; Ralph Manheim, trans.), p. 114.

3. "An initiate, 'one who through God sees in God with the eye of God'" (Corbin, 1969, p. 119).

4. See, as an example, Rodney Collins, *The Theory of Celestial Influence* (London: Vincent Stuart, 1954).

5. a: b; c: d

6. The German philosopher, scientist and mathematician, Leibnitz, made the notion of the monad accessible, and it will be useful to refer to his writings. He wrote, "the natural changes of monads come from an *internal principle.*" (In the case of the oyster, sand.) He says further, "besides the principle of change

there must be differentiation within that which changes," "Differentiation within that which changes" is a description of evolution. Elaborating upon differentiation, Leibnitz says it "must involve a plurality within the unity or the simple. This plurality within the unity is what is called perception." Putting this in the words I have been using, he is saying evolution must involve "plurality within unity," in other words: the ambiguity of knowing/being within unity. Careful analysis of what Leibnitz says shows Oneness/knowing/being to be precisely the anatomy of the monad. Let us make that analysis. Leibnitz introduces the monad by saying it is "nothing but a *simple* substance which enters into compounds; *simple*, that is to say, without parts." Simple without parts means Oneness, from which the particle of sand emerges. This, as we shall see in just a moment, makes it possible, and indeed necessary, for matter, life, and consciousness to evolve. He also says the monad is a "simple *substance*." I have preferred to use the term "being" instead of substance, although the etymology of the word substance, "that which stands under," would make it as eligible as "being" for what I have in mind. And, finally, he says evolution comes from "the plurality in the unity," which he says is perception; what I would say "knowing/being." Leibniz quotations are from Mary Morris (trans.) *Leibniz: Philosophical Writings* (London: Everyman's Library No.. 905, 1956), pp 4-7.

7. Ethologists have remarked, sometimes with surprise, that very rarely do these confrontations end in the death of one or the other of the contestants. But this is not surprising because the death of the other is not the point of the contest; the point is to get the other to recant. The point is not even to assert oneness, because this would be tantamount to its denial: oneness has to be taken for granted. This taking Oneness for granted is why wars are essentially "defensive" wars, wars against an aggressor. The famous chip on the shoulder was but a device to get another to be the aggressor, "to start something" and then force him to retract. Winning therefore would not be gaining superiority but letting superiority shine out by itself.

8. Let us not forget that the etymology of the word exist means "to stand outside of."

9. de Chardin op cit. p. 247

10. Von Franz says, the paradox, or ambiguity, of one/two is contained within the Pythagorean cosmogony in the "idea that the monad, sometimes represents the one original arche of the world and sometimes reveals itself as the generating single seed (thus revealing only one side of the its two antithetical series.)" The original arche is what we have called the field; the "generating single seed" is the null point. Marie-Louise Von Franz, trans. by Andrea Dykes, *Number And Time Reflections Leading Toward A Unification Of Depth Psychology And Physics* (Evaston: Northwestern University Press, 1974), note on pp. 62-63.

Chapter 9

On Awareness

We can be aware of certain things in a way that is quite different from focussing our attention upon them.
MICHAEL POLYANI AND HARRY PROSCH

I N THE LAST CHAPTER I said that we cannot know being. This means, more concretely, that I do not see the page in front of me. To say this may well seem absurd, and it is certainly contrary to common sense. Let me, therefore, spend a little time on understanding this apparent absurdity. To help with the presentation I will again generalize. Instead of saying "I do not see the book," I will say "I am not *aware of* the book," or, better still, "I am not aware of being." "Awareness-of" includes all the senses: seeing, hearing, smelling, touching, tasting, and thinking. What I call "being" is the object of these senses—that is, colors, sounds, smells, textures, tastes, and thoughts.

If, as common sense tells us, I see a page, but (as we have seen) knowing and being are quite distinct, how is interaction possible between seeing and the page, between knowing and being? Everyday experience seems to indicate they do interact. On the one hand, *being* impinges upon and modifies *knowing*: for example, the page (or, more precisely, the light waves reflected by the page) impinges upon the retina of the eye, and I see. On the other hand, *knowing* impinges upon and modifies *being*. This is demonstrated even as I write these words. Ideas flow from the mind and are translated, in some way, into movements of muscle, bone and flesh—all matter, in other words, "being." The results of these movements are words written on the page before me. Therefore, my statement "knowing does not encounter being" (or, do I not see the page) would appear to be false. How am I to justify making it then?

This is, by no means, a new problem. Rather, it is simply a restatement of the mind/body problem. Traditionally, two answers have been offered: on one hand, "it is not possible"; on the other, "the two, mind and matter, run parallel courses." The first alternative also has two sides: mind and matter do not interact because mind is simply the outcome of matter organized into complex structures. Seeing, hearing, smelling and so on can all be reduced to neurological structures and activity.[1] The other way of denying the interaction between seeing and the world is the idealist way promulgated by some Eastern and Western philosophers who say everything is a product of mind—everything is an illusion or a dream—and therefore being has no independent existence, and so cannot impinge upon knowing.

The other alternative (i.e. knowing and being run on parallel tracks) is the belief that mind and matter are like two rails of a train track—they never meet, nor do they influence each other in any way. This argument agrees with the idealist's view that human beings create their own worlds; for instance, the world of an aborigine and the world of a modern Westerner are vastly different. Both are different, self-contained worlds. The same argument also agree with the materialist's view that the atomic, molecular, and cellular activity, as well as the nervous system, are responsible on the physical plane for all that is known but without the help of consciousness or awareness. But as we have seen, the idealist and the materialist point of view cancel each other out; logically one can equally well justify holding either of them. But, if they are both true, as the parallellists feel, then why does commonsense insist on there being a connection between them.

Before we leave this discussion, I must point out that some scientists have tried to find such a connection. Wilder Penfield, the celebrated neurologist, felt that part of the brain was responsible for an interaction.

Penfield also helps us understand the problem and its difficulty of solution. In *The Mystery of Mind*, he wrote that two hypotheses are possible:

(a) that man's being consists of one fundamental element, and (b) that it consists of two. "However," as he says, "the brain mechanisms . . . would have to be employed on the basis of either alternative." But, he adds, "there is no good evidence that the brain alone can carry out the work that the mind does. I conclude that it is easier to rationalize man's being on the basis of two elements than on the basis of one."[2]

Unfortunately, he then, tantalizingly, goes on to straddle both alternatives. On the one hand, he says that all through his life as a scientist, "I have proceeded on the one-element hypothesis . . . that activities of the highest centers and mental states are one and the same thing, or different sides of the same thing."[3] On the other hand, in his foreword to Penfield's book Yale Professor of Moral philosophy Charles Hendel says that he found a "convincing justification of your hypothesis and belief that the mind has a distinct being from the body, although intimately related and dependent on the body."[4] But the question remains, when does mind become body, or body become mind. When we put the question in this way, we have to admit that either mind is always body, or it is impossible for mind and body to interact.

A New Way of Understanding Awareness

So now let me try to justify this startling statement that we cannot be aware of the world. To do this, I need to make an analysis of awareness itself, and show that, in addition to pure awareness and awareness-of, another awareness exists which we will call *awareness-as*. Unfortunately, as you will see, I will have to strain the language a bit to accommodate this new insight. However, let me stress that the insight comes not from a philosophical necessity but from many years of meditation, and cumbersome expressions seem a small price to pay for this understanding. The distinction between the three types of awareness, and we shall add a fourth on the way, is so important that we shall spend the next several chapters clarifying, explaining and showing the value of making it.

Touching and Feeling

First let me make a distinction between *touching* and *feeling*. Touching is quite innocuous; it contains no drama. But already, even in so slight a contact, a seed is sown. You will see what I mean if, instead of talking about *touching*, I talk about *feeling* something. Touching is not the same as feeling; they are qualitatively different. Although this difference may seem innocuous, it is fundamental.

A carpenter picks up a piece of wood, he holds it, then he passes his hand across its surface. He *feels* the wood. On the one hand is the carpenter (or, better still, the hand passing over the wood), on the other is the wood. The hand is active, the wood, passive, inert. Now, let me ask, does the feeling belong to the hand, or does it belong to the wood? To make the question more meaningful, let me ask you to participate in a simple exercise: Please pass your hand over the surface of this page. Then ask yourself the question, "Where does the hand end and the page begin?" [You might find this easier if you close your eyes as you do this.] If you do this, you will see that, although the page and the sensation in the hand are quite different and the one cannot be confused with the other, the feeling is *one*. To see better what is meant by this, ask yourself, "What in the feeling is given by the page, what by the hand?" In Zen a similar question is asked, "Does the ear go to the sound or does the sound go to the ear?"[5] Where does hearing end and sound begin? Or where does sound end and hearing begin? The feeling is one yet also two; the hearing is one, yet also two: hand and page, ear and sound, each irreducible to the other.[6]

Awareness-as and Awareness-of

When you feel the page, what do you feel? [I ask you to do this so you can see we are dealing with a reality and not simply with a semantic quibble.] Coolness, smoothness, the resistance of the page? Now let me ask another question. What are you aware of? You will no doubt say that one is aware of the coolness, the smoothness, the resistance and so on, believing all the while that the two questions—"what do you feel?" and "what are you aware of?"—are exactly the same question. However, close attention will reveal a fundamental difference between feeling the coolness of the page and being *aware of* feeling the coolness of the page.

Feeling and touching are often looked upon as synonyms, but within the context we are proposing they are quite different. On one side is simple touching without any awareness-of touching. On the other is feeling: touching with awareness-of this touching. Awareness-of transforms touching into feeling. In order to help with the discussion I will use the word feeling to mean specifically "touching with awareness-of touching," and the word touching to mean one is "not aware of touching." Similar distinctions can be made between hearing and listening, and between looking and seeing: in these cases listening is *awareness-of* hearing, seeing is *awareness-of* looking. For example, one can *hear* a noise and then *listen* to see whether it is repeated. One cannot doubt one *hears* the music at a movie, but how often does one *listen* to it? Also, it makes perfect sense to say "I was *looking* right at it but did not *see* it." Again, awareness-of transforms looking into seeing and hearing into listening.

Now let me introduce the notion of "awareness-as" because, although touching might be said to occur without the accompaniment of awareness-of touching, nevertheless touching is not *unawareness*. Touching is awareness, but not awareness-of the page. Instead it would be better to say it is awareness-as the page; or, better still, 'awareness-as coolness, as smoothness, and so on. This brings us to the heart of the matter because, as we saw above, we cannot separate touching into what comes from the hand and what comes from the page. Touching is one seamless whole, even though on the one hand is "awareness" as knowing, and on the other is page as being, and the two are quite distinct.

It could be said that touching combines these two: when I touch the page it seems that awareness and page are brought together. Yet immediate experience refutes this superficial view that they are "brought together," because no boundary exists to say where awareness ends and the page begins; nor where the page ends and awareness begins. Awareness/page are just one—or, better still, awareness/smoothness is one; awareness/coolness is one, and so on. The bringing together occurs *after* the fact of touching, not before. There is awareness/smoothness and then, "What is smooth?" "Ah yes! The page." "What is awareness?" "Oh, I am aware of the page." In truth, even to say touching is awareness/smoothness, awareness/coolness is too much. Touching is upstream of all verbalization and is not in any way dependent upon consciousness, language and thought.

British philosopher F. H. Bradley put it this way:

> We in short have experience in which there is no distinction between
> my awareness and that of which it is aware. There is an immediate feel-

ing, *a knowing and being in one* [my emphasis] with which knowledge begins; and though this in a manner is transcended, it nevertheless remains throughout as the present foundation of my known world.[7]

So, I can say, "I was looking at it but did not see it"—which means I was looking at it but was not aware of looking at it. If we were to use more precise language, instead of saying "I am aware of the world," we would say "I am *aware of awareness-as* the world." If you will look around the room what you are aware of is not the room; you are aware of awareness-as the room.

I appreciate that the expression "awareness-of awareness-as the room" may seem strange and, because of its strangeness, you might be tempted to believe that it is unnecessarily cumbersome and complex. However, it is much less complex and cumbersome and much more precise than the terminology used by psychology: preconscious, subconscious, conscious, unconscious processes, the unconscious, subliminal, ego, super-ego and so on. Indeed, awareness-of awareness is quite a common expression. All I am doing is showing that *two qualitatively different kinds* of awareness are clearly involved.

Even this is not new. In their book *Meaning*, Michael Polanyi and Harry Prosch speak about two different kinds of awareness and, although there are some minor differences between what they say and what I am saying, yet the similarities far outweigh the differences. In the extract below, the comments between the square brackets are mine.

A striking feature of knowing a skill is the presence of two different kinds of 'awareness of' the things that we are skillfully handling. When I use a hammer to drive in a nail, I attend to both, but quite differently. I watch [am aware of] the effects of my strokes on the nail as I wield the hammer. I do not feel that its handle has struck my palm but that its head has struck the nail. In another sense of course, I am highly alert to the feelings in my palm and fingers holding the hammer [awareness-as]. They guide my handling it effectively, and the degree of attention I give to the nail is given to those fingers to the same extent. But in a different way. The difference may be stated by saying that these feelings are not watched in themselves, but that I watch something else by being aware of them . . . I may say that I have a subsidiary 'awareness of' the feelings in my hand which is merged into my focal 'awareness of' my driving the nail.

The two different kinds of awareness which we found interwoven in the use of a hammer are present in the same way in our 'awareness of' any set of particulars perceived a as whole.[8]

An Example of Awareness-as

Because the distinction between awareness-as and awareness-of is so basic to what I am going to say, let us look at some striking examples of awareness-as to show that the distinction is valid and not dependent upon definitions alone.

Indeed, several accounts are found in literature of the experience of awareness-as the Other. In fact, the experience is so common that, in Sanskrit, the word *samadhi* is used to denote it. Samadhi may appear spontaneously, or as the result of spiritual practice.[9] Here is an extract from an account of spontaneous samadhi: the writer said she was standing at the edge of a low cliff overlooking the sea where birds were swooping in the sky when suddenly her mind switched gears.

> I still saw the birds and everything around me but instead of standing looking at them, I was them and they were me. I was also the sea and the sound of the sea and the grass and the sky. Everything and I were the same, all one.[10]

The expression, "instead of standing looking at them, I was them" could be translated, using the terminology we have developed, as "'instead of standing, aware of [awareness-as] them, I was just aware as them." There was a diminution of awareness-of awareness as the birds, sea and grass, leaving simply awareness-as them.

Zen master Bassui put it this way:

> The universe and yourself are of the same root, you and every single thing are a unity. The gurgle of the stream and the sigh of the wind are [your voice.] The green of the pine, the white of the snow, these are [your color"].[11]

One might protest that the woman must have been residually aware of the situation; otherwise, how could she both remember and report upon the experience? This is true, and the objection only points out more clearly that, while a clear distinction can be made between awareness-of (which is focused awareness) and awareness-as (which is unfocused), they are, nevertheless, both pure awareness, or what I have called knowing. This diminution in awareness-of is possible because, as I have noted, awareness-of evolves out of awareness-as, and so the diminution is simply a reversion to this earlier condition.

Awareness-as is fundamental, undifferentiated awareness. It underlies looking, hearing, smelling touching, and so on in the same way the clay of a pot can be said to underlie its form. Even so, it should not be thought of as simply a feature of the senses. Although awareness-as *may* be manifest as the senses—as hearing, seeing, and so on—this is not always so, because it also underlies memories, dreams, imagination, even hallucinations and delusions. Not only this, it underlies awareness itself—as for example, when one is simply "aware as awareness," which is a state of deep samadhi.[12]

A difficulty arises when talking about awareness-as because when our attention is directed toward awareness-as we become aware of it. That is, we are now aware of and awareness-as is no longer apparent. This means that although it is ever present, even in sleep, it is only by under going special spiritual training that we can be aware as without the intervention of focussed awareness.

Interaction Between Knowing and Being

Now let us return to the question that started this chapter, which we have not yet answered: what, if anything, is the connection between knowing and being? How does mind interact with matter? It has not been possible so far to understand the interaction of mind and matter, or knowing/being, because of an unwillingness to come to terms with ambiguity. Once we are willing to come to terms with the possibility that the logic of ambiguity is a more fundamental logic than traditional logic—and once we recognize, as Bohm suggests, that the *law of identity* in logic is a secondary, but special case of ambiguity—then the question virtually drops away as we no longer have a body/mind *problem* but a body/mind *ambiguity*.

Let us take an ordinary, everyday situation as an example, so we can be sure that we know what the problem is. Let us suppose that you are driving and come to a traffic light which is yellow and a about to turn red. You check in your rearview mirror and see that another motorist is within a few feet of your trunk. You decide not to stop and go across the intersection just as the lights turn red.

A commonsense way to interpret this is to say that the traffic lights emit light waves that enter your eye and send a stimulus to the brain, so you see a red light. (This could be understood as the activity of matter) At the same time you ask yourself, "Should I stop?" (This is the activity of mind.) You look into the rearview mirror and see a motorist. (This once again could be seen as the activity of matter.) At the same time you think, "No, he's too close. I dare not stop." (This could be seen as mind.) So you accelerate and go through the intersection. In this commonsense way of looking at the situation, mind and matter, knowing and being, are inter-mixed at will.

However, this would not be a very scientific way of looking at things. A neurologist might well say that all that business about decisions and thoughts is unnecessary, that what really occurs is the movement of mol-ecules from beginning to end. He would see it all from the objective point of view, the point of view of matter. He may well claim to be able one day to map exactly the route of all the stimuli and responses that pass through the brain, to prove his point. On the other hand, from a psychotherapist's point of view, what is important is what you felt, how you acted, what you decided, and so on. What you *thought* you saw would be as important as, perhaps even more important than, what you actually saw. The psychologist would not be interested in synapses, neural paths, brain chemistry, or molecular movements. A parallelist would say that both the neurologist and the psychologist are right: each of the two worlds has its own laws and processes, but neither impinges upon the other. Yet we still have to face the fact that a mental decision did have a physical effect—the car went faster. The yellow light, the proximity of the other car, the intersection, the speed of the car, all of which we could call physical, had an effect on the mind and brought about the mental question, "Should I stop?" Furthermore, at one moment equal pressure is on you to stop and to accelerate. The logjam was broken by a decision.

Once more it seems as though we are in a cul de sac, unless we use the logic of ambiguity. When we do so, a simple resolution of the whole affair falls into place. In one way it is regrettable that it is so simple. For a question that has racked the minds of so many, one almost hopes the so-lution should be very complicated requiring very arcane mathematics for its resolution. Because it is so simple, many will want to reject it. In another way, however, it is just as well that the resolution is simple; because, as the question touches on the most fundamental ground of existence, its resolution cannot be complex. It must be a resolution that is valid at the simplest of levels.

Resonance

We are interested in the interaction between body and mind, or, more generally, between being and knowing. So let us look for a while at the relationship of mind and matter in the evolution of life forms. In doing so we can call on the work of a biologist Rupert Sheldrake, who introduces an interesting notion of *resonance* as a possible answer to the question about how mind interacts with matter. Later we can adapt what we learn from this detour to the problem of the interaction of mind and body.

Researches in microbiology, particularly the researches in DNA and RNA, has led scientists to conclude that evolution is dependent upon genes [being], and the evidence is overwhelmingly in favor of this. But to claim that this research will provide answers to all the problems surrounding evolution is akin to an out of space visitor saying a symphony is simply the movement of various kinds of instruments which produce sound waves. What about the composer, what about the score?

Could it be, using the musical metaphor, that genes stand to evolution as tones stand to a musical composition? The tones of music are physical limits within which the intelligence of the composer works. Is this what genes are? Are they physical limits within which an intelligence works? Let us remember that when we listen to a piece of music we only hear the interaction of tones. We do not hear the intelligence of the composer. This must be inferred. In a similar way, when we look at an organism we see only the result of the interaction of genes. We do not see the "composer." Let us explore this as a way to understand the body/mind interaction without doing violence to the work of scientists like Monod, while, at the same time, satisfying those who recognize that awareness also must be taken into account.

Some evolutionary changes occur, Sheldrake suggests, because of the influence of what he called *morphogenic* (or *morphic*) fields, which have an influence upon genetic structures. Sheldrake says these fields "seem to be a new kind of field so far unknown to physics, but at the same time not to be new fields at all."[13] In our musical metaphor, these fields would play the role of the composer of the symphony of existence.

One of the characteristics of the field, Sheldrake says, is me-mory, and this ties in closely with what we are saying. According to Sheldrake:

> If morphogenic fields contain an inherent memory, their evolution can be conceived of in a radically different way. They are not transcendent forms, but are immanent in organisms. They evolve within the realm of nature, and they are influenced by what has happened before.[14]

In other words, Sheldrake observes, the structure of the field depends upon what happened before, and what has happened before is held in memory. Furthermore, the field does not transcend the forms any more than the music transcends the tone.

The influence of memory occurs through what Sheldrake calls "morphic resonance," which he says, "does not involve a transfer of energy from one system to another, but rather a non-energetic transfer of information. However, morphic resonance does resemble the known kinds of resonance because it takes place on the basis of rhythmic patterns of activity."[15] The information he is referring to, which is now believed to be the origin of form, "is seen to reside in molecules, cells, tissues, the environment often latent but causally potent, allowing these entities to recognize, select, and instruct each other, to construct each other and themselves, to regulate, control, induce, direct, and determine events of all kinds."[16]

Sheldrake criticizes traditional biologists' view of information because they do not specify whether this information is physical or mental. Furthermore, as he says, "if information is indeed to explain the development of bodies, behavior, minds and cultures it cannot be regarded as static, but must develop and evolve."[17] Yet Sheldrake himself does not answer the question whether the morphic fields, which he says are fields of information, are physical or mental, being or knowing. He says, "Thinking of information as contained in morphic fields helps to demystify the concept, which otherwise seems to be referring to something that is essentially abstract, mental, or mathematical, or at any rate nonphysical in nature."[18] From this it would seem information is not mental, not knowing, but physical—"being." However, Sheldrake also insists, "these fields contain a built-in memory sustained by morphic resonance."[19] He is therefore trying to sit on the fence between the two, between knowing as memory on the one hand and being as the physical (molecules, cells, tissues,) on the other.

The notion of morphic fields is of great interest in our study because, if these morphic fields contain inherent "memory," then awareness is implied—although Sheldrake does not come out and say as much. Even so, even if memory is inherent and the memory in these fields does imply awareness, Sheldrake still does not resolve our question: how do knowing and being interact? Is the morphic field knowing or being, or is it an amalgam of the two? If the latter, what kind of amalgam? In either case, when does awareness appear on the evolutionary scene and how does it influence being?

Although peering through the mist of words one discerns "knowing" and "being" in this theory of Sheldrake's, they still seem to be running on parallel tracks. So we must conclude that Sheldrake has not shown how morphic fields interact with being. But this does not mean we have to reject his theory. One certainly wants to agree with him when he says, "The idea that morphogenetic fields contain an inherent memory is the starting point for the hypotheses of formative causation. The reason I am putting it forward is that I think it could lead to a genuine evolutionary understanding of organisms, including ourselves."[20] Is it possible for us to understand what he means by "inherent memory" using the terminology I have developed, in such a way that violence is not done to the point Sheldrake makes yet the contradiction between the two conclusions we have reached is resolved? (The two conclusions, of course, being that no interaction is possible between knowing and being, and that knowing and being interact.)

Resonance is an interesting phenomenon because it arises out of the "one is two; two are one" ambiguity with which we are now familiar. Strike the tone C on a piano, and the string of tone C an octave higher resonates. Why? Why does the higher C vibrate but the strings adjacent to C do not? The strings of tone C and C an octave higher vibrate in sympathy because they are One, they are both tone C; they are the same although they are different. Let us use this as an analogy and see where it leads.

Tone C1 and tone C2 are One, both are C

The tone C1 is one tone, the tone C2 is another; they are quite different.

However because of the unity underlying C1 and C2 resonance is possible between them.

Knowing/being is One: a quantum.

Knowing/being is two; neither knowing nor being is subordinate to the other, nor do they interact.

However, because of the unity underlying knowing and being, resonance is possible.

In his book *The Self Organizing Universe*, Erich Jantsch reports that it has been found that stroboscopic light of the frequency of about 8 to 14 Hz,

> induces alpha rhythm in the brain waves and sensitizes humans to resonances with other humans over a distance . . . . At the Stanford Research Institute in California it has been found that under such circumstance (stroboscopic light) resonances of these types occur when another person in a remote room lives a strong experience, such as an electric-shock. This seems to be the first experimental arrangement which has succeeded in making so-called parapsychological phenomena reproducible.[21]

As I have in reference to our young woman/old woman figure, when we see the young lady she can have no interaction with the old woman simply because the old woman is nowhere to be found. To say she is present in potential is simply to start weaving a verbal web. However let us change something about the young lady, let us give her a necklace.

The mouth of the old woman is changed. Even though no interaction of any kind has occurred between the two, a change in the one has brought about a change in the other. We now discover that

Fig. 3

each of the different theories, in its own way, is right. The parallelist is right: the two, matter and mind, have no interaction. The materialist is right: one can investigate the objective realm with the hypothesis that it is all a matter of molecules, because, with the objective viewpoint, no subject can be found. If we see the old woman, where could we ever find the young woman? So, from this point of view all talk about decisions, values, judgments, and so on is just sloppy thinking. The psychotherapist is right in a similar way: one can look upon the mind as an autonomous field. What is at issue is what you thought, felt, imagined, or feared. The interactionist is right: a change in the mind does make a change in the body, and vice versa, even though no communication exists between the two. Furthermore, every change registered by the knowing is reflected in being, and vice versa.

The reason for this magic is the ambiguity—One/(knowing/being). The change in the young woman is a change of the *one field;* because the one field is changed, the old lady, as manifestation of the one field is also changed. Furthermore the changes can occur via the young woman, via the old woman, or via unity itself.

Memory and Remembering

Now let us see how this relates to what we said earlier about the morphic fields. Remember that Sheldrake says morphic fields evolve within nature, they are influenced by what has happened before, and they are immanent in an organism. I would go further and say that morphic fields *are* the organism. Sheldrake says that morphic fields are influenced by what has happened before—that is, they are influenced by memory. French philosopher Henri Bergson says that there are not things that change, but that change is things:

> Reality is flowing. This does not mean that everything moves, changes, and becomes; science and experience tell us that. It means that movement, change, becoming is everything that there is, there is nothing else. There are no things that move and become; everything is movement, is change, is becoming.[22]

Everything is change. This is in agreement with the fundamental axiom of Buddhism, which says that all is impermanent. Furthermore, change is time. Time is not a framework of experience, but is experience itself. This is clearly brought out by a twelfth-century Zen master named Dogen in an article that he wrote on *Uji*, or being/time.[23] According to Dogen, being is time. Time, therefore, is not an interval between two points. Time is ongoing. The paradoxes of Zeno arise because of our need for a stable context, providing which is the main function of consciousness. One of these paradoxes for example, is that an arrow can never reach its target because to do so it must pass through half the distance. To pass through this half, it would have to pass through half that distance, and so on. So the arrow cannot move. This comes from the view that time is an interval between two points, which may be filled by some kind of action. The arrow leaving the bow, passing through space, arriving at its target— all of this is time. It is only in the abstract that one can extract time from the action. All of this is an elaboration on the basic idea that I have been suggesting, which is that evolution and memory are the outcome of dynamic unity One/(knowing/being).

Normally we believe that we see something, or hear something, and then remember it. Seeing and memory would, in this case, be two different "faculties." However, because the basis of all is dynamic unity, memory and awareness are not two different faculties but two different ways of looking at the same process. To understand this, we must distinguish clearly between memory and remembering. In the terms I have been using, *memory* is a mode of awareness-as, whereas *remembering*, which requires a focusing of awareness, would be a result of awareness-of. To remember something implies seeing it or hearing it again. From a panorama of memory, one focuses on some particular aspects or memories. This would mean *forgetting* is a result of awareness-of, because forgetting implies an inability to focus in quite the right way—or, in other words, an inability to remember. With memory, forgetting is not possible: everything we are aware as is already memory. This seems to be confirmed, at least as far as human beings are concerned, by hypnosis and various studies of the brain, notably those of Wilder Penfield. Buddhism has the notion of the *Alaya vijnana*, or the storehouse consciousness, because it is said to contain all memories of all individual lives and therefore the seeds of all phenomena.

All existence, including life, is essentially dynamic because of an insatiable hunger to restore lost unity. Physically, dynamic unity manifests as energy, as well as structures derived from energy such as particles, atoms molecules, and so on. Our inner life is also a manifestation of dynamic unity. This means that awareness is not static but 'ongoing, and ongoing awareness-as implies memory. Memory is not simply a series of static pictures, but is a continuous unending film.

What I have just said implies that memory is cumulative. This means one cannot listen to the same note played for some time, because each successive moment is affected by, or cumulative upon, all preceding moments. Suppose you listen to a single violin tone played for a number of seconds. You will hear it differently after each moment of hearing, because at each moment the way you hear the tone is *affected by* the past moments of hearing. In its turn, the future is affected because the very fact of hearing it differently changes your expectation about the future. A composer plays with the expectations of his audience, and the violation of these expectations is an important part of musical composition.

I am not simply repeating what Heraclitus said about not being able to step into the same river twice. Rudyard Kipling once observed, "Time, like an ever rolling stream / bears all its sons away. They fly forgotten as a dream dies/ at the opening day." That is one way of speaking. But perhaps it is not that memories fly away but that they are built upon and therefore supplanted by other, successive memories.

Let us return to the illustration of listening to a note being played. Our interpretation of the note—that is the way we hear it—changes from one moment to the next. Interpretation involves what has happened, what is happening, and what is likely to happen in the future. Interpretation, furthermore, is governed by the need for simplicity: we need the simplest explanations of what is happening. Memory, therefore, is not simply a record of what has happened. It involves an anticipation of the future. Additionally, evolution is not simply a response in the present to what has happened in the past, it is purposeful as well. It involves memory, as Sheldrake points out, but it is also conditioned by the need to absorb the null point.

This is quite likely what T. S. Eliot was thinking of when he said mind changes and,

> [T]his change is a development which abandons nothing *en route, . . . this* development, refinement perhaps, complication certainly, is not from the point of view of the artist, any improvement. . . . But the difference be-

tween the present and the past is that the conscious present is an awareness of the past in a way and to an extent which the past's awareness of
itself cannot show."[24]

Eliot went on to say, "Someone said: 'the dead writers are remote from
us because we know so much more than they did.' Precisely, and they are
that which we know."[25]

The change that occurs in the quality of a tone played on a violin for
a period of time is something comedians exploit. Imagine someone standing on a stage playing one long drawn-out tone. After you hear the tone
for a while, it can suddenly seem funny, even though up to that moment
one could well have been listening to it in all seriousness. Indeed, the more
seriously you listen to the tone, the funnier the switch around can seem.
If the tone stops or changes before a critical moment, there is nothing at
all funny about it, but if it continues, then after that moment, it could well
become funny. If the tone continues to play even longer still then one
could well get restless, even angry. The humor and the anger occur after
a while because the one tone is both changing and not changing. It is
changing because of the cumulative effect of memory; it is not changing
because it remains the "same" note. Therefore, two conflicting interpretations of the same phenomenon occur: the one based on the appreciation of change, the other based upon the recognition of no change.
Creativity occurs when a single situation or idea is perceived in *two self-
consistent but habitually incompatible frames of reference*. Humor, as I have already pointed out, is a creative reaction; anger is failed creativity.

Let's look at another physical analogy. When you strike a gong, the
sound does not issue in a steady and unvarying stream, but in an undu-
lating way which is known as the beat phenomenon. This occurs because
sound is propagated in waves. Striking the gong sets up wave motions,
which are of uniform length. They start off in phase but, because of the
passage of time, they become completely out of phase, then become in
phase again, then out again, and so on. This creates the surge and diminution typical of the beat phenomenon. The wave length is constant, and
as such represents unity. The wave out of phase represents unity divided
against itself. This would be a period of maximum tension.

In a roughly similar way, dynamic unity creates its own beat phenomenon. One important difference between the sound issuing from striking

a gong and the knowing/being forms arising from dynamic unity, is that the sound dies away and the initial impetus is used up. Dynamic unity, as we have seen, cannot die away and so evolution must be unending.

Because dynamic unity is unchanging in its thrust to restore lost unity, and because at the same time it is subject to the cumulative effects of memory, it will become ambiguous. Because of this ambiguity, a creative leap will be necessary and memory will be structured in a new way. Re-structuring memory by way of creative leaps is what we call learning and will result in a learning curve which is not simply a smooth curve but a series of plateaus. Furthermore, restructuring memory in this way could be called "time binding," because the subsequent structures are built upon previous structures. Therefore, they are crystallized time. Finally, insofar as resonance occurs between awareness and being, being also will be modified. The crystallization of awareness we call ideas; the crystallization of being is what we call matter in all its varies forms: particles, atoms, molecules, cells etc. All of what we have been saying is similar to Sheldrake's thought, but it has the advantage of not requiring the addition of something called a morphic field.

Notes

1. This belief is again gaining greater credence with the development of what is called A.I., artificial intelligence, with the claim that, given sufficient complexity and sophistication, there will eventually be no reason why one should not regard computers as conscious and intelligent.
2. Wilder Penfield, *The Mystery of the Mind* (Princeton, NJ: Princeton University Press, 1978), p. xxi.
3. ibid.
4. ibid.
5. The *Surangama Sutra* poses this question.
6. I have used the word "hand" to stand for knowing. Of course the neurologist would tell us that electrical impulses travel from the hand to the brain, and this creates the "feeling." However, this just makes the question more complex, because the question still remains: how do electrical impulses, which are what we are calling "being" become knowing?
7. F. H. Bradley, *Essays on Truth and Reality* (Oxford: Clarendon Press, 1914), pp. 159–160.
8. Michael Polanyi and Harry Prosch, *Meaning* (Chicago: University of Chicago Press, 1975), p. 37.

9. The word *samadhi* covers a wide field in Eastern thought, and the way I use it is one of many.

10. Meg Maxwell and Verena Tschudin, *Seeing the Invisible* (London: Arkana, 1990).

11. Philip Kapleau (ed.), *The Three Pillars of Zen* (New York: Harper & Row, 1966), p. 183.

12. In Sanskrit, another word that is similar to what we are calling awareness-as being is *rupa*, and Lama Govinda says, "*Rupa* literally means 'form,' shape, without indicating whether this form is material or immaterial, concrete or imagination, apprehended by the senses (sensuous,) or conceived by the mind." But he also points out the ambiguous nature of *rupa* when he says, "The question regarding the essence of the so-called external phenomena is not decided beforehand; the possibility remains that the sensuous, *rupa*, and the mental thought correlatives, cannot be dissolved into each other, but may nevertheless have the same source." In other words, the sensuous *rupa* and the mental correlates are two but may nevertheless be one. Lama Govinda, *Foundations Of Tibetan Mysticism*, (London: Rider, 1960).

13. Rupert Sheldrake, *The Presence of the Past* (New York: Vintage Books, 1989), p. 106.

14. Ibid.. p. 107

15. ibid.. p 108

16. ibid.

17. ibid. p. 113

18. ibid. p. 113

19. ibid. p. 107

20. ibid. p. 107

21. Erich Jantsch, *The Self-Organizing Universe* (New York: Pergammon Press, 1980), pp. 213–214.

22. H. Wildon Carr, *Henri Bergson: The Philosophy of Change* (London: People's Books, 1911).

23. See Joan Stanbaugh, *Impermanence is Buddha Nature: Dogen's Understanding of Temporality* (Honolulu: University of Hawaii Press, 1990), pp. 24–71.

24. T. S. Eliot, *The Sacred Wood* (London: Methuen, 1969), p. 52.

25. ibid.

Awareness-of

I live in the understanding of writing, lighting things up,
walking in and out and the like. More precisely I am... speaking,
walking, understanding, intelligible dealings.
MARTIN HEIDEGGER

ALREADY WE CAN BEGIN to see an evolution emerging. I started by saying that the source and origin of all is a dynamism, a dynamic unity, for which we must use a logic of ambiguity: One/(knowing/being). We then saw that a null point emerges that gives direction and purpose to the dynamism. This purpose is to reabsorb the null point and so restore unity. Then knowing/being differentiates into knowing as being, and later awareness itself differentiates into awareness-as and awareness-of. We could illustrate this evolution as follows:

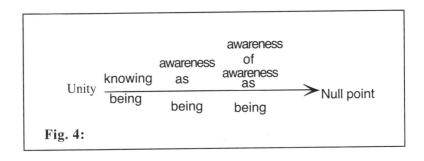

Fig. 4:

Scientific research has shown that being also differentiates into increasingly complex structures such a photons, particles, atoms, molecules, and so on and one could suppose that some correspondence must exist between the evolution of the two realms of knowing and being, because, we have said, every change in knowing is registered in being and vice versa. However, we do not want to complicate matters by trying to guess what this correspondence would be. Our concern is primarily with the evolution of consciousness, and it is with this that we must remain.

"I" and "Me"

In order to be as precise as possible, we must make another distinction, this time between "me" and "I." Most people are able to make this distinction readily when it is brought to their attention. When asked about the difference, they say that me is intimate and more inclusive than I, which they often perceive as being more objective and more divisive. Most people can conceive of animals having a me, but not I which, they feel, depends upon language. Using this distinction let us explore me, leaving aside for the moment what I means. We shall return to I later.

Me is the *viewpoint*. In Chapter 4 I used the word *weltenschauung* and said that it means a world idea. Moreover, I said that each of us has a world idea. This world idea can be seen as a field under tension, not passive but dynamic, not a window through which we look but a magnifying glass that concentrates the ray of Unity. Now I'd like to make a small but important change: instead of saying that I *have* a world idea, I would now say that me *is* the world idea.

Etymologically idea means "to see." Seeing is an action, something that is going on and this is true of me. Me is not something, an entity such as a person, soul or a ghost in the machine, but a process.[1] Me is, furthermore, quite evidently not nothing—an unnecessary postulate, as the behaviorists and positivists would say. Me, the subjective center of a world, can be likened to a whirlpool in a stream. The stream is dynamic unity, and the force of the whirlpool, its whirling, comes from the fact that, although me is the subjective center, it is also the object of me, something like a dog chasing its own tail. The viewpoint me is the unique subjective and dynamic center of a world; it is the One and as such it is the only center, everything else is object or peripheral to it. But, me can be object to itself, peripheral to itself. Me-as-center is then also me-as-periphery. Yet, as emissary of the One, *only one me is possible*. Thus we encounter, again, this impossible situation of One that is two, this time as me, divided against itself. Thus a fundamental schism lies at the very heart of our being.

The Birth of Me

In the next few chapters, I will elaborate upon this in more detail to show how the whirlpool is born and also how me is both subject and object. I will show how consciousness evolves out of the schism that this causes. This will not be easy, as what I will be describing is preverbal. For this reason, I ask you to try to get beyond the words, to return to your own immediate experience when reading what I am going to say.

In the last chapter I distinguished between awareness-as and awareness-of. Awareness-of differentiates out from pure knowing and is focused awareness, focussing makes concentration possible. The word concentration means "with a center," and awareness-of therefore is awareness focused on a center. Awareness-as, on the other hand, is without focus or center. It is not directed but, on the contrary, completely responsive to all within its field. Me is yet unborn; therefore awareness-as is not personal; it is not *my* awareness. To help the reader carry the burden of new and unfamiliar expressions, we will now and again use the expression "focussed awareness" in stead of awareness-of.

As you read this page, awareness-as the page must first be present. Included in awareness-as the page is awareness-as each individual letter, awareness-as the words (both as black shapes on a white page and as meaning), and awareness-as sentences and their meanings. All this is what the psychologist calls subliminal, preconscious, or even unconscious. The problem with these kinds of expression is that they imply a deficiency in awareness-as. They suggest that consciousness is the "real" state and that awareness-as is pre-, sub-, or unreal. In fact, it would be more true to put it the other way around. Consciousness is far more ephemeral, far more dependent than is awareness-as. This latter is constant and immutable. It is known as the "eye that never sleeps." It is the condition which is known as mindful (sometimes mindless) in Buddhism, recollection in the Sufi tradition, and as self-remembering in Gurdjieff's work. Gurdjieff insisted on a clear distinction being made between self-remembering, awareness-as, and self-observation, a condition in which one is aware-of awareness-as.

You are not normally aware of‡ the letters, words, sentences, and their meaning. What you are aware of is the overall meaning of what is being written about, the argument that is being made or, if it is a novel, of the plot, the characters and so on. Sometimes, if a letter or word is badly printed, you may become aware of them as objects. Or you might not know the meaning of a word and have to look it up in a dictionary and so again be aware of the word. Sometimes you get tired or lose the gist of what is being said, and then you find that you are just reading words and the overall meaning is lost—you are no longer aware of the meaning. However, none of this is what you normally do, normally you are aware of awareness-as a whole, a gestalt. This sense of a whole, of a gestalt, therefore comes from awareness-of, not awareness-as.

In a similar way, you have awareness-as the room in which you are at the moment without being aware-of any particular aspect. However, if you decide to turn on the radio, or look for a book, or want to feed the cat, for a while you become aware-of awareness-as the radio, or as the book, or as the cat, and in this way attention is focused on one or other of them. After you have accomplished what it is that you set out to do, the radio, or book, or cat will slip back into the general totality of which you are aware-as, and now your awareness-of will be of an undefined whole, the total situation.

However, it is possible for awareness-of to become more sharply focused on awareness-as itself, and one becomes, as it is said, "self-aware." Normally this is difficult to sustain because, after a very short time (seconds in most cases), awareness-of becomes drawn to some image or sound, and you are again aware-of awareness-as image or sound. Furthermore, you are not simply aware-as sights, sounds, smells, and so on but also as thoughts, feelings, sensations all of which flow constantly as a stream of awareness-as. Within this stream is an additional incipient awareness-of in the form of an inner monologue, which sometimes is called the stream of consciousness. When the woman, whom we quoted in Chapter 9 said she became the sea, the birds, and so on, it meant that the surface turbu-

---

‡ I have deliberately lapsed into the usual way of speaking rather than pedantically repeating awareness-of awareness-as. However, it may be as well for the reader to remind him or herself of the more precise formulation.

lence caused by awareness-of was put to rest and she was simply mindless, aware-as all that is.

The possibility of a sharper focus for awareness-of enables us to discover a further step in the evolution of consciousness. As I have said, it is out of awareness-of awareness-as, or self-awareness, that consciousness evolves. Awareness-of can be further turned back upon itself. This means that, with self-awareness, the self (or me) that is aware will be precisely the same self (or me) of which it is aware. Put differently, awareness-of will then be aware-of awareness-of., and this in turn would be awareness-of-awareness-of-awareness-of . . . in a kind of vicious circle. To help talk about this vicious circle, I will refer to it as *iterative awareness*. Webster's Dictionary defines iteration as "to say or do again and again and again." This captures very well the nature of iterative awareness. The vicious effect of iterative awareness can be seen with anxiety. One is anxious. Then one becomes anxious at being anxious. Then anxious at being anxious at being anxious. One then starts to panic at being anxious, and then one panics because one panics and so on. The ancients referred to iterative awareness as the *uroboros*, or the snake that swallows its own tail. However, the situation is a lot more complex than this symbol suggests because the tail that is swallowed is also the head that swallows.

Iterative awareness is pure process, and me is born out of process. The emergence of me is a major leap forward in the evolution of consciousness because awareness-of, henceforth, is no longer tied to being in the same way that awareness-as is tied to being. An "inner" world is now possible, with an "outer" world made possible by awareness-of awareness-as being.; because of this, an apparent separation occurs between the inner and outer worlds. Me begins to have a life of its own. However, this inner world is fraught with danger because me can swallow me. This is the horror of which I spoke in Chapter 1. It may well be what Nietzsche meant when he said that if you gaze into the abyss, the abyss will gaze back into you. This feeling of being swallowed, or of being engulfed, is fairly common and underlies panic attacks. Because it is an incipient threat that underlies human life, we live constantly on a crumbling edge of existence. So anxiety, worry, and the feeling of carrying a perpetual burden are common ingredients of our daily life.

Awareness-of as Intention

When I discussed the emergence of the null point, I said it was neither knowing nor being, but instead it was a reality in an intermediate realm between the two. I also said that the tension between inclusive and exclusive unity generates a tension, or energy, that also is neither physical nor mental but arises in the intermediate zone.[2] Let me now go further and say that spirituality, creativity, and *intention* emerge out of this intermediate zone. Physical movement—for example, the movement of my hand as I type—requires caloric and electrical energy. Caloric energy is energy carried by the blood and comes from the food we eat. It is energy burned by the muscles as they move. But electrical energy is also necessary; it is electrical energy, generated chemically within the body, that passes through the nerves and the synapses of the brain. Without these two energies, no movement is possible. In some sense, we are like cars that need the caloric energy of gasoline and the electrical energy of the generator to function. Without them, the car will not start. But just because a body can move, it does not mean that it will move. What converts the possibility of movement into movement? The behaviorist will protest here, saying that nothing extra is necessary, that caloric and electrical energies are enough. But many people have felt that, somehow, they are not enough. In view of what I have said so far, both are right. In other words, it is not necessary to conjure up an additional energy—a life energy, a libido, or something like that—but, even so, caloric and electrical energy are not enough to account for the movements of a dancer or of a cat stalking a squirrel.

De Chardin was among those who felt that an additional energy was necessary. He opined that two energies were operating in the universe: one he called tangential energy, which is the energy recognized by science. The other energy is what he calls radial energy, "which draws the [world] towards even greater complexity and centricity — in other words forwards."[3] It could be said, therefore, that radial energy is a centering energy, an energy that comes from concentration, or from having a focus, more normally known as intention. This is precisley the way I described dynamic unity. De Chardin's radial energy arises directly out of the tension inherent in unity being divided against itself. The centering of this energy comes from what de Chardin called the Omega point, and what I have called the null point. Radial energy then can be considered to be One/(knowing/being) centered upon the null point with the intention of restoring lost harmony. The heaven after a life of travail that most religions offer shows that this very idea of restoring lost harmony is embedded deeply in the psyche of human beings. However, all this is simply a way of speaking. A special energy is not involved because all is the expression of dynamic unity. One cannot therefore measure or find it in the physical world because this world is a way that unity is manifesting.

Intention could be said to be a special case of dynamic unity and is always directed towards the future. Intention could be called *will*, the future tense of being; but intention is also closely associated with purpose which is normally considered a mental phenomenon, as well as being closely associated with having a point to life. This suggests that we recognize intuitively that intention is neither physical nor mental, but that it comes out of the intermediate zone and is directed towards the null point. Let me also point out that intention is not *my* intention, nor is it something added to the organism. Although intention is focussed by me—just as light that is focussed by passing through a magnifying glass, does not belong to the magnifying glass—so the intention that passes through me is not mine. We shall have more to say about this in Chapter 16.

Henri Bergson also suggested something similar to both radial energy and dynamic unity. By using the term *durée*, Bergson shows the connection with time. Bergson elaborated on this in several places:

> The universe endures. The more we study the nature of time the more we comprehend that duration means invention, the creation of forms, the continual elaboration of the absolutely new.[4]
>
> Wherever anything lives, there is, open somewhere, a register in which time is being inscribed.[5]
>
> Continuity of change, preservation of the past in the present, real duration—the living being seems then to share these attributes with consciousness.[6]

If, for example, you see a cat leap onto a shelf without disturbing any of the things on the shelf, or see it stalk a squirrel, you see a purpose, intention, and intelligence at work. It is this that has persuaded many people that some controlling agency—a soul—must be at work. Writing about the dancer practicing her art, I said "When a dancer practices her art she simplifies her movements, eliminating the extraneous, retaining only the essential. She refines and integrates these, with each movement flowing into the other, following a continuous and subtle shift of a center of gravity." All of this suggests an agent, a self. We talk about *her* doing this, *her* simplifying that, and so on. We must do this because of the demands of language. Our language forces us into a subject/object mode of expression. The awkwardness of my explanation of "me" earlier, the ugliness of the expression me-as-center/me as periphery, the difficulty of phrase One/(knowing/being) all come from the fact that our language does not allow us to speak about dynamic wholes but only about parts in relation to other parts. When I was using the word me, the language cried out for me to use I instead. In fact, because of these very demands, occasionally I do use I. But If I yield to language in this way, I obscure what it is that I am trying to clarify.

No controlling agent is at work in the dancer or in the cat. Both cat and dancer are One/(knowing/being), pure dynamic unity. Intention is not something that an organism has. A cat does not *have* the intention to catch a squirrel. The intention is the cat, and therefore the cat is not put into motion; the cat is motion. The cat is intentional which means already in motion; rest and sleep these are special kinds of motion. Recall what Bergson says: it is not that things constantly change, but things are constant change.

Notes

1. I have elaborated on this in Appendix 3.
2. For a fuller discussion of the "intermediate zone," see Henri Corbin, *Creative Imagination in the Sufism of Ibn 'Arabí* (Princeton, NJ: Bollingen Press, 1969); and Henri Corbin, *Temple and Contemplation* (London: KPI, 1986). In Arabic, the intermediate zone is *'alam al-mithál*, "the world . . . between the corporeal and the spiritual state (Corbin, 1969, p. 47). According to Corbin (1986, p. 188), "With the exception of the school of Jacob Boehme and the Cambridge Platonists . . . the Western world has lost sight of the intermediary world."
3. De Chardin (1959, p. 70).
4. Henri Bergson, *Creative Evolution* (New York: Modern Library, 1944), p. 14.
5. Bergson (1944, p. 20).
6. Bergson (1944, p. 27).

Chapter 11

Me and You

I require a You to become;
becoming I, I say You.
MARTIN BUBER

I N THE LAST CHAPTER I spoke about "iterative awareness" and of "me"; me as both subject and object, me-as center/me-as-periphery. "Iterative awareness" and "me" are not two and distinct. They are both manifestations of the basic ambiguity. This ambiguity, the source of what it means to be a person, has the potential for opening a wound at the very heart of us. This wound underlies not only our deepest horror but also the stress, frustrations, and irritations of daily life. It also underlies the highest ecstasies as well as our daily joys. The horror, however, is a constant threat, and humans have developed two ways to avert it. The first way is by awakening to "you"; the second by discovering a center. Let us first deal with awakening to you; we shall return to establishing a center later.

*Awakening to You**

How do I know that "you" are there? Consider another every day occurrence: we are sitting in a cafe chatting about this and that. But how do I know that I am talking to *you*? Let me put the question in a slightly different way: Are you just the body that sits in front of me, or is "something" more involved? The behaviorist would answer, "No, there is nothing more. You are just the body. You are, it is true, extremely complex. But it is simply because of this complexity that you appear to be something more than the body." A similar response would also be given by those working in computers, some of whom also believe that intelligence, sentience, and what we call a person, come from matter which has simply reached a sufficient degree of complexity.

One of these, Frank Tipler, in his book *The Physics Of Immortality: Modern Cosmology, God and the Resurrection of the Dead,* has even calculated the complexity of the human brain in units called *flops*. On the basis of this calculation, Tipler estimates that, at the present rate of growth in the complexity of computers, a mere seven years is all that is necessary before we have machines that rival humans in complexity—machines complex enough to be consider not just machines but persons.[1] One might hope he made this prediction with his tongue firmly in his cheek—but no, Tipler claims to be a serious. His books sports an appendix full of erudite formulae for the scientist, and it attempts to show that machines will be our saviors. According to Tipler, these intelligent machines will "enhance our well being, even if they are our superiors in every way. Without the help of intelligent machines the human race is doomed. With their help we can and will survive forever." He adds that, to reject such an idea, "to regard the creation of such people—I call intelligent robots people because that is what they are" is racism.[2] Tipler defines racism as "a belief in the inherent superiority of any group of intelligent beings."[3] Presumably, then, politeness would require that in our conversations with machines we would address machines as *you*.

But how will we know that machines are intelligent, have consciousness, are alive? Why will we have to address them as you? Because, says Tipler, they behave as though they are intelligent and alive. He draws upon

---

*   In order to make the presentation easier, I will be using the words *I* and *me* interchangeably in this chapter. Later, I will distinguish between them again.

Turing's test in support. Let me quote Tipler at length:

> How could we tell if a computer was intelligent? For that matter how
> do we know if a human being we see is intelligent?. . . . The answer in
> the case of the human being is simple: talk to them. If they make a co-
> herent reply to a question you pose, then you immediately conclude that
> they probably have full human intelligence. The great British scientist Alan
> Turing proposed that we apply the same criteria to the computer intel-
> ligence: if you talk to the machine — really talk to it, carry on a con-
> versation with it just as you would with another [sic] normal human be-
> ing — then the machine is intelligent. If after interacting for years with
> the machine it acts as if it has a personality, has consciousness (and a
> conscience), then it really does.[4]

In other words, I know you are you because I habitually interact with
you as if you were you; if I can be conditioned to believe that you are you,
what would stop me from being conditioned to believe that a machine
is also "you"?

Tipler speaks in the name of science in much the same way as the
behaviorist Watson spoke in the name of science. It is difficult to know,
however, whether in Tipler's hands science has advanced or retreated.
According to the behaviorist, if I cannot prove you are conscious, I may
not assume that you are conscious. In fact, I must not even assume that
you are you or that I am I.[5] According to Tipler and Turing, however, if
I cannot *disprove* that machines (and presumably you) are conscious, then
I must assume that they (and you) are conscious.

One of Tipler's great failures, a failure important enough to nullify the
whole book, is his failure to address the question of knowing and awareness. Many people feel that somehow knowing—awareness and consciousness—and life, intelligence, immortality, and God are all connected in some
way. Tipler talks about the latter four in a context that supports his point
of view, but he ignores the first three. For example, he attempts to define
Buddhist Nirvana, but he does so without any reference at all to "knowing," even though Nirvana is pure knowing. Nirvana, says Tipler, means
blowing out the candle, extinction. This is so. Nirvana does mean extinction, it means extinction of desire and intention, including the intention
to exist, as well as the intention to exist eternally. But, what is left after
extinction is not "nothing" but pure knowing, knowing without reflection,

pure peace. The words *Buddha* and *Bodhi*, two common words in Buddhism, are both related to intelligence, knowing, and awareness. But, even though he presumes to be able to use Buddhism as a support for his theory, nowhere does Tipler address the question of awareness. On the contrary, a human being he says, "is a finite state machine, and *nothing but* a finite state machine." This is his emphasis. He quotes with approval a Japanese roboticist who says, "to learn the Buddha way is to perceive oneself as a robot."[6]

Integrity

Earlier, I referred to Bridgman's plea for *integrity* and his saying that the first person report becomes increasingly necessary if we hope to describe faithfully what occurs, let alone understand it. Turing also concedes the importance of 'the first person report' because, as he says, if I want to know whether a human being is intelligent etc. *I* talk to him. If I want to know whether a machine is intelligent and alive, *I* talk to it. It is not the behavior of the machine alone that determines whether it is intelligent. To this behavior must be added *my conviction* that the machine's behavior is intelligent.

Awareness of the Other

As we all know, we can be mistaken about this and become convinced that something is conscious when it is not. In years past, a London Bobby stood in a darkened corner by the entrance to Madame Tussaud's Wax Museum in London. It was not unusual for people to ask the Bobby for directions or information, and then to recoil with slight horror when they realized the Bobby was made of wax. We must ask ourselves, "Why does the recognition of our mistake create horror?"

The experience described in the quote below is not by any means an unusual one:

> There was just the room with its shabby furniture and the fire burning in the grate and the red shaded lamp on the table. But, the room was filled by a Presence, which in a strange way was both about me and within me, like light or warmth. I was overwhelmingly possessed by Someone who was not myself, and yet I felt I was more myself than I had ever been before. I was filled with an intense happiness, and almost unbearable joy, such as I had never known before and have never known since.[7]

One of the Apollo astronauts, I think it was Sheppard, encountered God when he was on the moon. People who have near-death experiences sometimes encounter what they call "a being of light." Paul met Christ on the road to Damascus, also as a being of light. I could multiply examples like these a hundred-, a thousand-fold. But do I need to? All of us have had a faint shadow of what is implied by this presence. Who has not had that eerie feeling, when in a house alone or walking along a dark path, of another presence nearby? If *you* are simply the result of conditioning, why do we have these experiences, from whence comes the uncanny feeling of someone else being present when there is no one?

Watson could have dismissed these, as he dismissed any other evidence contrary to his theory, by denying consciousness altogether. But Tipler and Turing cannot do that. They have allowed into the discussion the idea that to know that the behavior of a machine is intelligent *someone* must be there to know it. The quote above about the room filled with a presence suggests that one can know you just by your presence, without your being physically present in any form at all.

The question of what constitutes "awareness of you" is important. If someone truly believes that machines are alive and aware, as some primitive people believed that idols carved of wood were truly alive, then surely we must be able to account for this in some reasonable way—just as we must be able to account for the experiences people have of a living light or an encounter with Christ, Buddha, Krishna, Kali, and so on. Simply condemning these people—calling them stupid, ignorant, or wrong—is not a reasonable response. Nor is simply dismissing the experiences as imaginings, illusions, or self-suggestions. However, a more important reason for getting a satisfactory understanding is that this could show there is a "reality" that does not need physical support of any kind, but at the same time is not imaginary nor illusory. For most societies in the past, this would not have come as any surprise. However, it is something that many of our society's leading thinkers, if they did not simply ignore it, would scoff at as mere superstition.

I say, "I see you." What do I mean? I see your body and its behavior, and in this way I know your body and behavior. However I also know that you are *you*. How do I know that you are not simply a body, a set of responses, a repertoire of behavior, or even you, a name, but *you*. A man who is in love with a woman is pervaded by her whole presence, whether she is with him or not. Or course he may recall certain mannerisms she has—her smile, her way of leaning forward when she speaks, the way she brushes the hair from her eyes—but beyond all of this, is *you*, the woman he loves. What does that mean? Who is this you who lies beyond mere memory of detail? The same question arises when we consider the mystic's encounter with his beloved as we quoted above. What, or who, was encountered? In the article in which he speaks of the encounter, the author says that he could describe the presence as "Christ coming to him"—in other words, the presence he felt was a person.[8]

A famous mystical saying attributed to the Prophet Muhammad put it this way: "He who knows himself knows his Lord." In other words, to know oneself is to know You. Christ, the Lord, you are not objects among other objects, but *subjects*. We have difficulty understanding this because we believe that even we, ourselves, are objects, separated and isolated in a world of objects. "Alone and afraid in a world I never made," as someone put it. We know this world through causal relations, through sensory data which create in us images, sounds, smells, and so on. As objects we are inhabited, some believe, by souls or spirits, and these are also, in their own way, objects. Associated with this belief in being a separate, isolated object among objects is the tacit assumption that my world could exist without me, an assumption that many physicists today are questioning (see Appendix 1). Because of this belief, moreover, when confronted with the mystery of you, we ask ourselves, "What stimulus from the outside, what causal relation, which of my senses tells me of your presence?"

If we are, indeed, separate, isolated individuals, then, as Tipler pointed out, all we have left of you is behavior: the twinkle in your eye, the smile, the toss of your head, and so on. But what about that presence that has no accompanying form or behavior, the presence that is just presence? What about the beloved who pervades yet transcends all of her manifestations? We could dismiss these as imaginings, dreams, the effects of too good a meal. But this would surely be to lack integrity. A good scientist would not reject data because they challenged his theory, but would use the data as levers to make his theory more embracing.

Though "you" may not have a material counterpart, this does not mean that you must be a product of my imagination; on the contrary, you may well be as real as me, which, as we have seen, arises with awareness-of and has no material basis. What it means is this: because you have no material counterpart, my awareness of you is not dependent on sensory data. If my knowledge of you is based solely on sensory data, this would be best described in the terminology developed in Chapter 10 as *awareness-of awareness-as you*. But we cannot use this expression, because awareness-of awareness-as you *is already you,* in the same way that awareness-of awareness-as me is already me. *I* am not aware of you. I do not see *you;* you and me come out of the seeing, out of awareness-of awareness-as. Furthermore, although I have used words to describe this encounter between you and me, let me stress that the encounter is in no way dependent upon words, thoughts, or even ideas. Neither you nor me is an idea; you are you without any need of words, just as me is me without needing the word me. An animal as well as a human being is aware-of aware-as, so what I have said about me and you applies to animals as well as to humans.

Martin Buber, the well-known Jewish philosopher, also said that to know the self is to know the Lord. He put it this way, "God is the eternal you whom men address and by whom they feel that they are addressed." He said it again another time, in a slightly different way but with the same intent, "I-you is basic; it is not derived. Another does not cause the relation I-you, but gives it expression. We are content with this I-you evocation until it is shown that we err." Thus, I-you does not tell us anything about what evokes it other than what evokes it has the power of evocation. This means that if someone *truly* believes that a machine is alive, when he addresses this machine as "you," he does not thereby confirm the aliveness of the machine; he confirms that the machine can awaken a genuine and primordial experience, an experience me-you which is at least as real as the experience of the world.

The me–you relation to which I refer is not simply a relation known only by human beings. Animals, birds, and fish are capable of reflexive awareness, awareness turned back upon itself, which is the basis for me–you. Some people will no doubt object to the idea that animals have reflected awareness. Ever since Descartes, it has been maintained rigidly that animals are simply machines. However, recently some people working in the field with animals have had second thoughts and are more willing to attribute consciousness to animals. For example, reflective awareness, or self-awareness, has been demonstrated in chimpanzees by a simply experiment. A chimp was anaesthetized, and while he was asleep an odorless and tasteless coloring was put onto his eyebrows. When the chimp awakened, he was given a hand mirror. The chimp immediately began inspecting the eyebrows reflected in the mirror and wiping his own eyebrows at the sametime.[10]

One can easily demonstrate this reflective awareness in a dog by simply looking it in the eyes. The dog will blink and look away, often with great discomfort. My daughter had a young dog and one day she happened to put a wooden owl with huge eyes on the floor near the dog. The dog saw the owl and immediately fled, whimpering, to hide under the nearest chair. When she covered the eyes of the owl, the dog lost its fear.

Even birds have reflective awareness. My wife and I once stayed in a cottage in the country, and we used to feed the birds seeds as well as leftover bread. No sooner did we put the food out than the birds would come flocking to eat it. On one occasion I had some biscuits, round ones with red jam in the center. Because they had become stale I put them out for the birds. Not a single bird came, either for the biscuits or for the other food. It stayed this way for several hours, until I suddenly had an idea. I broke the biscuits up into small pieces. No sooner had I done this than the birds came flocking. The circular biscuits with the red circles inside must have looked like eyes and frightened the birds. This idea is borne out by the fact that nature herself uses false eyes as a way of frightening away predators. Butterflies, caterpillars, fish, insects, and frogs all have species in which eyes are "painted" on as a way of frightening predators.

How often do you look into the eyes of another? Even in the best of times we most often look another in the eyes for only a few seconds, then look away, then look again, and so on. When I visited New York a short while ago, a friend who was meeting me there said, "Just avoid eye contact with others as you walk along the street." To look another in the eye for too long is considered rude, aggressive, or dangerous, depending on the circumstances. In most cultures, people who occupy a lower social rank keep their eyes down or averted when they are in the presence of a person of higher social rank. (There is, of course, a well-known exception to this unwillingness to look too long into the eyes of another: Lovers may gaze for hours into each others' eyes. Indeed, they seem not to be able to look long enough. But we'll leave aside this phenomenon for the moment, and return to it later.)

Underlying the hostility that is aroused when one looks too long into the eyes of another is the uroboros, the snake swallowing itself. When I look at you and you look back at me, who is looking, and who is looked at? Who is the subject whom is object? Who is swallowing and who is swallowed? In the presence of another more powerful than me that same *me*, the source of iterative awareness, can be swallowed, sucked dry, annihilated. Under these circumstances, looking and being looked at is a question of being and not being, a matter even more serious than life and death. This is the origin of the myth of the evil eye, a myth that all societies have.

But in the case of the owl's eyes, or the biscuits, where were "you"? What was it that looked back at the dog or the birds? Obviously, it was not the owl or the biscuits. The eyes that stare from the wings of the moth, where do they get their malevolence? It was the dog's and the birds' own awareness-of that evoked you; it is in this way that the eyes get their malevolence. You and me are born out of the same awareness-of. As Meister Eckhart said, "The eye with which I see God is the same eye with which God sees me." The eyes—whether the eyes of a predator or those nature paints on the rump of a frog—act as a trigger, but they are not the cause of the explosion. The horror I feel when I look into the eyes of a psychopath and the horror I experience when I am lost in a dark forest and start feeling presences close in are both the same horror; they both arise out of awareness-of. The slight horror I feel when I realize the Bobby is made of wax is the same.

Just as the snake can swallow its tail, and so contract toward annihilation, the reverse is also true; expansion into infinity is possible as well. If the first goes toward ultimate horror and negation, the second goes toward ultimate bliss and affirmation. The lover seeks this bliss and affirmation through the eyes of the beloved, and, in seeking bliss and affirmation, grants them at the same time. Women (and men) have enhanced the seductive power of the eyes by using various cosmetics and ornaments. Until quite recently, one way was to put Bella Donna in the eyes to enlarge the pupils. It is said that the eyes are the windows of the soul, but whose soul do they open onto? Yours, mine, yours and mine? Or do they open onto a unity that embraces both?

The encounter with the other occurs upstream of consciousness and experience; I do not encounter you in the same way that I encounter your body. Your body parts, and in particular your eyes, are triggers that evoke the awareness, but the awareness does not take place in the same world inhabited by your body and mine. Love songs attest to this, singing of "you" coming from heaven, "you" coming from a dream, and so on. Again, literature, myth, and folklore are filled with accounts of gods, ghosts, and ethereal beings that inhabit another world and whom one can meet and even converse with. We must be careful, however, in how we understand what is meant by this other world. We should not interpret it to mean another world of objects: of spirits and ghosts, which are simply things alongside tables and chairs. Nor does this other world mean another, higher world of ideas and images, nor a collective unconscious.

A man looks into the eyes of the woman he loves and is transported into a rapture of bliss. This means that iterative awareness is reflected back on itself, but this can occur also without the trigger of the eyes. Indeed, as we saw in the quote about the Presence filling the room, when it occurs spontaneously in this way the bliss and rapture are far more intense. Sometimes people feel that they are in the presence of a beautiful, living, loving light at other times people know just the presence without it being transmuted into light. In both cases the result can be truly ecstatic. What we have said about iterative awareness can help us understand this presence as well as an allied phenomenon which has caused much interest, the phenomenon of the Near Death experience. Just as a lover looks into the eyes of the beloved and can be transported in a rapture of bliss so the iterative awareness reflected back on itself can bring about the same intense bliss.

Most of us do not experience this bliss because we are immersed in a flow of thought and tied down by awareness-as being. In a dying person, however, the brain—which is the repository of thought and sensation—loses its hold on awareness-of, which, reflected back upon itself, manifests as love and light.

This suggests that focussed awareness, which may be both subject or object, seer or seen, in its objective mode, might well be light. Light accompanies the presence because, in this experience, awareness is seeing itself objectively. Light, one could say, is awareness known objectively. The connection between knowing and light has been known for millennia, and one will find the connection mentioned repeatedly in spiritual literature. Just a few of a myriad of possible references are: Arjuna was aware of Krishna as a blazing light[11] and the resurrection body of Christ was light. *Pistis Sophia,*[12] which tells of Christ's resurrection drips with light. The Hermetic tradition[13] and the Sufi tradition[14] are pervaded by awareness as light.

Max Pulver in his Eranos lecture "The Experience of Light in the Gospel of St. John, in the *Corpus hermeticum* of Gnosticism and the Eastern Church," makes an important observation.[15] Pulver says that the Gnostic illumines because he himself is illumined. He quotes St. Paul saying, "For God, who commanded the light to shine out of darkness, hath shined into our hearts, to give the light of the knowledge of the glory of God in the face of Jesus Christ." Pulver adds, "Christ is the Thou to God's I." Finally, Pulver comments, "This illumination is no poetic image. It is, rather, a technical term for the experience gained in a technical exercise *photizan* means not only illumine but also to turn into light."

But to return to more immediate experience, "you" and "me" are inextricably bound. We are closer than brother and sister and the Gospel's injunction to turn the other cheek and love our enemies is simply giving us a way by which to avoid tearing ourselves apart. Psychology has insisted for some time now on the importance, for the psychological development of a child, of a nurturing relationship. Furthermore, men who have been made a prisoner and isolated from others often go to heroic limits to stay in communication. Many ex-prisoners have written accounts of the struggle to communicate with others despite the punishment that they endured in trying to do so. Solitary confinement is one of the most painful of experiences. In all this we can see how important "you" are to my mental well being: you ward off the ghosts, enable me to grow psychologically, and support me in my anguish. You help me to be me by carrying half of my burden, in this is your love for me. Romantic love is pure iterative awareness, pure presence, out of which you and me are born. In the you-me relationship, love may become impure in possessive love or in appetitive love. It may also sparkle in the play of erotic love of you as me, me as you, giving, while taking, affirmation, or it may become simply the mundane feeling of friendship and affection that one has for those around us.

The more we can reciprocate—that is, the more I can become one with you and you can become one with me, without losing our autonomy—the greater the chance love has of retaining its purity. Trouble begins when I identify you with your body and behavior so that you become an object, something among other things. The freedom you inspired, the sense of eternity is lost, and you become an experience among other experiences, bound by time and space. The same deterioration occurs when we begin to believe that the idol *is* God. The nouminous is lost and, instead of spontaneous awareness-of reflecting back upon itself in free play, the relationship becomes a commercial one in which I will adore you if you will give me protection, peace, love, whatever. I become prey again to the lurking ghosts and must face the anguish without you taking up half the burden. In short, I am lonely.

Before leaving this subject we must look at several objections. If you and me are upstream of experience, upstream of objects, does this not make both of us unreal? If the experience I have of you is not the same as the experience of your body, why is it that few people seem to be aware of this? Finally, awareness-of awareness is an everyday occurrence; anyone can, if they wish, become aware-of being aware. Why do you say, then, that to be aware-of awareness is replete with so much drama?

Let us deal with the third objection first. Our everyday experience of awareness-of awareness is already filtered through the sieve of experience, and experience is centered on a stable point, I. Consciousness, experience, and its social counterpart culture all have evolved to contain the conflict inherent in awareness-of and to provide vehicles for its expression. And all of these vehicles are dependant on this stable point. For lovers and mystics, poets and artists, this stable point is attenuated, and the structures dependent on it dissolve and so lose their containing power. So these people fall into uncertainty and ambiguity. Sometimes, indeed often, this fall is accompanied by feelings of anxiety, dread, fear, and even panic. It is not for nothing that lovers and artists have been compared to madmen.

People normally are not aware that the encounter with the you occurs in "another world," because they rarely experience this encounter in its purity. Indeed, many people never experience it at all. Those who do will experience it a few times at most. When one does experience it, one never forgets it. But this is not to say that the me–you encounter does not occur. It does so constantly. But I associate you with your body in much the same way that I associate the soundtrack of a film with the shadows that dance across the cinema screen. We do not live in the present much; we usually live in the past, in memory and association, in thought and judgment, all of which filter out the impact of the immediacy of you. Even so, beyond this curtain of mental activity, the encounter with you is made in a timeless world, an encounter which in itself has no thought, no words—as with the lover struck dumb.

In his poem *The Waste Land*, T. S. Eliot sums up some of what I have being saying this way:

Yet when we came back, late, from the hyacinth garden,

Your arms full and your hair wet, I could not

Speak, and my eyes failed, I was neither

Living nor dead, and I knew nothing,

Looking into the heart of light, the silence.

Oed' und leer das Meer.[16]

Notes

1. Frank J. Tipler, *The Physics of Immortality: Modern Cosmology, God, and the Resurrection of the Dead* (New York: Doubleday, 1994).

2. Tipler (1994, p. 86).

3. Tipler (1994, p. 86).

4. Tipler (1994, p. 20).

5. D. Dagobert, *The Dictionary of Philosophy* (Boston: Littlefield, Adams, 1962): "Behaviorism is a contemporary American school of psychology which abandons the concepts of mind and consciousness, and restricts both animal and human psychology to the study of behavior. Thinking and emotions are interpreted as implicit behavior: the former is implicit or subvocal speech; the latter implicit visceral reactions."

6. Tipler (1994, p. 88).

7. F. C. Happold, *Mysticism: A Study and an Anthology* (Harmondsworth, UK: Penguin Books, 1970), p. 133.

8. The author was not in any way a mystic and the encounter came quite unbidden.

9. Martin Buber, *I and Thou* (New York: Scribner's, 1974; Walter Kaufmann, trans.).

10. Frans de Waal, *Peacemaking Among Primates* (Cambridge, MA: Harvard University Press, 1989).

11. See the *Bhagavad Gita*.

12. See *Pistis Sophia* tr. G.R.S. Mead (London: John Watkins, 1963).

13. See, for example, Brian P. Copenhaver, *Hermetica* (Cambridge, UK: Cambridge University Press, 1996).

14. Corbin, Henri, *The Man Of Light In Iranian Sufism.* (Boulder and London: Shambhala, 1978).

15. Max Pulver, "The Experience of Light in the Gospel of St. John, in the *Corpus hermeticum* of Gnosticism, and the Eastern Church," in *Spiritual Disciplines: Papers from the Eranos Yearbooks* Bollingen Series XXX. (Princeton: Princeton University Press, 1985), p. 4.

16. T.S. Eliot, *The Waste Land* (New York: W.W. Norton, 2000).

Chapter 12

The Birth of Trauma

Here we have the paradox, the potentially tragic paradox,
that our relatedness to others is an essential aspect of
our being, as is our separateness, but any particular
person is not necessarily part of our being.
R. D. LAING

Hell is other people.
JEAN-PAUL SARTRE

WHY DO WE SUFFER? Where does the pain of psychic trauma come from? That we do suffer is obvious. That both suffering and trauma are painful one cannot doubt. Both are often associated with physical pain, although physical pain is not always present. Both, however, always involve you and, as we saw in the last chapter, you are not contingent. You do not just happen to be associated with me, you are an intrinsic part of me, or rather me and you are neither one nor two.

I-thou, I as Thou, I am Thou, Thou art me; are we two, are we one? I encounter you constantly during the day: now you are a wife, now a daughter; now you are a friend, now an enemy. You are always there; even when I'm alone I talk to you in that never ending mono-duologue of the mind. You are always there lurking in the shadows. As my boss, as the waiter in the restaurant, as the stranger in a queue, you are you and I am I. But, this is because Thou art veiled, hidden behind the forms in which

I have invested thee. When I meet you in these forms I feel a tension, I feel awkward. If I hold your eye too long, I am embarrassed. I cover this up with talk, with raillery, playing the fool; or else I "communicate" with you—formal, efficient, structured, machine talking to machine. I turn our communion into a matter of commerce, of getting and receiving. But who are you, who art Thou? Who am I?

To Feel May Be to Violate

Let me take an everyday experience, traveling on a subway, and use it to illustrate some of what I said in the last chapter and show how the fundamental wound to being is inflicted. This illustration will also help show how further differentiation in awareness comes about. I will have to ask you to do more than simply follow the words; you must also try to enter into the situations described. In this way you can appreciate the different nuances of awareness-of and awareness-as. Later I will build upon these distinctions and, unless you have been convinced of the validity of the distinctions between the two modes of awareness, these later developments will seem to be so many empty words.

When traveling by subway, we are touched by many people, and we in turn touch many people. Although sometimes we get fed up with the pressure of so many others around us, the fact of being touched does not upset us. But, if someone on the subway were to *feel* us, then we should certainly be upset, even offended. Physically no difference is experienced between being felt and being touched. In both cases the hand of another is against, or on, part of my body. Wherein, then, is the difference? Why should the one upset me and the other not? Moreover, if on the subway instead of being felt, we were caressed by a stranger, we should no doubt get very angry indeed and wish to do something drastic to make him desist. Why this offense, why this anger and revulsion?

If we go back to the example of the carpenter feeling a piece of wood, we can see that what he feels is inert, an object. When I am felt I am turned into an object; or, more exactly, I am known as an object. But leaving this aside for the moment, what is important for us is to ask, by *whom* am I known? This question, too, is crucial to what I am saying; so let me spell out, step by step, my reply, even though this reply will transform an experience that is spontaneous and alive into something pedestrian and dull. I will use the distinction I have made between feeling and touching—the distinction, that is, between awareness-of and awareness-as—to help give this reply.

Originally I am simply aware-as in the same way the woman above was awareness-as herself and awareness-as the birds, the sea, and so on. The awareness is global and seamless, One/knowing/being. And this global awareness—this awareness-as—is not *my* awareness. It has been the basis of countless mystical and spiritual experiences and, in all the accounts given of these, the absence of me as an agent is always remarked upon. Awareness-as is not a higher consciousness but a more elementary condition out of which our consciousness emerges. When using the expression, "I am simply aware-as" I am using the word "I" as an expedient.

In the diagram below (Figure 5), awareness-as is shown by a dotted line. The dotted line, rather than a continuous line, indicates that the boundary does not exist in reality but is there as an illustration. "Me" and "stranger" are also indicated by dotted lines. Both are potential, and neither has yet been actualized or differentiated out. Throughout the sequence of diagrams that follow, the dotted line is used to indicate awareness-as, and to remind us that this awareness is a constant condition, out of which our conscious experience emerges like a crystal out of a gel.

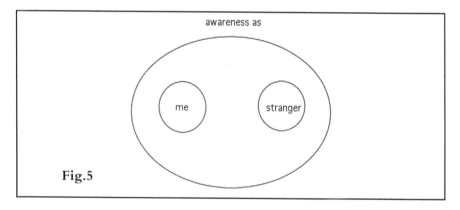

Fig.5

Awareness-of

Awareness-of is focussed awareness. Unless otherwise noted, it must always be understood that focussed awareness arises out of awareness-as in the same way that waves arise out of the sea. For the rest of this chapter we shall generally take this as a given and so will not have to use the cumbersome phrase "awareness of awarenss as." Focussed awareness has a source and a destination. It has variations such as *attention, interest, concentration* and so on. When focussed awareness appears, the viewpoint "me" appears simultaneously. Indeed awareness-of and this viewpoint are not separate, in much the same way that the sun and the rays of the sun are not separate.

This viewpoint is illustrated in Figure 6

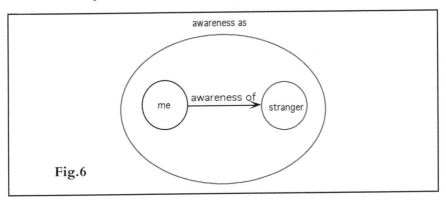

Fig.6

In Figure 7 we go a step further. With the appearance of awareness-of, I can also become aware *as the stranger* who is feeling me (is aware of touching me). This gives rise to a situation quite different from that shown in Figure 6. When I am aware of the stranger, I am aware of him as an object, as something in the surroundings. Now, however, as Figure 7 shows, the stranger is aware of me. These two situations are quite different: A tension arises in the situation shown in Figure 7 that was not there in Figure 6. We have all had the experience of looking at someone who then turned to look at us, and have experienced the tension that this created.

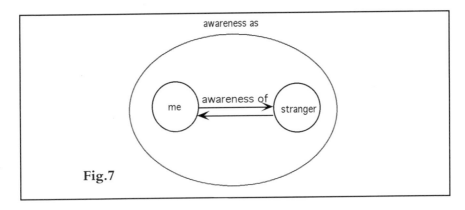

Fig.7

The first important point is this: In all of this, I have not moved out of the original awareness-as illustrated in Figure 5. The following may help you to appreciate what I mean: Suppose you are sitting alone in a room reading a book. Suddenly you have the feeling that someone is looking at you, someone is aware of you. You get up, look around, and find no one there. Now, suppose you are sitting alone reading, you have the feeling someone is looking at you, and you look up to see a friend standing there. Before the verification, the feeling "someone is looking at me" *is the same in both cases*. Little children who are afraid of the dark are convinced that someone is looking at them. One leaves a light on so that, if necessary, they can look around to see that this is not so. People who are alone in a strange house often have the feeling of someone else being present. This is why it is said that both you who are looking at me, and me being looked at, emerge from awareness-as. Your physical presence is simply the trigger.

Thus, instead of saying "I am *aware of the stranger* who is aware of me," it is more precise to say "I am aware of the stranger, and I am aware as the stranger who is aware of me." Let me try to make this clearer.

Me and You

We have the expression, "to see ourselves through the eyes of another." This could be made broader by saying, "To be aware of myself through another's awareness-of me." For example, seeing ourselves through the eyes of another, or being aware of ourselves through another's awareness-of us, is the basis of stage fright. But stage fright is often worse *before* one meets the audience. Stage fright is the clash of two awarenesses, but not the clash of my awareness-of the audience and the audience's awareness-of me.[1]

Let me return to the stranger to clarify this point. Suppose I am convinced the stranger is feeling me, but I am mistaken. Unless I am made aware of my mistake, *the perception of the situation* is unchanged. I am still aware *of* the stranger and aware *as* the stranger who is aware of touching me.

Putting this as precisely as possible, when I am felt by a stranger I am aware of being felt and I am aware of feeling. In the normal course of events I attribute the first to myself and the second to the stranger. I say, "I am being felt" and "He is feeling me." Nevertheless, both are "my" awareness. I am *aware-of* being felt as me *and* I am *aware-of* feeling as you (the stranger).

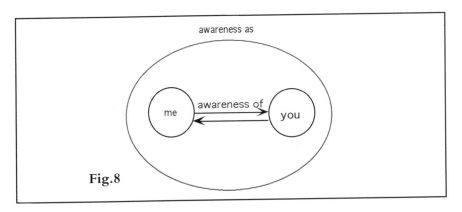

Fig.8

Note that I have changed the word stranger and used *you* instead. With the transformation of the stranger into you, the tension I spoke of earlier appears at the same time. But, and this is the heart of the matter, there are not two *awarenesses-of* because *awareness-of* being felt is the same *awareness-of* feeling. In other words, there are not two awarenesses-of, but awareness turned back or reflected onto itself. It is indeed out of this "turning back" that you emerges.

The word *you* refers to quite a different phenomenon than the word *he*. In French the word *he* is *il*, and the same word *il* is used for *it*.

What I have shown in Figures 5–8 is the anatomy of me-as-center/ me-as-periphery, of which I spoke in the introduction—Me:center, you:periphery; you:center, me:periphery. In other words, you do not just happen to be associated with me, you are an intrinsic part of me—or, rather, me and you are not one nor two.

The Origin of Suffering and the Birth of Trauma

So now we come to the crucial point of this chapter. If I wish to break the contact, it is not the contact between me and the stranger I must break, but the contact between *me* and *you,* I must divide me/you. This means, in effect, that *me will be separated from itself.* This break will be either at the level of awareness-as or at the level of awareness-of. First let me say what happens at the level of awareness-of and then elaborate upon it.

At the level of awareness-of either me or you are suppressed. This leads to what could be called *self-denial,* on the one hand, and *suppression* on the other. Let us repeat, only one awareness-of is at issue. Focussed awareness is reflected back onto itself, like two mirrors reflecting each other. However, with focussed awareness, the two mirrors, me and you, emerge out of the reflection. With suppression, the mirror "you" is done away with; with self denial it is "me" that is done away with.

You do something to annoy me. Annoyance, anger, and violence escalate in an attempt to break the connection. To overcome 'you.' I may try to break the connection by walking away from you. However, as we well know, this strategy is rarely effective. When I walk away from you I take you with me. I continue to fight with you "in my mind," so to say. You and me have our origin in awareness-as, in what we sometimes call the "mind." You, and the tension generated by the emergence of 'you', are always present to a greater or lesser degree. The inner monologue that goes on endlessly comes out of focussedawareness reflected back upon itself. What makes those rare moments of pure awareness-as so precious, is that for the moment the inner monologue and the tension that causes it are laid to rest.

Let me return to the scene in the subway when the stranger feels me. I am annoyed. This annoyance is caused by the feedback between me and you (the stranger), like the feedback that occurs when a microphone is held up to a loudspeaker. If I were to use the language with which we are now familiar, I would say my awareness-of tries to overcome your awareness-of. *But only one awareness-of is possible,* and this clash would be a clash within awareness-of itself. This means that the success of my awareness-of, as it overcomes yours, brings an increase in the level of intensity of the awareness-of. But this increase in intensity causes a reciprocal increase in the level of your awareness-of also. This creates a feedback and leads to the buildup of a vicious circle of annoyance and then anger, until the tension becomes intolerable. This might end in my trying to overcome you physically through an act of violence. Or, I could turn the violence onto myself in feelings of guilt and shame, still with the end in view of suppressing awareness-of.

To escape the pain of this division in awareness-of, I could also tear awareness-as apart. To do this I would create an entirely different viewpoint, an entirely different me. This would, at best, create a pseudo-viewpoint, called by Jung *a complex.*[2] At worst, it would create multiple personalities. Thus, this resolution is potentially more drastic, and to uderstand it we need to probe a deeper layer yet. At this deeper level we will see why abuse, sexual harassment, date rape, and even actions that might seem innocuous can be so devastating to the victim, and why this more drastic strategy would be resorted to. At this deeper level our inquiry will also provide the groundwork for showing how consciousness has emerged both for the human species and for each individual human being.

The Caress as Betrayal

Suppose that a woman visits her doctor for a checkup for possible breast cancer. To make his examination the doctor must feel her breasts. She has no trouble with this because she has faith in the doctor, and therefore has no need to break the contact. Me-you is in harmony. Nevertheless she is likely to be embarrassed. This embarrassment has to do with being "made into an object." It comes out of an ambiguity in awareness, similar to the ambiguity we have just considered, but it has the potential to be far more devastating .

To understand this embarrassment we must first make the distinction between being caressed and being felt, because this time the faith the woman has in the doctor is the faith that he is *feeling* her breasts and not *caressing* them, whereas in the subway we have faith the stranger is simply touching us and not feeling us.

If I caress someone, I want to feel her and not just touch her. But I also want to be aware-of her being aware-of being felt. This reciprocal awareness-of turns feeling into caressing. However, while I caress, the reciprocity is within the same awareness-of. This is shown in Figure 9.

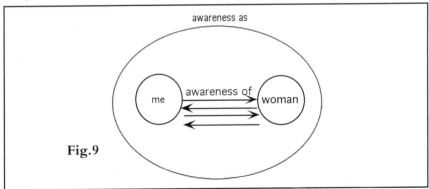

Fig. 9

As we see in Figure 9, a feedback occurs but, in the case of the caress, it is not an increase in *volume* of awareness but in *intensity*; it is heightened awareness. But even so, the feedback is not between the woman's awareness-of the situation and my awareness-of. It is feedback between me/you, as shown in Figure 10.

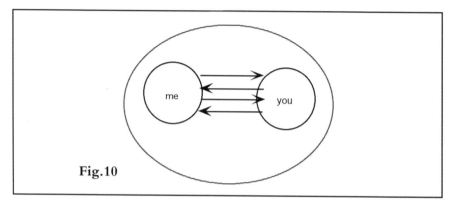

Fig.10

As I have already shown, me/you is not dependent upon another person being present. The encounter can be simply me/you, but it is important that this not be construed as simply imagination or illusion. On the contrary, what is illusory is the belief that me/you *must* mean me involved with another physical person. Thus another way of illustrating Figure 10 is shown in Figure 11.

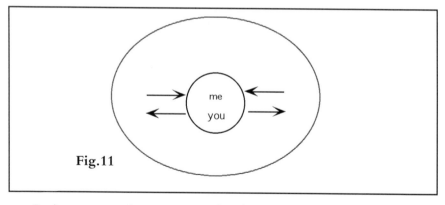

Fig.11

Let's return to the woman in the doctor's office. During the physical examination, the more she insists on the absence of being caressed, and the more professional the doctor‡ is, the more she must turn herself into

‡   A "doctor" is not so much a person as a role that a person adopts. The more completely one is able to fulfill the role, to more professional one is.

an object. If either she or the doctor shows awkwardness about what is happening, disaster threatens. Were the doctor to act unprofessionally and betray his patient's confidence by *caressing* instead of *feeling* her breasts, she would have to break away, not simply from him but *from herself*. The break in this case would be much more severe than the break with the stranger because it occurs at a heightened intensity. In addition, to break away from the caress, the feedback must be interrupted at another level beyond the one described in the subway episode.

In the doctor's office, the woman must deny awareness-of being felt by becoming an object to herself and to the doctor. She does this by blocking, or interrupting, the feedback process. This means she has denied herself as subject. An object is not aware-of being felt. The greater the trust she has in the doctor, the more she is inclined to make this denial, and therefore the more she accepts being an object. Nevertheless she is, of course, still a subject—a person. Thus a separation occurs between her awareness-of herself as a subject and her awareness-of herself as an object. The feelings of embarrassment and awkwardness during the examination are due largely to this separation. But this means the intensity of pain she will experience if she is betrayed is proportionate to the degree of trust she has. As she becomes aware-of being caressed, and not just medically examined, she will have to increase her acceptance of being an object, along with her denial being a subject. In other words, she must say that she is no longer *me*. This denial could reach a point at which it can no longer be sustained. The woman's "old me" would then be abandoned and an entirely new one would emerge. This would cause a profound inward tearing. Women who are abused in this way may take months or even years to recover. Violence and self-hatred can result from this rupture of her self, which occurs at the deepest spiritual levels[3] and could even cause the woman to go mad or commit suicide.

The Caress as Love

If we now consider two lovers caressing, we can see more clearly that we are talking about *Oneness* divided against itself. From the purely physical point of view, the caress of a lover and the caress of a sexual abuser can be exactly the same; but in the case of the lover, instead of the outcome being a violent separation held in place by hatred, there is an increased sense of union, a coming together in a paroxysm of love. Instead of division, there is enhancement. The woman is caressed by the man and in turn caresses the man. The feedback is compounded by the awareness-of the feedback of the other in the following way:

I am aware of you
I am aware of you being aware of me
I am aware of you being aware of me being aware of you
I am aware of you being aware of me being aware of you
being aware of me being aware of you
I am aware......................[4]

Writing about the onset of the orgasm, Murray Davis describes it thus:

[One reverses] the polarity of one's identity with that of a real or fantasized partner — alternately looking through at the partner through one's own eyes and at oneself through the partner's eyes. (One can also look at both through the imagined eyes of some observing third party. Mirrors facilitate this last, omniscient point of view.) These oscillations of identification increase in frequency and intensity as orgasm approaches. When orgasm occurs, the self is experienced as a mixture of both identities.[5]

Sex without 'love' is most often a tawdry affair. To love another, in the context of the erotic, is to want to be *aware of* the other's *awareness-of*, and aroused by one's own arousal. Put in simplistic terms, the man who simply seeks his own pleasure in the erotic relation makes a poor lover, as does a woman wanting to give pleasure without enjoying it. Furthermore, most people agree that the erotic situation is 90% "in the mind," which in our terms means the erotic situation is essentially one in which there is a feedback of awareness-of.

Oneness/Twoness/Oneness

Thus two situations that are identical from a physical point of view can lead to diametrically opposite results. A man caresses a woman. In the first instance (the doctor's office) it arouses violence in the woman which she often directs at herself through the sense of guilt, self-hatred, and anguish. (More rarely, she directs this violence at the man through physical or verbal abuse.) In the second instance (the lover's caress) the caress can lead to a paroxysm of ecstasy. The same mechanism—feedback of "awareness-of awareness-of"—is present in both. Although for a woman a man may be instrumental in the feedback, nevertheless the feedback is between the me/you of the woman, not between the woman as a person and the man as a person. Simply remembering or imagining the lover's caress can set in motion erotic buildup. Thus awareness-of leads to an ambiguity, an identical situation leading to opposing results; me is both the subject and the object at once—or, in both, oneness is divided against itself. In the first case the division leads to violence, hatred, and hell. In the second this division leads to greatly heightened awareness-of oneness, to heaven.

I chose for these examples the sense of touch because it has an immediate quality. Most people register repugnance at the very idea of being felt and readily recognize the difference between being touched, felt, and caressed. But the same feedback occurs through the sense of sight. Two lovers looking into each others' eyes can set up an erotic cycle; on the other hand, two enemies looking into each others' eyes can bring about an explosion of violence. Looking often is associated with the arousal of intense energy; this has given rise to the myth of the "evil eye," which is widespread in our own and other civilizations.[6] This is the power to inflict damage on another's person and property and sometimes even to inflict death simply by looking—the encounter of awareness-of with awareness-of. The look is also associated with beatific experiences, particularly in connection with falling in love and in the encounter with the look of the guru.

This detour has shown how unity can be divided against itself. Now let us return to consciousness and show how this division of unity occurs at the most fundamental level.

Awareness-as is not *mine*. Awareness-as is without the least trace of subjectivity or objectivity. It is neither inside me nor out-side me; it does not come or go. Furthermore, it was only because of the constraints of language that I call the viewpoint "me." However, a viewpoint does imply subjectivity, and we could say the viewpoint is the original subjectivity. This subjectivity could be that of a human being or of an animal. (We have analyzed subjectivity in some depth but because of the complexity of the description have decided not to include it at this point as it would slow down the flow too much. The results of the analysis are in Appendix Three.)

However, the viewpoint is not simply subjective. It also implies the *other*. This is why I do not just talk about me-as-center, but always insist on including me-as periphery. These two cannot be separated. Me-as-periphery involves the other as much as me, indeed at this original level the other is me. These two are one. Thus "me" and "you" have equal status, the one equally independent yet dependent upon the other, and both are at the center as awareness-of and at the periphery of awareness-of at the same time.

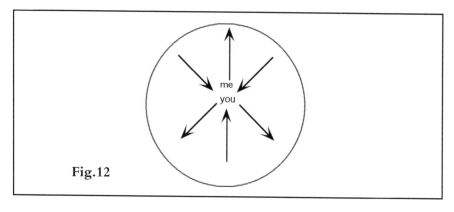

Fig.12

Me and you, or, to use the biblical term which is more intimate, I and thou, *are the outcomes* of divided awareness-of; awareness-of turned back onto itself. Awareness-of is *not an attribute* of me or you as personalities. The look is the encounter of awareness-of within itself, upstream of consciousness, which is why we can never grasp the other as a form of consciousness. You are, as it were, a hole through which I can fall into heaven or damnation. Consciousness is a series of buffers by which the threat of hell and the promise of heaven is attenuated. The function of consciousness is to provide ways by which a direct encounter with you can be avoided. I take ready made words and names, stereotypes, phrases, ways of acting and reacting: buffers against reality, ways by which to transform you into an it. But, these buffers sometimes collapse, the veils tear and I stand outside myself in ecstasy or horror. You and I together are as a mirror and image, a perfect unus-ambo, but who is the mirror and whom the image cannot be determined. Love, human love, the love of a man for a woman, releases me into other moments of standing outside, of ecstasy, when you and I are two but one. But so does love of man, and woman, for God, the Love of I for Thee.

Notes

1. Instead of saying, "My awareness-of my awareness-as the audience before actually encountering" the audience one would usually say " my awareness-of an imaginary audience," but this would lose the precision we need to understand what is happening.

2. Jung says that the complex consists of "a nuclear element and a large number of constellated associations. The nuclear element consists of two components; first a factor determined by experience and causally related to the environment; second a factor innate in the individual's character and determined by his disposition. The constellating power of the of nuclear element corresponds to its value intensity, i.e., to its energy." C.G. Jung, *The Structure and Dynamics of the Psyche* (London: Routledge & Kegan Paul, 1960; R.F.C. Hull, Trans.), pp. 11–12.

3. On the very day this was being written a report appeared in the Montreal Gazette saying "The sexual abuse of patients can lead to very serious consequences. . . .In extreme cases, you have suicide attempts and outright psychotic episodes."

4. Again the statement has been simplified so that the point can be made.

5. Murray S. Davis, *Smut Erotic Reality/Obscene Ideology* (Chicago: University of Chicago Press, 1983).

6. See Alan Dundes, *The Evil Eye* (Madison: University of Wisconsin Press, 1992).

Part 3

Chapter 13

Yearning for Unity:
The Frog Voice

How came I to be? Whence am I? To serve what purpose did I come? To go again? How can I learn aught – naught knowing?

I N THE NEXT FEW CHAPTERS I will talk more specifically about the evolution of consciousness, the third creative leap in evolution. (The first leap was the creation of matter, and the second the creation of the cell.) The creation of consciousness comes out of the creation of the world idea, which gives form to the field I call me. In human beings the world idea and me are one. Before we can understand the creation of the world idea and then consciousness, we must understand creativity itself—what inspires it, why it is often so abrupt, and what controls it. Each of these will be the subject of a chapter of its own. The creation of consciousness was the major step in the evolution of human beings, and so it must be at the human level that we consider creation. However, we must not forget that the force which creates *in* a human being is the same force that creates the human being.

Underlying the deepest needs and yearnings of the human being is a germ common to all. These yearnings give rise to creativity, spirituality, and romantic love; when they are frustrated, they give rise to violence. But they have a common source. This source or germ is simple in structure but far-reaching in its effects. In this chapter, we will get to know this germ, the inspiration of our yearning that has been called by the poets "the frog voice"; it will help us in our exploration of consciousness.

The chapter will show the influence of unity as a force in human affairs in creativity, love, spirituality, and violence. In Chapter 15, we'll consider why creation is so often abrupt. And Chapter 16 will show the anatomy of the frog voice, which is the anatomy of the idea as the eye of unity. But first let us see unity as a force calling out for expression.

Creativity

Vincent van Gogh, the great Flemish painter, once wrote to his brother, "I can do without God in my life and in my painting, but I cannot, ill as I am, do without something which is greater than I, which is my life— the power to create."[1] This statement is all the more remarkable when we realize that at about this time van Gogh also wrote that he had had in recent months only three warm meals. He had eaten so poorly because he was unable to sell even one of his paintings, and he was living off the benevolence of his brother. Nevertheless, he was so driven by the power to create that most of the money he received he spent on paint, canvases, and fees for models.

This power to create of which van Gogh speaks is not simply a human need; it is the power that created humanity as well as all human culture and civilization. Only by accepting creativity as inherent in the universe can we attribute it to human beings. Yet if we deny it to human beings, not only is the universe not the same but, as de Chardin pointed out, no universe is possible.

The power to create has its source in the yearning for unity. One way this yearning appears in a human being is as a longing for his or her life to be meaningful. Van Gogh expressed this longing poignantly, saying that he was one of those people "who are somehow mysteriously imprisoned, prisoners in an I-don't-know-what-for horrible, horrible, utterly horrible cage. Such a man often does not know himself what he might do but feels instinctively: yet I am good for something. . . . How then can I be useful, how can I be of service! Something is alive in me: what can it be!"[2]

"Something is alive in me: what can it be!" The poet Beddoe echoed this sentiment when he called the power to create that comes from the yearning for unity:

A bodiless childful of life in the gloom
Crying with frog voice, "What shall I be?"[3]

This proved so apt as a description of the creative urge that it was subsequently used by a German poet, Gottfried Benn, in a lecture he gave on creativity in poetry, and later still by T. S. Eliot in *Three Voices of Poetry*. Eliot's article can help us understand this creative power of van Gogh, and this understanding in turn sheds light on the question of the human situation and on life in general, because creative powers are not simply vested in a few select individuals but are the blessing, and the curse, of us all.

Eliot starts his article by asking, "What is it that prompts a poet when he or she starts writing a poem?" We can read this to mean, "What is it that underlies both creativity and evolution?" In other words, "What is the source of inspiration?" Quoting Benn, Eliot says: "first *an inert embryo or creative germ is conceived* and then comes the Language, the resources at the poet's command."[4] Van Gogh, instead of the language of words, used the language of painting. Generalizing further, we can say that in all creation first an inert embryo is conceived, which then finds a form. Eliot insists that not only does the poet find a form for the embryo, but the poet *must* find the form, he or she *has* to find the language in order to give life to this inert embryo. Thus, still quoting Benn, Eliot says, "The poet has something germinating in him for which he *must* find words."[5] Creativity is not a luxury but a necessity, an imperative. Many people think of the artist's life in a romantic way, not realizing that creativity can be tyrannical, demanding, and painful. Conversely, many do not realize that their own sense of being oppressed, of being burdened by life, may well come from an unfulfilled urge to create, the frog voice calling in vain, as it did when Van Gogh cried out in pain.

Novelist Henry James also used the notion of a germ that incites an author to write, but he said it is both an infection that sends the hapless author into a literary fever *and* a seed cell ready to germinate into full-blown literary life. For example, a chance comment at a dinner party was the seed of his novel, *The Spoils of Poynton*. This comment made him instantly aware of the "whole of the virus."[6]

Poet Denise Levertov describes this "whole virus" in sensory terms when she says, "You can smell the poem before you can see it. Like some animal . . . the smell of a bear; you know, you might begin to hear it kind of going . . . pad . . . pad around the house."[7] Levertov adds that she waits until the germ feeling unfolds itself "into some phrases, some words, a rhythm, because if I try to push that into being by will before the intuition is really at work, then it is going to be a very bad beginning, and perhaps I'm going to lose the poem altogether."[8]

These germs, this whole virus, "contain for the creator the qualities of wholeness, nuance, ambiguity, open-endedness and also concrete specificity."[9]

Although the poet has something germinating in him for which he *must* find words, he cannot, Benn says, know what words he wants *until he has found them.* Benn goes on to say, the poet cannot identify this embryo "until it has been transformed into an arrangement of the right words in the right order,"[10] (or, for the painter, until it has been transformed into an arrangement of the right forms and colors in the right order). "When this has been done the 'thing' for which the words had to be found has disappeared, replaced by the poem."[11]

This unknown knowing, or mystery, comes from the utter inconceivability of Unity. Stravinsky refers to it, "This foretaste of the creative act accompanies the intuitive grasp of an unknown entity already possessed but not yet intelligible, an entity that will not take definite shape except by the action of a constantly vigilant technique."[12]

As Gregory Bateson said in his *Ecology of Mind,* "Sometimes—often in science and always in art—one does not know what the problems were till after they have been solved."[13]

In discussing the unknownness of the thing that compels an artist to work, Benn says that what you start from is nothing so definite as an emotion, in any ordinary sense; it is still more certainly not an idea; it is, and this is where he uses the quotation from Beddoes, "A bodiless childful of life in the gloom/Crying with frog voice, 'what shall I be?'"

Eliot takes over at this point in his article, saying that he agrees with Gottfried Benn and would go even further to say that the poet uses all his resources to express this obscure impulse.

> He does not know what he wants to say until he has said it... He is not concerned, at this stage with other people at all; only with finding the

right words or, anyhow, the least wrong words. He is not concerned whether anybody else will ever understand them if he does.[14]

This is similar in kind, although perhaps not in intensity, to having something on the tip of your tongue—an author's name, perhaps—you want to say but just cannot remember: an inert embryo arises, a creative germ with a struggle to find words. This germ is something *and you know what it is.* When someone asks, "Is it Conrad?" you answer, "No, not Conrad." Yet you don't know what it is, as it is not yet consciously integrated with other experience. By knowing we most often mean a thought or image, or perhaps even an emotion. Although all of these may well be brought into play when trying to express the creative germ, it is not any one of them. Indeed, it is not an experience at all. What is at issue modifies experience, creates emotions, and releases thoughts, but it is itself none of these. However, if one says that it is *something* and then proceeds to reject all possible contents of the mind as not being it, one must come to wonder what kind of something it can be. The frog voice, the bodiless childful of life in the gloom, is unity—and we refer to it as something simply as a linguistic device. Unity is the womb of all things, but unity is not a thing.

To return to the analogy between this creative embryo and the struggle to remember an author's name, in both cases the struggle is accompanied by tension. This tension seems to vary according to how close we are to remembering the name and how important it is for us to remember it. If it is very important and if the name seems imminent, it can cause frustration, anxiety, grief, and even anger. On TV game shows that test people's inexhaustible supply of trivia, contestants go through all kinds of tension when they "know the answer—but do not know it." Indeed, it could be the vicarious enjoyment of this tension and its release in a cathartic orgy of excitement that causes people to watch these shows. If it is not important that you find the name, you might feel only discomfort, a slight nagging tension that somehow will not go away.

When the right name or the right word does come a "snapping," a sudden release takes over; in Eliot's words "a moment of exhaustion, appeasement, of absolution and of something very near annihilation." Of course, for someone remembering a name it would be a much milder release of tension and feeling of relief. But, it must be the *right* word.

Sometimes during the struggle, amid the flow of thoughts, a pseudo solution may be offered and accepted, and although the struggle may abate,
however, the snap of release does not occur and the vague nagging feeling continues.

Eliot says that while struggling with this inert embryo the poet is *not
concerned with making other people understand anything.* This is important to
emphasize because so often people confuse creativity with communication; and, while communication may well require creativity, creativity in
itself is not communication. This distinction will be vital later, when we
distinguish between the creation we call *language* and communication.
Some evidence for saying that creativity and communication are not
necessarily connected is seen in the struggle to find the elusive name of
the author. Even though the impasse could well have appeared during a
conversation, nevertheless the struggle to remember may go on long after the conversation has ended. In the struggle to find the releasing word,
one retires, as it were, into a private world. Indeed, if one gets locked into
trying to remember, the conversation and surroundings can fade away
completely.

Eliot echoes the cry of Van Gogh, "Something is alive in me: what
can it be?" when he says:

> He is oppressed by a burden which he must bring to birth in order to
> obtain relief. Or, to change the figure of speech, he is haunted by a
> demon, a demon against which he feels powerless, because in its first
> manifestation it has no face, no name, nothing; and the words, the poem
> he makes, are a kind of form of exorcism of this demon.[15]

The creative power of Van Gogh was also a form of exorcism of a
demon, a demon that keeps him bound *"in a horrible, horrible, utterly horrible prison."*

In other words, Eliot says, the poet or painter is going to all that
trouble not simply to communicate with someone else but to gain relief
from acute discomfort (in the case of Van Gogh. we would have to say
from indescribable anguish). When the words are finally arranged the right
way—or in what he comes to accept as the best arrangement he can
find—the artist may experience a moment of exhaustion, of appeasement,
of absolution, and of something very near annihilation, which is itself in-

describable. And then he can say to the poem: "Go away! Find a place for yourself in a book—and don't expect me to take any further interest in you."

Van Gogh, Gottfried Benn, Beddoes, and T.S. Eliot were driven by an unknown demon that has all the characteristics of a curse, a cross, a burden. This curse is the curse of unity, a curse shared by all humankind. We are driven to discover unity, a unity that was ours and which seemed to have been lost when awareness-of turned back on itself. Unity is called paradise when seen to be in the future, or the Garden of Eden when seen in the past. Looking at unity this way gives new meaning to God's curse on Adam and Eve: "Cursed is the ground for thy sake; in toil shalt thou eat of it all the days of thy life." Not only the artist but all of us are driven by this nameless, formless demon, whose curse drives us to distraction until it has been exorcised. It is this same curse, or blessing, that impelled the first human being onto the road to consciousness. But let us see this impulse as it underlies the various aspects of being human.

Romantic Love

In both *The Iron Cow of Zen* and *The Butterfly's Dream*, I wrote at length about romantic love and so will deal with it but briefly now. Plato tells a myth to account for the arising of romantic love but it could also be interpreted as a myth to account for the curse laid upon human beings. According to this myth, beings with two heads, four arms and four legs once lived on earth. Because of their stability and strength, they became a threat to the gods who, in self-defense, cut them in half, compelling each half forever to seek its counterpart in an endeavor to return to lost unity. The myth tells us that the lover as well as the artist is driven by this demon of unity. Plato talks of the desire that the lover has for the beloved. He says, "The cause of this desire is to be sought in the fact that this was indeed our primitive nature when *we constituted one unit which was still whole*; it is really the **burning longing for this unity** which bears the name of love."[16]

The burning longing for unity bears the name of love. And it comes from an underlying feeling of separation, incompleteness. How often do we read stories about a lover being separated from his beloved. Love and death are the substance of tragedy; on the one hand is love, perfect unity— all conflict, all division are laid to rest. On the other hand is death, the ultimate divide, an abyss that has no bridge. One of the most famous instances of longing for unity haunted by strife and expressed in romantic love was the love affair of *Romeo and Juliet*, which as we know ended in tragedy. Shakespeare uses the separation of the clan of Romeo from the clan of Juliet to give concrete expression to the anguish of separation that underlies Romeo and Juliet's love, causing it to end in tragedy. But we do not have to turn to historic or legendary figures for examples of the separation that often leads to tragedy. Not so long ago the film *Fatal Attraction* portrayed a young woman driven to madness by her love for a man. In real life many know the sad story of a school headmistress who ended in prison accused of the violent death of the lover who betrayed her. Driven by fury, lovers end in destruction; a love affair gone awry through an inability to transcend separation. Oneness which is two, twoness which is one, unus-ambo, which we explored at length in Chapter 12, is at the very root of romantic love.

Lovers are often said to be living in a dream. How many songs have this as a theme? The dream comes out of the sense of no separation, of one mind embracing the two lovers. But the dream threatens constantly to erupt into a nightmare of separation, and the lover becomes tormented, restless, driven. A song from the 1940s sums up the feeling of some hidden and unknown force, a frog voice, at work:

> I'm restless as a willow in a windstorm,
> I'm active as a puppet on a string,
> I'd say that I had Spring fever,
> But it isn't even Spring.

Trite though it may be, the song expresses that feeling of oppression, of being driven by the demon to find Unity. Something disturbs, rages in a Lover, the same force that disturbs and rages in the artist. And what about spirituality does it too have the same demon?

Zen Buddhism[17]

Indeed, the literature of spirituality is flooded with cries from the heart of those seeking God, Love, wholeness, Unity. As just one example among a multitude, consider the opening lines of Psalm 22:

> My God, my God, why hast thou forsaken me?

Why art thou so far from helping me, and from the words of
my roaring?
O my God I cry in the day time, but thou answerest not;
And in the night season and am not silent.

Underlying the search for unity in Zen Buddhism is the "doubt sensation"—the sensation of hunger and longing. As a Zen Master said, when
one is working on Zen the important thing is to generate the doubt
sensation. He went on to say, "To all intents and purposes, the study of
Zen makes as its essential the resolution of the ball of doubt. That is why
it is said: 'at the bottom of Great Doubt lies great awakening. If you doubt
fully, you will awaken fully.'"[18] The doubt sensation, he said, underlies such
questions as why was I born, where was I before my birth, where do I
go after death, and the meaning of life itself.

The Zen Master says that the important thing is to generate the *ball
of doubt*. Seeing that he gives various kinds of questions that might generate this ball of doubt, obviously it does not arise from *any particular one
of them*. Indeed, several ritualistic questions that monks ask Zen masters
have evolved such as, "What is Buddha?" "What was the meaning of
Bodhidharma coming from the West?"[19] This means in effect that the *form*
of the question is unimportant; *the fact of questioning*, the ball of doubt, is
what is important.

The great doubt is none other than the inert embryo; the monk's
question, "What is Buddha?" is but a mask put on the face of Eliot's faceless demon to help in its exorcism. This word *doubt* is an unfortunate one
in that it has too much of an intellectual ring. In the New Testament the
expression occurs this way: "Blessed are they who *hunger and thirst* after
righteousness, for they shall be filled." This doubt sensation should be seen
as a hungering and thirsting after righteousness. When Van Gogh cried out,
"Something is alive in me, what can it be?" he was giving voice to the
doubt sensation.

Another name that we could give to the great doubt is great longing. The author of a Christian mystical text titled *The Cloud of Unknowing* put it this way:

I would rather weep till my heart should break because I lack this awareness of God and feel the painful heaviness of the self, and thus inflame

my desire to have and to long for that awareness, rather than enjoy all
the well-devised imaginative and speculative meditations that men can
tell of or find written in books, no matter how holy or worthwhile they
appear.[20]

Later in the same work he said, "Your whole life must now be one
of longing if you are to achieve perfection. This longing must be in the
depth of your will put there by God with your consent."

Yasutani-roshi, a contemporary Zen Master, said, "The ball of doubt
is a doubt as to why we and the world should appear so imperfect, so full
of anxiety, strife, and suffering, whereas our faith tells us exactly the opposite is true. It is a doubt that leaves us no rest."[21] This kind of doubt
is surely known to us all. Again we see strife infuse with unity. Our faith
is faith in unity; our anxiety, the outcome of conflict and separation—
oneness that is twoness.

Great Doubt is original chaos and disorder of the Being. Another Zen
master, Ta Hui, says that great doubt is generated at the very point at
which confusion arises. Confusion, bewilderment, anxiety and anguish—
such is the stuff of which great doubt is made. By using this chaos and
turning it into great doubt, the Zen Buddhist is able to use it in a creative way. Ghiselli wrote of creativity in the same way we could speak of
the the doubt sensation:

Chaos and disorder might be wrong terms for that indeterminate fullness and activity of the inner life. For it is organic, dynamic, full of tension
and tendency. What is absent from it, except in the decisive act of creation, is fixity and commitment to one resolution or another of the
whole complex of its tensions. It is a working sea of indecision.[22]

We are again reminded of van Gogh's "prisoners in an I-don't-know-
what-for horrible, horrible, utterly horrible cage."

The absence of "commitment to one resolution or another" is
stressed constantly in Zen in its insistence on avoiding good and bad.
Some famous lines titled "Verses on the Faith Mind" and written by an
early Chinese Zen master illustrate this:

The Great Way is not difficult
For those who have no preferences.

When good and bad are cast aside
The way stands clear and undisguised.
But even slight distinctions will
set earth and heaven far apart.

John Keats, the Romantic poet of nineteenth-century England, also made a case for absence of commitment to one resolution or another when he talked about the value of *negative commitment* in creativity. He said it occurs, "when a man is *capable of being in uncertainties*, mysteries, doubts, without any irritable reaching after fact and reason."[23]

So we have the artist, the lover, the spiritual seeker all striving for unity, a striving that comes out of conflict and, deeper still, out of the frog voice, the unus-ambo.

Before leaving this mystery of the frog voice, let's make one more call, this time on Marcel Proust. What he has to say puts succinctly the point I am trying to make. He had just drunk a spoonful of tea in which he had soaked a morsel of cake:

No sooner had the warm liquid mixed with the crumbs touched my palate than a shudder ran through me and I stopped, intent upon the extraordinary thing that was happening to me. An exquisite pleasure had invaded my senses, something isolated, detached, with no suggestion of its origin. And at once the vicissitudes of life had become indifferent to me, its disasters innocuous, its brevity illusory — this new sensation having had on me the effect which love has of filling me with a precious essence; or rather this essence was not in me, it was me. I had ceased now to feel mediocre, contingent, mortal. Whence could it have come to me, this all-powerful joy? I sensed that it was connected with the taste of the tea and the cake, but that it infinitely transcended those savors, could not, indeed be of the same nature. Whence did it come? What did it mean? How could I seize and apprehend it?. . .What an abyss of uncertainty, whenever the mind feels overtaken by itself; when it, the seeker, is at the same time the dark region through which it must go seeking and where all its equipment will avail it nothing. Seek? More than that: create. It is face to face with something which does not yet exist, to which it alone can give reality and substance, which it alone can bring into the light of day.[24]

This *"the mind feels overtaken by itself,"* is the key for unlocking the enigma of creativity, spirituality, and eros. Did I say unlock the enigma? That would be a foolish claim, unless *the key is the enigma;* the mind being, to use Proust's phrase, at one and the same time the seeker and "the dark region through which it must go seeking," the center and the periphery.

The key is the enigma. But, I am anticipating and much ground needs to be covered before we can enter this tiger's cave. We are exploring the germ of consciousness and in this chapter we saw a yearning, a longing, a will-to-be, a frog voice, precedes the birth of this germ. Is it the same frog voice for all? In the next chapters, we will explore that further.

Notes

1.   Vincent van Gogh, *Dear Theo: Autobiography of Vincent van Gogh*, eds. Irving and Jean Stone (New York: Signet, 1937), p. 382.
2.   Van Gogh (1937, p. 380).
3.   Cited in T. S. Eliot, *On Poetry and the Poets* (London: Faber & Faber, 1957), p. 98.
4.   Eliot (1957, p. 97).
5.   Eliot (1957, p. 97).
6.   Cited in John Briggs, *Fire in the Crucible* (Los Angeles: Jeremy Tarcher, 1990), p. 283.
7.   Briggs (1990, p. 283).
8.   Briggs (1990, p. 228).
9.   Briggs (1990).
10.   Eliot (1957, p. 228).
11.   Eliot (1957, p. 228).
12.   Briggs (1990, p. 289).
13.   Gregory Bateson, *Steps to an Ecology of Mind* (New York: Ballantine Books, 1972), p. 271.
14.   Eliot (1957).
15.   Eliot (1957, p. 98).
16.   Plato, *Symposium* XIV–XV, 192, d–e; italics mine.
17.   I am using the term Zen, although in this instance it might be preferable to use the word *Ch'an*, which is the Chinese equivalent. Indeed, in that Zen is derived from Ch'an, justice in a way demands that we use the Chinese term. However, Westerners are more familiar with the word Zen, and for this reason I have decided to use it.
18.   Chan Chen-chi, *The Practice of Zen* (London: Rider Books, 1959), p. 79.

19. Bodhidharma is reputed to be the founder of Chan in China and therefore the first Chinese Patriarch. The question could be loosely translated as, "What is the meaning of Buddhism?"

20. *The Cloud of Unknowing*. Translated by Ira Progoff (New York: Delta Books).

21. Philip Kapleau (ed.), *The Three Pillars of* Zen (New York: Harper & Row, 1966).

22. Brewster Ghisellli, *The Creative Process,* (Berkeley: Mentor Books, 1952).

23. John Keats, *The Selected Letters of John Keats,* ed. Lionel Trilling (New York: Doubleday, 1951), p. 103.

24. Marcel Proust, *Remembrance of Things Past* (Harmondsworth, UK: Penguin, 1983), p. 49.

Chapter 14

The Eruption of Unity

[Creation] occurs quite without volition,
as if in an eruption of freedom,
independence, power, and divinity.
NIETZSCHE

AT THE END OF THE LAST CHAPTER I quoted Proust: "No sooner had the warm liquid mixed with the crumbs touched my palate . . . " The experience he was describing came out of the instant; it was sudden. The eruption of unity is always sudden. The mark of the truly creative moment is the eruption of unity into what was previously an area dark with confusion. As Francis Crick said, "before, everything is in a fog." He went on to say, "It is not easy to convey, unless one has experienced it, the dramatic feeling of sudden enlightenment that floods the mind when the right idea finally clicks into place."[1] The "right idea" is the perception in the foggy field that dispels the gloom and brings everything into a clear and harmonious whole. Crick said, "one immediately sees how many previously puzzling facts are neatly explained by the new hypothesis."[2]

The eruption of unity is not only the mark of true creativity, it also is the moment of true love and spiritual awakening. It can also be the moment of the eruption of violence. According to de Chardin, an eruption is also responsible for the explosion that brought consciousness into being and so introduced into the universe an entirely new creation. He says, "reflection is, as the word indicates, the power acquired by [aware-ness] to turn in upon itself, to take possession of itself as of an object endowed with its own particular consistence and value." He added, "The being who is the object of his own reflection, in consequence of that very doubling back upon himself, becomes in a flash able to raise himself into a new sphere."[3]

First let's explore some examples of the eruption in creativity. In the next chapter we will explore why the creative idea—which is but another name for the germ of consciousness—is the eruption of unity.

The Suddenness of Creativity

The French mathematician Poincaré wrote an article about his own ex-perience of this moment of unity. He reported that for fifteen days he had struggled with a mathematical problem without success. Then one evening, contrary to his usual work habits, he drank black coffee and could not sleep:

> Ideas rose in crowds; I felt them collide until pairs interlocked, so to speak, making a stable combination. By the next morning I had established the existence of a class of Fuchsian functions, those which come from the hyper geometric series; I had only to write out the results, which took but a few hours.[4]

About this time he went on a geological excursion. The change of routine and scenery made him forget his mathematical work. Then "having reached Coutances, we entered an omnibus to go some place or other. At the moment when I put my foot on the step the idea came to me, *with-out anything in my former thoughts seeming to have paved the way for it.*"[5] This idea finally resolved the mathematical problem which had nagged at him for so long. He went on to say he did not verify the idea as he did not have the time but, instead, took his seat in the bus and went on with a conversation already commenced. Nevertheless he said that he felt perfectly certain. On his return to Caen, for conscience's sake, he verified the re-sult.

What is of interest here is the flash of recognition. There was a sud-den resolution. In the wings is the frog voice, the demon; but now, cen-ter stage, is the sudden recognition, and with it the complete certainty the problem is resolved.

Another famous mathematician, Karl Friedrich Gauss, reported:

At last two days ago I succeeded, not by dint of painful effort but so to speak by the grace of God. *As a sudden flash of light,* the enigma was solved...For my part I am unable to name the nature of the thread which connected what I previously knew with that which made my success possible. 6

Goethe reports, in connection with his writing *The Sorrows of Young Werther:*

I was collecting elements that had been floating within me for a number of years. I endeavored to retain a vivid picture of the cases that had been most urgent and most frightening to me. Yet nothing would take shape. What was lacking was an occasion in which they [these elements] could be embodied. All of a sudden, I heard the news of [a friend's suicide], and immediately . . . [my idea took shape] like water in a vessel, which on the freezing point, turns into ice at the slightest shock.[7]

Let me give one final story to round off these accounts: In 1879, Louis Pasteur was studying chicken cholera and had been preparing cultures of the bacillus. His work was interrupted and the cultures he had prepared were left unattended throughout the summer. In the autumn he was able to resume the experiment. He injected some chickens with the bacillus cultivated before the summer break. He found that the chickens became only slightly ill and so used another culture of the virulent bacillus. At the same time he injected another batch of newly bought chicks.

The newly bought chicks all died but, to his great surprise, the old chicks, who had been injected once already with the ineffective culture, survived. An eye witness in the lab described the scene that took place when Pasteur was informed of this curious development: He remained silent for a minute, then exclaimed as if he had seen a vision, "Don't you see that these animals have been vaccinated?"[8]

Remember our struggle in the last chapter to remember the name of an author? There was a sense of being burdened, of being under some kind of pressure. Then suddenly the name pops up from nowhere. It might be next day or two or three days later. And with its appearance is the release, the pleasure.

The Suddenness of Love

This sudden resolution not only comes in moments of creativity and discovery but also when falling in love. The suddenness of falling in love is legendary. A song in the 1940s put it this way:

> The first time I saw you,
> I knew at a glance,
> I was meant to be yours,
> Yours alone.

"I knew at a glance," in an instant. For this we do not really need the quotes. Who has not had the exhilarating moment of suddenly waking up in the midst of things and saying, "I'm in love!"

The Suddenness of Satori

At the basis of Zen Buddhist practice is what is known as *satori*. Someone once explained the meaning of the word to me this way: Suppose you are trying to explain something to someone, and at the end of the explanation the person looks at you somewhat bewildered. You try another explanation using a different tack. Again the bewilderment. You try a third time and then suddenly the other says, "Ah! Yes." In Japanese "Ah! Yes" translates as satori. Satori means, "Ah yes, I see it."

Although in Zen satori means the moment of spiritual awakening, which always comes in a flash, the meaning of the word ties it back directly to the examples of creativity given above. Let me quote a few examples of satori:

> Hsu Yun, a celebrated Chinese master who died in the 1950s, said about his awakening, "Instantly I cut off my last doubt and rejoiced at the realization of my cherished aim."[9]
>
> Yasutani roshi, a modern Zen master commented, "With the complete banishment of the I-concept, you suddenly experience Oneness. This is kensho (satori)."[10]
>
> Hakuin, a Zen master of the seventeenth century, put it more dramatically: "When the discriminating mind is shattered and the enlightened essence suddenly appears, the filling of the universe with its boundless light is called 'the great perfect mirror awareness.'"[11]

And lest you think spiritual awakening is instantaneous only in Zen, let me quote a Hindu and a Christian mystic:

Hindu teacher Nisargadatta said, "When one is fully matured, realization is explosive. It takes place spontaneously."[12]

The anonymous author of the Christian mystical classic *The Cloud of Unknowing* said, "The fruit of [meditation] is high spiritual wisdom, which is suddenly and without constraint belched forth by the spirit inwardly, within itself." The author added, "This work does not need a long time for its completion . . . [it needs] a time no longer than an atom of time, so short it cannot be analyzed."[13]

This sudden awakening, which is outside of thought, ties the experience closely with what French scholar Jacques Hadamard reported:

> One phenomenon is certain and I can vouch for its absolute certainty: the sudden and immediate appearance of a solution at the very moment of sudden awakening. On being very abruptly awakened by an external noise, a solution long searched for appeared to me at once without the slightest instant of reflection on my part.[14]

The Suddenness of Humor

Is there anything in our ordinary life that will give us an idea of what this sudden eruption is like? I mentioned the sudden remembering of a name. But an equally familiar experience is the joke. A group of people are standing around. One is telling a story. *Suddenly* the group members throw their heads back and laugh.

The following are some announcements taken from bulletins put out by various churches:

> Don't let worry kill you—let the church help.
>
> Thursday night—Potluck supper. Prayer and medication to follow.
>
> Remember in prayer the many who are sick of our church and community.
>
> For those of you who have children and don't know it, we have a nursery downstairs.
>
> The rosebud on the alter this morning is to announce the birth of David Alan Belzer, the sin of Rev. and Mrs. Julius Belzer.
>
> This afternoon there will be a meeting in the South and North ends of the church. Children will be baptized at both ends.

Tuesday at 4.00 P.M. there will be an ice cream social. All ladies giving milk will please come early.

Wednesday, the Ladies Liturgy Society will meet. Mrs. Jones will sing "Put Me in My Little Bed," accompanied by the pastor.

Thursday at 5.00 P.M. there will be a meeting of the Little Mothers Club. All wishing to become little mothers, please see the minister in his study.

This being Easter Sunday, we will ask Mrs. Lewis to come forward and lay an egg on the altar.

The service will close with "Little Drops of Water." One of the ladies will start quietly, and the rest of the congregation will join in.

Next Sunday a special collection will be taken to defray the cost of the new carpet. All those wishing to do something on the new carpet will come forward and do so.

The ladies of the church have cast off clothing of every kind, and they may be seen in the church basement Friday.

A bean supper will be held on Tuesday evening in the church hall. Music will follow.

At the evening service tonight, the sermon topic will be "What Is Hell?" Come early and listen to our choir practice.

Each of these items can be read two ways, a two which is one, an unus-ambo. Sudden recognition flashes, often accompanied by a release in laughter. A close connection exists between humor and Zen, so much so that the Buddhist scholar, Conze, once remarked, rather irreverently, that Zen is Buddhism with jokes. We will examine this connection more closely later. For the moment let me emphasize that once again, across the different areas of human life, a common thread can be found—this time the suddenness; the suddenness of resolution, the waking up to the moment of eureka! Two is one; one is two!

The Suddenness of Violence

Now let me recount some stories that show how this sudden eruption may be associated with hostility and destruction. The first is given by an observer who found himself in the middle of a family fight:

It started . . . sort of slowly . . . so I couldn't tell for sure if they were even serious. . . . In the beginning they'd push at each other, or shove, like kids—little kids who want to fight but they don't know how. Then, this one time, while I'm standing there not sure whether to stay or go, and them treating me like I didn't even exist, she begins yelling at him like she did. "You're a bust, you're a failure. I want you out of here! I can always get men who will work—good men, not scum like you." She pushes him, he pushes her, only she's doing all the talking. He isn't saying a word. Then *all of a sudden* she must have triggered off the right nerve because he lets fly with a right cross that I mean stuns. I mean she goes down like a rock! And he's swearing at her, calling her every name in the book.[15]

Another is told by a man who shot his wife:

I was a good provider for my family and a hard worker. . . . I told her if she stopped with the divorce, that I would promise to act better, but she wouldn't buy any of it. I got angrier and angrier. . . . I looked at her straight in the face and said, "Well, X, you better start thinking about those poor kids of ours." She said, "I don't care about them: I just want a divorce." My hate for her exploded then, and I said, "You dirty, no-good bitch," and started pounding her in the face with my fist.[16]

Paradoxically, this destruction too comes from the need for unity, a need that comes out of conflict and separation. In violence the need for unity can be satisfied only if one side of the conflict is destroyed or suppressed.

Summary

In Chapter 13, I talked about the frog voice, a haunting demon beyond words, thoughts, and images, indeed beyond all form, a demon that oppresses and has to be given some expression. In this chapter we have seen how this haunting call is resolved in a flash of transformation. Like the spark of electricity that unifies gases and makes them into water, a spark ignites: where previously unity was struggling in clouds of obscurity, confusion, and contradiction, it now shines in clarity, appeasement, and felicity. Eventually, I want to show that this spark is also a cosmic occurrence, leading to the birth of consciousness. But first, let's take a closer look at the creative germ and see whether we can tease out its anatomy.

Notes

1. Francis Crick, *What Mad Pursuit?* (New York: Basic Books, 1988), p. 141.
2. Crick (1988, p. 141).
3 de Chardin (1959, p. 183).
4. Brewster Ghiselin, *The Creative Process* (Berkeley, CA: Mentor Books, 1952), p. 36.
5. Ghiselin (1952, p. 36).
6. Ghiselin (1952, p. 36).
7. Briggs op. cit. p. 112
8. Briggs op. cit. p. 288
9. Charles Luk (Trans.), *The Autobiography of Hsu Yun* (Rochester, NY: Empty Cloud Press, 1974), p. 25.
10. Kapleau (1966, p. 137).
11. Thomas Cleary (Trans. and Ed.), *The Original Face* (New York: Grove Press, 19787), p. 130.
12. Nisargadatta op. cit. p. 113.
13. Clifton Walters (Trans.), *Cloud of Unknowing* (Harmondsworth, UK: Penguin Classics, 1961), p. 54.
14. Briggs (p. 17).
15. Jack Katz, *Seductions of Crime* (New York: Basic Books, 1988), p. 40.
16. Katz (1988, p. 33).

Chapter 15

Idea as the Eye of Unity

*We cannot have one and half actions. We cannot
decide to get up, vote, call a friend, speak or do
anything one-and-a-half-times.*
ARTHUR YOUNG

ARTHUR YOUNG, quoted above, is the author of *The Reflexive Universe*
and inventor of the Bell helicopter. He went on to say that wholeness is inherent in the nature of action, of decision, and of purposive
activity. Wholeness in action is implicit in the physical realm also. Young
said that the epoch making discovery of Max Planck was that "action
comes in wholes."[1] In perception, thought, and learning wholeness is
implicit, and this discovery is the basis of Gestalt psychology. In this chapter, I want to show it to be true of an idea and of consciousness itself.

To show that wholeness is implicit in consciousness I need to show
that the basis of consciousness is an *idea*, a world idea, and that idea has
a very precise anatomy. The anatomy of the idea can be expressed in terms
of the basic ambiguity, and, as well, in terms of me- as-center/me-as
periphery. This means that these three—idea, ambiguity, and me-as-cen-
ter/me-as-periphery—are but different ways of talking about the same
thing. An architect's drawing of a building has a plan, a side elevation and
a front elevation; no one considers these to be separate parts of the building. Likewise, a doctor may look at a body from the point of view of its

anatomy, its physiology, or its nervous systems. So, in this chapter I will be looking at consciousness from the point of view of Idea. But remember all that has been said about the basic ambiguity and about me-as-center/me-as-periphery, as this allows us to regard the source of consciousness from different points of view. Just as the architect can look at a building from three points of view, so we will be looking at the source of consciousness from three points of view.

I have said that the unfolding of the idea in creativity comes about from the force of dynamic unity. Taking my lead from the poets, I have tried to dramatize oneness by calling it the frog voice and the demon. I want to return to idea to explore it in greater depth. In doing so I hope also to show that both the force behind the idea and its sudden release come from oneness. To show what I mean, I'll use some practical exercises to help make the point.

The Hidden Man

What is the picture? This is not an ink blot test. The picture, when you see it, will be quite distinct and clear. The answer will come as a snap; the field will suddenly clarify and will take on quite a new significance. Bear

Fig.13:

in mind the purpose of this exercise is not so much to get to see the picture as to observe *the process involved in getting to see it*. So take note of this process of getting to see what the picture represents.

When you are first confronted with the picture ask yourself, "What *precisely* am I seeing?" Take note of your reactions and your feelings as you work at the picture; how do you feel about the exercise? Periodically, as you work at seeing the picture, ask yourself these same questions.

Discussion of the Exercise

The first impression most people have when confronted with this picture is of a confused field, a chaos of black and white shapes that may resolve into some kind of map or configuration. As they continue looking at the picture, trying to make sense of it, they begin to feel somewhat tense. Along with this tension a feeling of frustration or restlessness sometimes wells up, accompanied by a wish to give the whole thing up, to put the exercise to one side and get on with reading the book. This tension can become more and more acute, while the feelings oscillate between boredom, anger, frustration, and apathy.

Then, all of a sudden, the picture emerges; the tension releases. At this point people who do the exercise often smile or even laugh. This sense of relief waxes and wanes, becoming gradually less pronounced until the feelings become neutral.

Even after having seen it once, you can lose the picture and the field reverts again to chaos. The different stages of discovery will recur, although they are often less pronounced than during the first effort.

We can say the process is similar to what was described above as the frog voice. First the inert embryo, the creative germ arises when you are asked, "What do you see?" Then comes what Eliot called the "language." In our case this is the form the picture will take when we see it. We cannot know the word (or specific form) we want *until the form has been found;* this creative embryo, "*what* you see," cannot be given an identity until "what" has been transformed into "that." Eliot says the embryo cannot be identified "*until it has been transformed into 'an arrangement of words in the right order.'*" For our purposes, when the shapes have been arranged in the right order, "what is it?" disappears and is replaced by the picture.

Now what does one begin with? A question certainly, but what gives the question meaning? At the beginning of the search one has a certain faith, such as, "There must be something there, since he asked me to find it!" But this faith simply keeps the question alive. One cannot say that faith alone gives the question meaning. So again one must ask the question, "*What* is it one starts with?" This is a crucial question. Eliot says it is not so definite as an emotion, in any ordinary sense. He also says it is not an idea, that it is not a thought or an image. It is "A bodiless childful of life in the gloom / Crying with frog voice: 'What shall I be?'"

If you really do this exercise it will become obvious that, once the question "What is it?" has taken hold, one is locked in with it and nothing else; one is not concerned with other people. If the exercise is given to a group, some might feel they have to respond more quickly than others and so have a feeling of competition, but this is incidental to the question. One is "oppressed by a burden" from which one must find relief; or, to use Eliot's figure of speech, one is "haunted by a demon, a demon against which one feels powerless because in its first manifestation it has no face, no name, nothing." In other words, one goes through this exercise, once the question has taken hold, to gain relief from discomfort; and then one may "experience a moment of exhaustion, appeasement, or absolution, and of release, something very near annihilation, which is indescribable." Of course, such an extreme reaction would come only from someone who had labored long and hard; in the case of the exercise you are likely to feel some mild relief and pleasure. Eliot says to his poem, "Go away! Find a place for yourself in a book—and don't expect me to take any further interest in you." We say to the picture, "Oh, interesting!" and then forget it.

Of course, one can simply gaze at the picture without seeing it and then turn the page; then any talk of the tension and resolution makes no sense at all. Please do the actual exercise. It may be, as soon as your eyes light upon the black and white field, you will see the picture; it might leap out at you. This would be unfortunate, because we are interested in the *process* here.

The first question we must ask is this: what is this creative germ? The second question is this: was the face *created*, or was it *discovered*? To *discover* something means to uncover what is already there; to *create* is to have something new. We say the poet creates a poem, but a mathematician discovers a theorem. But is this really the case? Is there such a distinction between what the poet, painter, and musician do and what the scientist, mathematician, and philosopher do? Beethoven is reported to have said that music is "a higher revelation than all wisdom and philosophy." But *revelation* is simply to reveal what is already there—in other words, to discover.

If we say we *created* the picture in the exercise, then how is it that everyone else who truly sees the picture creates exactly the same thing? In a well-known psychological test, one is given an inkblot and asked to say what it represents. No *right* answer to the question is expected, and one is allowed, indeed encouraged, to be as creative as one wishes. But this exercise is not of that kind. A "right" picture is expected. When one "sees" this right picture, one realizes how unsatisfactory were the other pictures one might have come up with, how much more striking and present the right picture is. To say there is a right picture implies that one must discover it. But why does it take so long to discover it?

Although we may not be able to agree on whether the picture is created or discovered,[2] most people would agree that creation and discovery are quite different. Do we discover the world about us, or do we create it? Do we discover the thoughts swirling around in our heads, or do we create them? Do we discover God, or do we create Him? Remember, a God we discover would be quite different than a God we create.

Another Illustration

Let us try another exercise. Suppose I were to hold up a small wedge shaped piece of wood and ask you to tell me what it is, how do you think you would answer? I used this example during talks that I gave to managers showing the application to the business world of some of the things I am now writing about. When I held up the wood most of those present would say, "It is a piece of wood." I would then ask them, "How much is it worth?" and invariably the answer would be that it was worthless. I would continue to hold the wood up, and it would not be long before someone would say, "It is a doorstop." At this point I would pull out from my pocket a piece of rubber, more or less the same shape and size as the wood, which is sold as a doorstop in most dime stores, and then ask how much it was worth. Then people would say 25 cents or 50 cents. What was it that transformed the worthless piece of wood into a doorstop with some value?

A well-known story told by Gestalt psychologists is of a chimpanzee in a cage into which a stick was introduced. When the animal had become accustomed to the stick, some bananas were placed outside the cage, just out of arms' reach. The chimpanzee first struggled to reach the fruit with her hands. After having gone through a cycle ending in what appeared to be complete frustration, she suddenly turned to the stick and, after some trial and error, dragged the fruit within reach using the stick as a tool. What transformed the stick into a tool? First we see a piece of wood; then, as if by magic, it is changed into a doorstop; or we see a stick which becomes transformed into a tool. What was it that transformed the chaos of black and white into a clear picture? What was it that transformed a set of seemingly random information into the famous formula of Einstein's: $e = mc^2$. One is reminded of the fairy godmother who, with a touch of her magic wand, changes the pumpkin into a beautiful carriage and the mice into horses for Cinderella. What is that magic wand?

It is not a thought or a word, and it certainly is not nothing because, whatever it is, some people have it or get it and others do not. Beddoes says it is certainly not an idea, and if one uses the word *idea* as synonymous with *concept*, then one would have to agree. But the word idea can be understood in another way: An idea is the reason by which one sees the piece of wood as a doorstop, and the chimpanzee saw the stick as a tool.

Let me emphasize that when I use the word idea I am not talking about a thought or concept, nor is an idea even conscious. If I use the word in the way I have used it throughout this book, I would say idea is not simply in the realm of knowing. In his book *Intuition in Poetry and the Arts*, Jacques Maritain speaks of this idea:

> This determinative focus is what the Schoolmen called the *idea factiva*, that is to say the "*creative idea.*" They took care, moreover, to warn us that the craftsman's creative idea is in no way a concept, for it is neither cognitive nor representative, it is only generative; it does not tend to make our mind conform to things, but to make a thing conform to our mind. They never even used the word "idea" in the sense of "concept" as we have done since the time of Descartes. And so, if we may continue to speak of the craftsman's creative idea, it is on the condition that we be aware of the fact that this word idea is merely analogous when applied to that creative idea and to what we usually call idea.[3]

What Is an Idea?

One cannot say, *this* is what idea means, but we can say what it does not mean. The idealist school of philosophy, particularly the one advocated by Bishop Berkeley, says we do not see *things* but *ideas*. This is not the way I am using the word. When Plato used the word he meant to say that ideas are like templates that fit over form and allow form to become reality. But again, this is not how I am using the word. Nor am I using idea to signify a transcendent entity of which real or existing things are a kind of representation.

By idea I do not mean something opposed to reality, as when we say that such and such is *only an idea* and not reality; nor do I mean something alongside reality, as in having an idea *about* something. It is not a mystical or spiritual thing floating about in some otherworldly ether. Idea may be, but does not have to be, expressed in a thought; it can be expressed in painting, dance, gesture, symbol, and so on equally as well as in language and thought. Idea is neither unique nor general, and the words *it* and *something*, by which I have been designating it, are used only in deference to the demands of language. Strictly speaking, we cannot even refer to it as "an" idea or "the" idea, but sometimes, in the interest of style, we must do so.

Idea is not nothing. The very coherence of the world depends on the idea by which we perceive it. In *The Decline of the West*, Oswald Spengler hovered around this when he said:

> I distinguish the *idea* of a Culture, which is the sum total of its inner possibilities, from its sensible *phenomenon* or appearance upon the canvas of history as a fulfilled actuality. It is the relation of the soul to the living body, to its expression in the light world perceptible to our eyes. This history of a culture is the progressive actualizing of its possible, and the fulfillment is equivalent to the end.[4]

Spengler said he took this notion of idea from Goethe, who used also the term "prime phenomenon." He added, "to the spiritual eye of Goethe the idea of the prime plant was clearly visible in the form of every individual plant that happened to come up, or even that which could possibly come up."[5]

Etymologically, the word idea is derived from the Greek *idein*, which means "to see." In other words, we do not have an idea in addition to something of which we have an idea. *To perceive that something requires an idea.* When we see only a piece of wood, the piece of wood *is no less an idea* than the doorstop. Moreover, we do not see the piece of wood and then impose upon it the idea of the doorstop. When we see a doorstop, we no longer see a piece of wood. But we must not make the mistake of believing that the piece of wood vanishes and a doorstop appears, anymore than we should say the piece of wood underlies the doorstop or ask ourselves where the piece of wood goes when a doorstop appears.

Idea, therefore, is not a ghost-like existence and "piece of wood" the real thing; we cannot say, in this context, "it is only an idea," as though there were a higher reality. Nor are we using idea to mean a *representation* of reality. A representation is a picture and so, strictly speaking, in this case we should use the word *image* instead and, as a moment's introspection will show, a great difference exists between an image and an idea. Idea is that by which something is what it is, and is more akin to a window than a picture. Finally, idea is not an abstraction, what remains after an object has been stripped of some of its qualities. It is neither abstract nor concrete, it is neither something nor nothing, and so it does not dwell in the realm of being alone. This is made more difficult to grasp because I have been talking about idea, *and this very talking about it transforms idea into a concept. about something.*

As a first attempt to say something positive about idea, let me say it is "the eye of unity," that which "reveals relations within phenomena." Spengler spoke of idea as the sum total of possibilities. But careful reading of what he said suggests this is either a poor translation or carelessness on his part. Idea is not a sum total; it is not arrived at through a process of addition. The phenomena, moreover, whose relations are revealed by the eye of unity, are derived both from knowing *and* from being—or, more concretely, from thought and from the senses—and so we must not simply regard idea as simply mental. Idea, we could say, is the eye of one/(knowing/being) and so therefore emerges from what I have called the intermediate zone.

Look around the room in which you are sitting. You see a chair: That is someone's idea. You see a desk, a carpet, a book, the room itself: these are all someone's ideas in form. As we look we see more and more ideas: a wall, a lamp, some spectacles. The way the chairs are arranged, the way you are dressed, the clothes themselves, and so on—all of these are ideas. Now look around to find what is *not* an idea. But whose idea is it by which all of these, and the world, are seen? It should be made quite clear I am not talking about ideas in the mind. No box, spiritual or otherwise, exists in which ideas are "contained." The mind, me, and idea are one. This will become clearer as we proceed.

The Power of Idea

If you have ever painted the kitchen, or done something similar, you know the power of an idea. Once you get started you find you have a great deal of energy, enough to keep you at work sometimes with little to eat and for long periods of time. It might take two or three days to get the work done, but throughout the process a dynamism is at work. The time comes when it is finished. The paint brushes are cleaned; the ladder and drop cloths put away. The furniture is put back into place. Wonderful! It is finished. The next day, you see in a corner a spot no bigger than your hand, a part of the wall that was not painted. The whole kitchen is pale primrose, down there is a patch of blue. "Tomorrow," you say, or, "This weekend, I'll paint it." Two, three, four years later the sky blue patch, no bigger than your hand, is still there. You just cannot get down to doing it. Too much effort is involved, the idea has evaporated, the energy is lost.

So we must not see idea simply as something passive, inert, suspended in the atmosphere of the mind. On the contrary, many people have changed the course of history with an idea. Indeed, it is said nothing is so powerful as an idea whose time has come.

I have likened idea to a window. But when I was talking about the world idea I said it was akin to a magnifying glass, able to focus the rays of the sun and so produce fire. Idea so focuses the power of unity that it creates a whole universe and all the diverse forms within. This dynamic quality comes from an inherent tension in idea, a tension between intuition and analysis or between inclusive and exclusive unity—that is, between one and the null point.

Analysis and Intuition

Before I say more about this tension, we must understand what analysis contributes to this dynamic quality. Suppose, for example, you wanted to describe Figure 14 to a friend, and you can only use words to describe it.[6] Perhaps you are talking to your friend over the telephone and you want to get the message across in as few words as possible. What would you say? How would you describe Figure 14 so that your friend got an accurate picture of it in his mind?

Fig.14   Fig.15:

You might say it is a pair of parallel lines, as in Figure 15. Slide the top horizontal line down and the bottom line up, and you will have the form.

Suppose now you had to describe not only Figure 14 but Figure 16, as well. Now how would you do it?

Fig.16:

The parallel lines are the simplest way of describing Figure 14 but cannot describe Figure 16. The building block is now a cross instead of being a line. [**+**] If you were to use this building block, you could describe both Figure 14 and Figure 16 with a minimum of words.

Now consider Figure 17 How would you describe 14, 16 and 17. What would you now use as a basic building block?

Fig.17:

The cross will no longer be adequate and we shall now have to use **L** .

If we include Figure 18 in the group we have to describe, we must use still a smaller building block. If we add yet another form, a further analysis is necessary. As is evident, this continued analysis could go on until we have only the tiniest point left.

What we have been doing is a process of analysis. The word *analysis* comes from the Greek word *Analyeiun,* which means "to break up. In breaking up we go toward elements that are the same; in other words, we go toward *one* element which is reproduced a number of times and re-

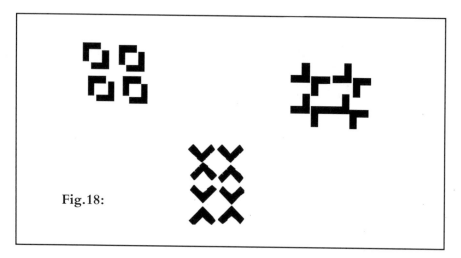

Fig.18:

lated in different ways. A recent example of extreme analysis is the superstring theory, in which the building block of all matter is no longer the atom or the particle, but a vibrating string. The *one* we go toward is a numerical one: *a quantity,* what I earlier called simple, which is not-composed. It is what de Chardin referred to when he spoke of the "profoundly atomic nature of the Universe." However, although the elements may be simple, the relationship between the elements can become very complex. Indeed, it can be so complex that in superstring theory researchers have found it necessary to add six additional dimensions to the four traditional dimensions of space–time.

If we refer back to the picture of the hidden man at the beginning of the chapter, we see quite the opposite. The relationship is essentially simple: we see one face; but each of the elements (the black and white areas) is unique, and unrepeatable. With analysis we isolate simple elements and combine them in complex relations. With this other kind of approach (which for the moment we will call *intuition*) we isolate simple relations but go toward unique, unrepeatable, and complex elements.

Two different kinds of thinking now appear: *intuitive,* which aims at simplicity of relations, and *analytical,* which aims at simplicity of elements. Intuitive thinking could be said to be toward *qualitative* simplicity, or not-complex simplicity, whereas analysis goes toward *quantitative* simplicity (one element), or not-composed simplicity. Both forms of thinking imply a drive toward oneness, but this drive goes in two opposed directions. Intuition goes in a centrifugal direction, from the center outward, incorporating more and more in a single grasp or comprehension. Analytical thought goes in a centripetal direction, reducing complexity to simple elements. In logic this element is a term; in physics it used to be the atom and now is a vibrating string; in language it is a letter; in medicine a virus. The ultimate analysis is to reduce everything down to a single point. We can depict these two tendencies as a spiral, but a spiral going in two opposed directions, as depicted in Figure 19.

Idea as a Force Field

Throughout this book I have claimed that unity is not simply a static, dead word but a dynamic and vibrant mystery. Idea is oneness; its dynamism and vibrancy come out of the tension inherent in oneness, a tension I have described between quantitative and qualitative simplicity and as me-as-center/me-as-periphery. Now we see the same tension at work between the centrifugal tendency of analysis and the centripetal action of intuition.

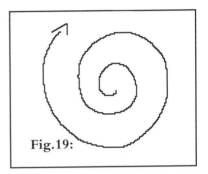

Fig.19:

A moment's reflection will show that we never use pure intuition or pure analysis; our perception of a situation is always the result of both. The two together create a dynamic field. This dynamic field is what I have called idea. But both analysis and intuition also emerge from the dynamic field called unity.

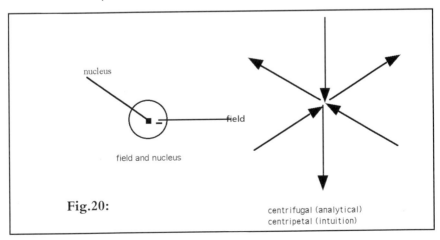

nucleus

field

field and nucleus

Fig.20:

centrifugal (analytical)
centripetal (intuition)

The diagram in Figure 20 is the same as the symbol I spoke of in Chapter 6 when I quoted de Chardin:

> The living element, which heretofore has been spread out and divided over a diffuse circle of perceptions and activities, was constituted for the first time as a center in the form of a point at which all the impressions and experiences knit themselves together and fuse into a unity that is conscious of its own unity.

The ancients saw this clearly and made the symbol for consciousness, for the sun, and for gold. Each of these three was an emissary of the life force. This same symbol is the symbol for me-as-center/me-as-periphery.

Notes

1. Arthur M. Young, *The Reflexive Universe* (Mill Valley, Calif.: Robert Briggs Associates, 1976), p. 20.
2. "Art for [William] James is at once invention and discovery, the production of a system of relations, and the revelation of immediate experience" (Schwartz Sanford, *The Matrix Of Modernism* [Princeton, NJ: Princeton University Press, 1985], p. 48).
3. Jacques Maritain, *Creative Intuition in Art and Poetry* (New York: Meridian Books, 1955), p. 100.
4. Oswald Spengler, *Decline of the West* (London: George Allen & Unwin, 1959), p. 104.
5. Spengler (1959)
6. The diagrams are adapted from a series of diagrams used by Edward de Bono, which appeared in his book *The Use of Lateral Thinking* (Harmondsworth, UK: Penguin Books, 1967).

Chapter 16

The Null Point as the Center of Consciousness

But for the point, the still point,
there would be no dance and there is only the dance.
T. S. ELIOT

All that exists, without exception, each and everything,
the whole (of reality), has sprung from the one point-instant
that is the (operational) source.
DZOGS-CHEN

The work of works for man is to establish, in and by each
one of us, an absolutely original center in which the universe
reflects itself in a unique and inimitable way.
TEILHARD DE CHARDIN

What is the Center?

CONSCIOUSNESS IS A CREATION; moreover, creativity has some re-
curring characteristics: It is preceded by a tension, and the product
(that which is created) is preceded by an eruption. The tension comes from
the imperative "Let there be one!" The eruption comes from the same imperative, because oneness must always emerge full-blown, it cannot emerge
in fractions. The original creation is the creation of the null point, which
comes out of the tension between knowing and being. The birth of the
null point creates an ambiguity in unity and a new, constant tension is thus
maintained coming from the need to reabsorb the null point. To remind
ourselves of the inherent dynamism or tension in unity, I have used the

expression "dynamic unity." This same tension makes it possible for know-ing to be focused into awareness-of, which I usually refer to as intention, interest, or attention, depending on the circumstances.

I said further that awareness-of could be reflected back upon itself and that from this arises me and you, with another tension inherent in that relation. Two important points must be reiterated: Awareness-of is no longer tied to being, and it is a highly unstable condition, on one hand exploding into love and ecstasy, on the other into violence and horror. Love and ecstasy are closely associated with creativity, and some violence is a form of failed creativity. I also said that the emergence of me and you were ways by which the burden inherent in self-reflection is made more bearable. However, two other possible ways are available: the first is shared with animals, the second is peculiar to humans. The first of these possi-bilities is the creation of a stable point of reference; the second is the stabilization of me by metaphor and so the creation of consciousness. However, the latter possibility is dependent on a stable point having been created. I made reference to the stable point in Chapters 9 and 16.

The stable point of reference is a harmonic of the null point. The creation of the null point is a *cosmic* creation, and the thrust of evolution of both matter and life arises from the need to reabsorb the null point. The creation of a stable point of reference, on the other hand, is a *life* creation, because it comes out of me-as-center/me-as-periphery.[1] Cre-ation that involves metaphor I'll call *human creation*. All three forms of creativity are isomorphic, the form being given by the basic ambiguity: an ambiguity, one face of which says there is no ambiguity, this face in itself is not unambiguous. We can now add to the evolutionary diagram a further step, as shown in Figure 21.

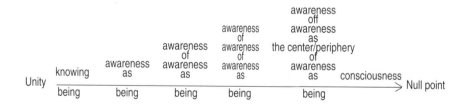

Fig. 21

Earlier, I introduced the symbol ⊙ for consciousness used by the ancients, which I said could be seen as a symbol for me. The point in the circle is simultaneously both the source and the destination of the same awareness. In order to deepen our understanding of both evolution and human consciousness, we must deepen our understanding of what part the stable point or *center* plays in our lives. This will throw light upon what de Chardin meant when he said, "The work of works for man is to establish, in and by each one of us, an absolutely original center in which the universe reflects itself in a unique and inimitable way."

Before going on, I must point out that the hunger for clarity and understanding, the wish to "get it all sorted out, defined, and well-formulated," is itself a product of evolution. This, in turn, makes such a clarification difficult to attain. Evolution is the outcome of the yearning to reabsorb the null point, which is the yearning to arrive at the center. This yearning, as I have said, can never be satisfied. For example, the search for some ultimate truth is a search for the center, and this search has given rise to all kinds of myths, including the crock at the end of the rainbow, the philosopher's stone, the holy grail, the promised land, Shangri la, the pure land, and heaven. In behavior this same search is the search for perfection, as well as the search to be unique, to be the one and only. This yearning can be seen in animals as well as in humans: the contest to be the alpha animal and the need to establish and maintain territory come out of this same urge. Furthermore, the impossibility of attaining the center (that is, of reabsorbing the null point) is the source of the loneliness and frustration that haunts humanity and makes us forever restless and dissatisfied. However, this very impossibility of attaining the center also makes it impossible for me to seize hold of the center and so make it accessible for you to grasp. This no doubt will be a source of frustration for some readers, who may feel that the fault lies not with the subject of discussion but with the author.

If, for example, you ask me what I mean by the word center, *I am at a complete loss how to respond*—and yet, until you ask, I know very well what it is. However it is only when talking about the *dynamic center* that difficulty arises. If you ask me what is meant by a *geographical* center I could point to it with ease as in Figure 22.

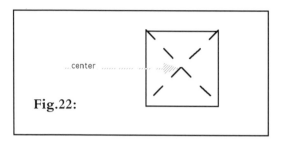

Fig.22:

center

I could again respond if you ask me where the center of gravity of a seesaw is to be found, as in Figure 23.

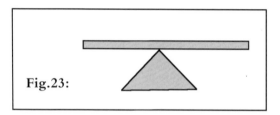

Fig.23:

I could also find the *center of gravity* of a stone or rock. But when it comes to the dynamic center, I am at a loss because it is *dynamic*; that is, it is not only at the center but, at the same time, it is at the periphery, not only the viewpoint but also the null point. Yet it is even beyond these also, because it is one. So my difficulty in talking about the center is aggravated because the idea of location itself arises from space and time, which in turn only have meaning with reference to a center—or, to use a more familiar term, to an observer. The center is not to be found in either the physical or the mental realm. It is neither mind nor body, so can be neither sensed nor known; it resides in the intermediary zone. Let me emphasize that I am not talking about a symbol, an archetype, or a concept, although most Western writers consider it one or other of these. Yet it is real, and its importance cannot be doubted.

The Center as World Center

In an article in *The Encyclopedia of Religion*, Mircea Eliade and Lawrence Sullivan wrote:

> The importance of the symbolism of the center can hardly be overstated for it establishes the order of the universe, drawing together the spiri-

tual destiny of collective humankind and that of the individual human being. The term center of the world refers to that place where all essential modes of being come together.[2]

The *symbolism* of the center does not have this function; the *center itself* has it. Symbols—such as the cross, the totem pole, temples, sacred mountains, and the flag—are created to embody or articulate the center, but *to relegate the center to a symbol is to relegate it to a creation of the mind or awareness,* which it is not. The center is not-knowing/not-being; it is "where all essential modes of being come together," the source of all power, both physical and psychological

Eliade and Sullivan go on to say that the center is always "*a sacred place,* qualitatively different from mundane space." Sacred space is that which is enclosed by unity, in contrast to mundane space, which is enclosed by boundaries and limits in experience. Sacred space, like the center, is neither knowing nor being. Even so, the ancients considered sacred space to coincide with physical space, whereas for the modern person it coincides with behavioral space.[3] But for both ancient and the modern peoples, sacred space is being/knowing centered upon the null point. The space is sacred because it is derived from the center, and what is derived from the center is of utmost concern, that which has supreme significance.[4]

I have said that the cosmic center comes out of the ambiguity in unity, an ambiguity which is echoed at the level of life by the clash between me-as-center/me-as-periphery. By reconciling this opposition, the field contains immense forces that are often illustrated by the symbols used to articulate the center. For example, Eliade and Lawrence write, "In the Branches of Yggdrasill [the Scandinavian cosmic tree] which spread out across the heavens and earth, live supernatural animals. At the foot of the tree lies the enormous cosmic serpent, Niohoggr, who threatens the very existence of the tree by gnawing continually on it. At the very top of the tree perches an eagle who does daily battle with the destructive serpent."[5] Niohoggr is a fine metaphor for the null point, and the eagle for oneness.

That the center contains tension is also shown in its various embodiments, which, Eliade and Lawrence say, depict an ambivalence:

> The spatial images themselves suggest two things at once: communication and distant separation. The very cosmic mountain and tree that join

heaven and earth together also hold them apart from one another. This ambivalence of the center describes well a primary quality of religious experience. On the one hand, the journey to the center may be arduous and dangerous. No-one may have access to the center, to different states of being, without careful preparation and spiritual strength. The journey to the center may require a complete transformation of one's spiritual being. On the other hand the image of the world center is replicated in multiple forms. This ensures that communication with the fullness of reality is everywhere possible.[6]

The authors also point out that the center is essentially connected with creation and, "just as the primordial moment of creation underlies all creative instances, so too does the place of origin become the point toward which all other life filled space is oriented."[7] The primordial moment of creation is the creation of the null point, which serves as a paradigm for all other creativity.

The center is not only connected with creation but with curing as well. "Curing rituals are often performed at the center, where life can be regenerated, powerful and fresh, just as it was once generated for the first time at the moment of creation."[8] Curing, or healing, originally meant to restore wholeness.

The Center and Western Psychology

Generally speaking, Western psychologists, apart from Jung, have not had much to say about the importance of the center in the ecology of the psyche. Even Jung did not think of the center as independent of knowing, but subsumed it as an archetype, together with wholeness, self, and ambiguity, which he also thought of as archetypes.

Part of the reason for ignoring the importance comes from the wish to make psychology a science, which requires terms to be defined in a clear and distinct manner, unambiguously. But another reason yet underlies this reluctance to deal with the center. In the preface to *Zen and Creative Management*, I made the point that when a culture reaches maturity its dilemmas rise to the surface, and the Hegelian-Marxist tenet, that all systems carry within themselves the seeds of their own destruction, is a variation of this point. Dilemmas, as I pointed out in that book, as well as in *The Butterfly's Dream,* come into being because of the fundamental ambiguity. This is in keeping with what we have been discussing so far. The evolution of human consciousness goes through cycles from a center, through a period of maximum tension and ambiguity with its attendant dilemmas, and then to a new center. We are undoubtedly living in a time of maximum ambiguity when the center has lost its hold and so it is not surprising that it has more or less slipped completely out of view of people of this time. All this adds to the difficulty of making clear what is meant by the center.

As I said, Jung is the only Western psychologist who has given much attention to the importance of the center, and even he did not see it as having a reality and power in its own right. Echoing Eliade he said, for example, that the ego is a complex factor "to which all conscious contents are related. It forms as it were, the center of the field of consciousness."[9] He said later that the ego is not a simple or elementary factor but a complex one which, as such, cannot be described exhaustively: "Experience shows that it rests on two seemingly different bases: the *somatic* [which I have called *being*] and the *psychic* [which I have called *knowing*]."[10] Finally, he added:

> The ego is acquired during the individual's lifetime. It seems to arise in the first place from the collision between the somatic factor and the environment and once established as a subject it goes on developing from further collisions with the outer world and the inner.[11]

In contrast to its treatment in the West, the center has always been recognized in the Orient. In Japan the center is called *Ki*, and it is both spiritual and material. It is also an energy and a point. The Japanese consider it a vital factor in the activity of the body/mind. The expression body/mind is used because the clear separation between body and mind that has occurred in the West in the last 500 or so years did not occur in some parts of the East.

Yet another reason that Western psychologists have given scant attention to the center is that they have taken the subject–object dichotomy as given. "I am here, the world is there," with its attendant naive realism, was the metaphysical foundation of Freud and his followers. That I–thou, and later I–it emerge out of a common ground under extreme tension is only now beginning to take on meaning in the West, mainly through the influx of Oriental spirituality[12] on the one hand and subatomic physics on the other. For Freud, the ego was the outcome of an instinctual force called *libido*, which was "inside" the individual, encountering the reality of the world, which was "outside." In other words, both he and Jung recognized that a *conflict* or *collision* underlies the development of ego. Freud believed these instinctual forces were essentially rooted in biology, and he looked forward to the day when all the insights of psychoanalysis would be explained by a biological understanding of the human psyche.

For Jung, the center was a subjective factor. He said, "the ego is the subject of all personal acts of consciousness."[13] On the other hand, Nisargadatta Maharaja, a highly developed Hindu thinker who died recently, said in reply to a question about the center of consciousness, that it was that "which cannot be given name and form, for it is without quality and beyond consciousness. Beyond consciousness is to be beyond the subjective."[14]

Maharaja went on to say:

> You may say that it is a point in consciousness, which is beyond consciousness, like a hole in the paper is both in the paper and yet not of the paper, so is the supreme state in the very center of consciousness and yet beyond consciousness. It is as if an opening in the mind through which the mind is flooded with light. The opening is not even light, it is just an opening.[15]

On another occasion, he explained further:

> You are the perceiving point, the non-dimensional source of all dimensions. Know yourself as the total. . . . First we must know ourselves as witnesses only, dimensionless and timeless centers of observation and then realize that immense ocean of pure awareness, which is both mind and matter and beyond both. The light by which you see the world, which is God, is the little tiny spark.[16]

Unity is both mind and matter, knowing and being, and beyond both. But as viewpoint, unity is a tiny spark, the tiny spark which is God—oneness.

The center is both the One and the null point and is neither subject nor object, neither consciousness nor unconsciousness, neither created by the mind nor the outcome of physical forces. The center is real and through it we grant reality to things, situations, and ideas—not only physical reality, but moral and ethical reality as well. Again Nisargadatta said, "There is a center which imparts reality to whatever it perceives."[17]

The Importance of the Center to de Chardin

I said the center emerges from a ground under extreme tension, and this can be illustrated by reference to de Chardin's biography. De Chardin was obsessed by the center. He believed that the whole of evolution tends toward the Omega point, the cosmic center, which for him was Christ. The tension from which this understanding came is highlighted by N. M. Wilders, who, in his short biography of de Chardin, said that de Chardin was haunted by unity yet lived for a long time in a state of "intellectual and spiritual schizophrenia."[18] Wilders said that de Chardin's experience was wholly governed by what he called "cosmic sense" and "Christian sense." He was inwardly torn by the simultaneous presence in his heart and mind of cosmic consciousness and Christ consciousness. This feeling of being inwardly torn arises, of course, from the ambiguity. Wilders explained:

After much unremitting strain and effort on his part, the cosmic and the Christian consciousness which had arisen in his mind in total independence of each other came to disclose their convergence and fundamental unity, and this involved the recognition that Christ had a cosmic function and that the evolution of the cosmos had to be seen as a movement oriented upon a cosmic central point. He called this "the Omega point."[19]

The *Phenomenon of Man* is a creative struggle by which de Chardin transcended his intellectual and spiritual "schizophrenia." Throughout the whole of the book one feels his deep excitement, which at times becomes almost desperation. This excitement sometimes leads de Chardin to write passages that are nearly incoherent unless one is prepared to read what he says with deep sympathy. Critic Peter Medawar was not so prepared, and he slashed and hacked at de Chardin in an unmerciful fashion, writing that de Chardin "is forever shouting at us: things or affairs are, in alphabetical order, astounding, colossal, endless, enormous, fantastic, giddy, hyper, immense." Medawar claimed that *Phenomenon of Man* was only for second- or third-class minds "which have been educated far beyond their capacity to undertake analytical thought."[20]

One has to agree with Medawar that, from an analytical (that is, from a purely objective) standpoint, the book gets low marks, but this does not mean that it is simply "fictional philosophy," as Medawar would call it. It is unlikely that a Jesuit would be educated beyond his capacity for intellectual thought; rather, analytical thought is of no use in what de Chardin was trying to do. Medawar's insistence that what de Chardin says must be analytically pure is just scientific dogma, a dogma that has completely stultified real attempts to understand life and consciousness. One must admit, however, that de Chardin called for such a criticism by his erroneous belief that he was writing as a scientist in *Phenomenon of Man*.

Anyone so obsessed with unity cannot be satisfied with reducing a whole down to its constituent parts. Some entirely different way of thinking is called for, a way of thinking that was offered in the past, to some extent, by religious dogma. But de Chardin had considerable integrity, and simple dogma would have been of no use to him either. This put him in the unfortunate position of being rejected by dogmatists in both camps, religious and scientific. His works were proscribed by the Church and published only after his death, and he thereby fell foul of both ecclesiastic and scientific bureaucrats.

In purely scientific matters, in times when his whole system of value was not threatened, he could no doubt have maintained an impartial and objective view of his material. But, as Wilders pointed out, de Chardin's system of values *was* threatened. He was brought up as a Christian and he looked upon Christ as the cosmic center. His scientific education, on the other hand, made him realize that another center was possible, a center which, because of the insatiability of the scientific appetite, would be forever receding into the future. It is the nature of analytical inquiry to be always finding new elements into which the world can be divided, and so the promised land can never be reached. The quarks of today will simply be precursors to more analysis tomorrow. Nevertheless, scientific thought is always converging in much the way one experiences convergence when driving through swirling snow on a winter's evening; it seems one is forever about to touch center, but the center always recedes. How fascinating is the Big Bang theory, with the center, the origin of it all, only nanoseconds away! Whereas it was possible for de Chardin to be at one with Christ as the cosmic center, he was thrust into the outer darkness of the periphery of the center chased by science. Only one center is possible, but which was center and which peripheral to it? It was being both at the center and at the periphery that was so intolerable.

For de Chardin the world of value and the world of fact were at odds and he had to find some way out of the unendurable tension this must have been generated in him. The Omega point was a tour de force, as it reconciled for him the two centers: the stable center that gave to his life value, importance and the sacred; and the promised dynamic center backed by facts, the evidence of science, and of the great minds of our civilization—that dynamic center which, though it gave direction and promise, gave neither significance nor any possibility of the sacred.

In *Phenomenon of Man* de Chardin wrote:

> As soon as a child is born it must breath or it will die. Similarly the reflective psychic center once turned in on itself can only subsist by means of a double movement which in reality is one and the same. It centers itself further upon itself by entry into a new space and at the same time it centers the rest of the world around itself by the establishment of an even more coherent and better organized perspective in the realities which surround it. . . . We are not dealing with an immutably fixed focus but with a vortex which grows deeper as it sucks fluid at the heart of which it was born. The ego only persists by becoming ever more itself, in the measure in which it makes everything itself.[21]

This is precisely the kind of writing that sent Medawar rushing for a fly swatter. He saw it as inexcusable evidence of shallow thinking. And clearly, if we try to understand this paragraph from the viewpoint of the traditional logic of non-contradiction, we can make neither head nor tail of it. If we want to understand it, and I suggest it is well worth the effort, we must first try to understand what de Chardin means by "the double movement" coming from the reflective psychic center turning in on itself: that is, the "movement" of the centering on itself and also the "movement" of centering the world.

Remember our example of the person in the subway being felt by a stranger. In that example two awarenesses-of were at work: my awareness-of and the stranger's awareness-of. (I have deliberately reduced the verbal complexity for the moment.) *Me* corresponds to what de Chardin calls "the psychic" center, and *the stranger* corresponds to the center "of the rest of the world." Now de Chardin talks of "a double movement which in reality is one and the same." In my account of the subway incident I came to the conclusion that there were not two awarenesses-of (my awareness-of the stranger and the stranger's awareness-of me) but *one* awareness-of. So now, instead of two awarenesses-of there is a double movement in which me is simultaneously the *source* and the *object,* both the *center* and the *periphery* of this awareness-of. The one dynamic center, the original viewpoint, is divided against itself.

This division does not occur only in situations like the subway scenario. Me, the psychic center described by de Chardin, de Chardin himself, and all sentient beings are divided in this way; all are simultaneously the source and object, at the center and at the periphery. De Chardin, no less than me, was inwardly torn by the simultaneous presence in his heart and mind of these two centers—or, rather, by the double movement of being *both center and periphery simultaneously.* Unremitting strain and effort are necessary to find a resolution. For de Chardin, this resolution was the omega point. Each of us makes the same creative tour de force when we first pronounce *I.*

The Center as I-It

The Omega point arose from irreconcilable tension within de Chardin's mind. I maintain that *I* (or ego) arises from the same tension. De Chardin wrote, "The work of works for man . . . is to *establish,* in and by each one of us, an absolutely original center in which the universe reflects itself in a unique and inimitable way."[22] This absolutely original center is I. In *The Closing of the American Mind* Allan Bloom wrote:

> [Non-Western cultures] think their way is the best way and all others are inferior. . . . One should conclude from the study of non-Western cultures that not only to prefer one's own way, but to believe it best, superior to others, is primary and even natural."[23]

In the heart of each of us lurks the assurance of our own superiority.[24] I is the reflection of original unity; because of this, each person necessarily feels unique: the absolute, original One. This original One is not the inclusive but the exclusive One. However, and this is the twist of the knife, for I to accomplish its work and bring inward peace, the null point, the exclusive One, must be absorbed.

Unfortunately the story of travail does not end here. As even as "I" claim to be the center of the world, the world makes the same claim as "I". I–it is the origin of the ambivalence that we find surrounding the center and to which Eliade returns frequently in his writings. Although "it" is the center, we can never pin down, never know, what "it" is. We say "it" is raining, "it" is time, I want "it," "it" makes me sad. The center to which I am at the periphery is essentially unknown and *can only be unknown*, because "I" is that it of which I am the center as well as being that same "it" to which I am periphery, and so on. Yet this is precisely the same vortex from which the center must rescue me. So we *assert* the center: the flag, the church, the leader, the cause. I is then sacrificed to this center in order to end the eternal vicious cycle generated by I–it. But in order for this sacrifice to be a viable solution, the center, the flag, the church, the cause must be *mine*. As such, because I am unique and superior, it too must be unique and superior. Hence, on one hand we see the national, ideological, and religious fanaticism and intolerance that mark our world. And on the other hand, we see the incessant squabbles, jealousies, enmities, and backbiting that pit and corrode our lives and lead to struggles, conflicts, competition, and wars over prestige, possessions, and power.

Thus, in our search for rest and peace, all we have succeeded in doing by establishing a center is set the stage for the endless human drama. I, the psychic center, and it, the unknown center, are in a perpetual dance around the null point, each claiming the center for its own. De Chardin said, and this is where the Omega point becomes more of a perpetual dance than a stable center, "We are not dealing with an immutably fixed focus but with a vortex which grows deeper as it sucks fluid at the heart of which it was born." This could also be expressed, perhaps less poetically but more understandably, as drawing power from the null point as source.

The birth of consciousness focused around the null point takes place in each individual. That this is always in process as a continuing saga is exemplified by de Chardin's own struggle. About the birth of consciousness he wrote, "[It] corresponds to a turning point in upon itself not only of the nervous system, but of the whole of being. What at first disconcerts us is the need to accept that this step could only be achieved at one single stroke."[25] He repeated this idea of suddenness later, adding, "access to thought represents a threshold which had to be crossed at a single stroke."[26] The emergence of the omega point echoes the emergence of the null point which also emerges from a field of insupportable but irreconcilable tension.

On one occasion when discussing this sudden emergence, de Chardin drew an analogy between it and a kettle of water coming to the boil. On another he drew an analogy between the emergence and taking sections of a cone from the base to the summit:

> With the primates an instrument was fashioned so remarkably supple and rich that the step immediately following could not take place without the whole animal psychism being as it were recast and consolidated on itself. Now this movement did not stop, for there was nothing in the structure of the organism to prevent it advancing. When the anthropoid, so to speak, had been brought mentally to boiling point some further calories were added. Or when the anthropoid had almost reached the summit of the cone a final effort took place along the whole axis. No more was needed for the whole inner equilibrium to be upset. What was previously but a centered surface became a center. By a tiny tangential increase the radial was turned back on itself and so to speak took an infinite leap forward. Outwardly almost nothing in the organism had taken place but inwardly a great revolution had taken place.[27]

The boiling point must have occurred when the anthropoid reached a point of intense anguish, similar, although no doubt more intense, to the deep anguish de Chardin himself suffered. From this intense pain the great human leap into consciousness was made. For the anthropoid this great leap gave birth to what I call *the word*; for de Chardin a similar great leap gave birth to the omega point. Awareness-of was doubled back on itself. As de Chardin wrote, the anthropoid becomes the

> object of his own awareness in consequence of that very doubling back [and] becomes in a flash able to raise himself into a new sphere. In reality another world is born. Abstraction, logic, reasoned choice and circumvention, mathematics, art, calculation of space and time, anxieties and dreams of love—all these activities of inner life are nothing else than the effervescence of the newly formed center as it explodes onto itself.[28]

At one moment there is profound anguish; at the next a new manifestation of the center is born. This creation (or discovery?) of the center is then the paradigm for all human creativity. The new manifestation appears, whole and complete, as one. This appearance must be *sudden,* out of time, because there cannot be a gradual appearance of one. But what was this new center for that first anthropoid?

I'll let Helen Keller—a woman who was deaf, blind, and mute, lost in a realm of endless twilight until she met her teacher—speak for the anthropoid who made the great leap and experienced the miraculous birth of the word:

> Someone was drawing water and my teacher placed my hand under the spout. As the cool stream gushed over my hand she spelled into the other the word *water*, first slowly, and then rapidly. I stood still, my whole attention fixed upon the motion of her fingers. Suddenly I felt a misty consciousness as of something forgotten . . . and somehow the mystery of language was revealed to me. I knew then that w-a-t-e-r meant the wonderful cool something that was flowing over my hand. That living word awakened my soul, gave it light, hope, set it free.[29]

Notes

1. One cannot help wondering whether this is the dynamic that initiates mitosis.
2. Mircea Eliade and Lawrence Sullivan, "Center of the World," in *The Encyclopedia of Religions* (New York: Macmillan, 1993; Mircea Eliade, Ed.), p. 166.
3. For more on the notion of behavioral space, see Kurt Lewin, *Field Theory in Social Science* (New York: Harper-Torch Books, 1951).
4. That which is of utmost concern is what Paul Tillich calls Holy, and it is in this sense that I use the term.
5. Eliade and Sullivan (1993, p. 161).
6. Eliade and Sullivan (1993, p. 161).
7. Eliade and Sullivan (1993, p. 161).
8. "According to Levi Strauss what holds for totemism . . . holds for all communication systems, since these always embody pairs of opposites that express distinction within unity, opposition within solidarity. What we have seen in totemism is a manifestation of a general characteristic in all human thought" (Brian Wicker, *The Story Shaped World* [Notre Dame, IN: University of Notre Dame Press, 1975], p. 39).
9. C. G. Jung, *Aion* (London: Routledge & Kegan Paul, 1959; R.F.C. Hull, Trans.), p. 3,

10. Jung (1959, p. 3).
11. Jung (1959, p. 5).
12. With his notion of field theory in psychology, Kurt Lewin could be looked upon as anticipating the idea of a field under tension.
13. Jung (1959, p. 6).
14. Nisargadatta, *I Am That,* (Durham, NC: Acorn Press, 1986; M. Frydman, Trans.), p. 34.
15. Nisargadatta (1986, p. 34).
16. Nisargadatta (1986, p. 205).
17. Nisargadatta (1986, p. 344).
18. N.M. Wilders, *An Introduction to Teillard de Chardin,* (London: Collins, 1968), p. 21.
19. Wilders (1968, p. 23).
20. Peter Medawar (Trans.), *Plato"s Republic* (Oxford: Oxford University Press, 1984), pp. 242–251.
21. de Chardin (1959, p. 191).
22. de Chardin (1959, p. 184).
23. Allan Bloom, *The Closing of the American Mind* (New York: Simon & Schuster, 1987), p. 36.
24. See more on this in *The Butterfly's Dream, The Iron Cow of Zen,* and *Zen and Creative Management.*
25. de Chardin (1959, p. 189).
26. de Chardin (1959, p. 191).
27. de Chardin (1959, p. 184).
28. de Chardin (1959, p. 184).
29. Helen Keller, *The Story of My Life* (Garden City, NJ: Doubleday, 1936), pp. 23–24.

Part 4

His word, which proceeds like a storm
The word which destroys the heavens above
The word which shakes the earth beneath
His word is a rushing torrent
against which naught can stand.[1]
PRAYER TO MARDUK-ELLIL

Chapter 17
_____

The Word

*"[L]ogos" signifies both the outward form by which the inward
thought is expressed, and the inward thought itself. . . . As
signifying the outward form, it is never used in the merely
grammatical sense, as simply the name of a thing, but means a
word as the thing referred to . . . a word as embodying a
conception or an idea.[2]*

M. R. VINCENT

AT THE END OF CHAPTER 16 we quoted Helen Keller, "That living
word awakened my soul, gave it light, set it free." But what of the
first living word? Did not the living word, spoken by the first human being
in the dim distant past, give light to the whole world, set the whole world
free?[3] We, for whom words are so much junk food, who despise the poets,
forget the prophets, pollute and despoil the language—what does this first
word mean to us? Sunk as we are in the quagmire of words—newspapers,
journals, magazines, books, soap operas, advertisements, commercials, the
words of politicians and priests, salesmen and charlatans, the endless chatter
of mindless millions—how can we ever arouse the mind to drink in the
wonder, the light, of that first word? How can we imagine the anguish
and torment, the terror and the violence that must have preceded its
uttering? We who now long for silence cannot know the relief of escaping
forever the clutches of the still terror of not quite being, the desert of

silence dwelling in the land of half-seen shadows and lurking fear, the twilight zone of suffocating tensions, of the inexpressible.

"In the beginning was the Word": the word, the first human creative act. What is the word? Chimpanzees have been taught to communicate, taught to use words, and can even generate words of their own. Language, however, is more than communicating, more than using words or generating words. Something more, much more, is involved. Language, as the Word in its origins, differed fundamentally from communication.

We cannot doubt chimpanzees, dogs, cats, cows, even trees, communicate.[4] Nor can we doubt this communication sometimes reaches high levels of sophistication. One small example of animal communication can be given from my own experience: I used to drive home for lunch. One day the car broke down halfway home, and I had to walk the rest of the way on foot. When I got home, and as I started to walk up the driveway, our dog came barking aggressively at me. And then, he realized it was me. He stopped in his tracks, completely puzzled, embarrassed. And then he found the solution. He rushed back to the house and then came bounding down towards me, barking, but this time with obvious pleasure.

It is fairly obvious (except for those enmeshed in doctrinal Puritanism[5]) that animals can run a whole gamut of emotions, which they can communicate. But according to Chomsky, "Communication is only one function of language and by no means the only one."[6] Heidegger is even more explicit: "[T]he essence of language does not consist entirely in being a means of giving information.... language affords the possibility of standing in the openness of the existent. *Only where there is language, is there world* (my italics).[7] The creation of the word is not only the beginning of language; it is also the birth of the world. We 'create' the world with the Word.

"In the beginning was the Word, and the Word was with[8] God and the Word was God." This passage from the Gospel of John expresses so well the ambiguity inherent in the word. *The word was God!* St. Anslem talks of "the word by which thou sayest thy very self," which is another way of saying that the word is God. This is how we must understand that very first word. God is intelligence, wholeness, being, love; and all of this is focused, brought down to earth, fixed in and by the word. In this first word nothing was communicated, nothing given from voice to ear, from mind to mind but a condensation, a crystallization, or (to use the words of de Chardin) "the newly formed center exploded upon itself," and by this the One was focused and freed. What power, then, must have come to the one who spoke the first word? What genius would have made the utterance possible? Nothing preceded it in kind; it was the first human creation. Just as the creation of the cosmos was made possible by the null point, and the creation of life by the center, so the creation of consciousness was made possible by the word.

Who was the first creator who brought down from heaven the power of the word? The poet, says Heidegger: "The poet names the gods and names all things in that which they are." Naming is not simply sticking labels on things that already exist *but is the very act of bringing into existence.* "This naming," said Heidegger, "does not consist merely in something already known being supplied with a name; it is rather that when the poet speaks the essential word, the existent is by this naming nominated as what it is. So it becomes known as existent." He added, "Poetry is the establishing of being by means of the word."[9]

In Chapter 2 I wrote of the *weltenschauung*, a world view or idea which brings a world into existence. I said the world idea is not static, inert, or passive—as, for example, a window is inert and passive with respect to all that passes through it—but is intensely active, purposeful, and dynamic. Instead of being a passive window, the world idea is like a field of forces under tension, a field in dynamic equilibrium. It is fluid but within limits; fluid with a fluidity that is elastic; a dynamism capable of arousing intense energy, excitement, and stress. This dynamic comes from the weltenschauung, which is not simply world idea but also world view. What I am now suggesting is that the word fixes the world idea, in the same way that certain chemicals fix a photographic print. By fixing the world view in this way, the word creates a stage upon which the drama of existence and experience can play out.

Creation is not *ex nihilo*, because discovery is equally involved. The word is essentially creative, but it also uncovers what is already there. God *said*, "Let there be light!" This is the primordial imperative, the creative act by which all creativity of human beings is foreshadowed. Because of the word, light shines in the darkness. Some say language is merely a tool developed by humans in the struggle to survive, a tool useful to the hunter; in such a context, the first word could have been "kill!" But, as Heidegger said, language is not a tool at man's disposal; rather, "it is the supreme event of human existence."[10]

"I can do without God in my life and in my painting," said Van Gogh, "but I cannot, ill as I am, do without something which is greater than I, which is my life—the power to create."[11] Now it seems the power to create *is* God. This power to create created Van Gogh's paintings; for the poet it creates the poetry, and for that first human being it created the word and thus the world. It was also the same power that created Van Gogh, the poet and the first human being.

Om

What was the original, living word? Could it have been *Om*? This word has reverberated down the ages, surrounded by mystery and tradition, passed from teacher to student in archaic rituals. Om, in this case, would be the center. This was affirmed by Lama Govinda, who wrote, "Om stands like the sun in the center of the mandala, the place of Vairocana the 'Sun Buddha,' the Radiating One."[12] Mandala means both center and periphery. Om would have been the living word, standing as the sun in the center. He also said, Om is "the point of ultimate unification and spiritualization," words very similar to Eliade's description of the center as being "where all essential modes of being come together." Lama Govinda went on to say this point that is one "contains the latent properties of all the previous stages, just as the seed or germ (*bija*) does. In this sense Om is the quintessence, the seed syllable (*bija-mantra*) of the universe, the magic word par excellence."

Just as the center is not a symbol so we must not look upon the original word as *standing for* something. Rabindranath Tagore wrote:

> Om is the symbolic word for the infinite, the perfect, the eternal. This sound as such is already perfect and *represents*[13] the wholeness of things. All our religious contemplation begin with Om and end with Om. It is meant to fill the mind with the presentiment of eternal perfection and to free it from the world of narrow selfishness.[14]

This, perhaps, is how we in the twenty-first century understand Om, but originally Om *was* the infinite, the perfect, the eternal, and not merely its stand-in. Only in its degenerate form, after it has been caged in the zoo of words, does Om become a denatured symbol "representing" the wholeness of things. As Lama Govinda said, "The *sabda* or sound of the mantra is not a physical sound (though it may be accompanied by such a one) but a spiritual one. It cannot be heard by ears but only by the heart, and it cannot be uttered by the mouth but only by the mind."[15] We for whom God is dead; for whom the word has been decon-structed, castrated of its meaning; for whom, as Yeats says, "The center cannot hold," how can we ever see the word "stand like the sun in the center?"

Perhaps "God" is the nearest we can come to it, if we are looking for a modern counterpart to Om. But only if we remember that the word *God* comes from the Sanskrit *huta*, the past participle of a verb meaning "to beseech or implore." The word *Allah,* interestingly enough, means "sadness," its etymology being in a word connoting sad, "to be overwhelmed with sadness, to sigh toward, to flee fearfully toward," which is the emotional counterpart to yearning. Henri Corbin, whom I have been quoting, goes on to say this:

> For Ismalian Gnosis, the supreme godhead cannot be known or even named as "God"; Al-Lah is a name which indeed is given to the created being, the Most-Near and sacrosanct archangel. This name then expresses sadness, nostalgia eternally to know the Principle which eternally initiates it: the nostalgia of the revealed God (i.e., revealed for man) yearning to be once more beyond His revealed being.[16]

This is stated succinctly in "I was a hidden treasure and I yearned to be known. Then I created creatures in order to be known by them," or "in order to become in them the object of my knowledge."[17]

This yearning to rediscover lost unity, to find wholeness, to discover the holy beyond the null point and the binding contradiction it implies, expresses itself constantly in the search for the center, the hidden treasure. This yearning underlies all evolution. It was not for nothing that Gurdjieff called God "Our all-suffering Creator." Yearning is the *feeling* counterpart to dynamic unity. Van Gogh spoke of this same yearning when he talked of those "who are somehow mysteriously imprisoned, prisoners in an I-don't-know-what-for utterly horrible cage. Such a man often does not know himself what he might do but feels instinctively: yet I am good for something. . . . How then can I be useful, how can I be of service! Something is alive in me: what can it be!" Something is alive in me, an unspoken word yearning for a voice, a treasure yearning to be known.

What depth of sadness, of yearning, of conflict, of anger, what white terror there must have been before that voice was found and the first word spoken. Some inkling of this world without a center is given in the following account by a man who had bouts of mania:

> Psychosis, [we could substitute ambiguity] leaves you with fear; you lose all sense of yourself as a person among other persons. You feel yourself dissipating; your distinctiveness vanishes. No voice in the universe sounds like your voice; yet all voices sound like your voice. You see yourself as a vast multitude; and all these millions in the multitude become you. This voice, this multitude that is me has a detached quality to it without substance or body. This multitude drowns me; it swallows me up. With its persistent hollowness, the voice blots out any sense of an I and this hollow sound, like drums beating in a huge cavern, encircles me and paralyzes my thoughts.

The voice is lost, the voice that can pronounce the saving word. "No voice in the universe sounds like your voice; yet all voices sound like your voice." Without this "you lose all sense of yourself as a person among other persons." You dissipate, your uniqueness is lost. You are drowned, swallowed up in the voice that is a multitude without substance or body, a voice without the saving word.

This voice, both absent and all too present, "blotting out any sense of an I, any sense of a center," this "hollow sound, like drums beating in a huge cavern, encircles me and paralyzes my thoughts," this is Eliot's demon multiplied a thousand fold, ten thousand fold. Eliot wrote of it:

> [One] is oppressed by a burden which he must bring to birth in order to obtain relief. Or, to change the figure of speech, he is haunted by a demon, a demon against which he feels powerless, because in its first manifestation it has no face, no name, nothing; and the words, the poem he makes, are a kind of form of exorcism of this demon.

Renée, a young girl who had recovered from schizophrenia, spoke of this invasion by demons, and their exorcism by words:

> When, for example, I looked at a chair or a jug, I thought not of their use or function— but as having lost their names, their functions and meanings; they became 'things' and began to take on life, to exist...In the

unreal scene, in the murky quiet of my perception, suddenly 'the thing' sprang up. The stone jar, decorated with the blue flowers, was there facing me, defying me with its presence, with its existence. To conquer my fear I looked away. My eyes met a chair, then a table; they were alive, too, asserting their presence. I attempted to escape their hold by calling out their names. I said, chair, jug, table, it is a chair.[18]

Even the eloquent accounts of Renée and the man who suffered mania cannot approach the profound dream or nightmare of that first creative moment.

I believe the appearance of the word on the world stage was not an accident, although nothing can be found in the realm of being to account for it or even to anticipate it. To understand its emergence I have tried to follow the evolution of awareness. This would be a vast undertaking if it were done in depth, a task beyond my competence. However, let me now add one more tentative step to the evolutionary diagram, shown in Figure 24.

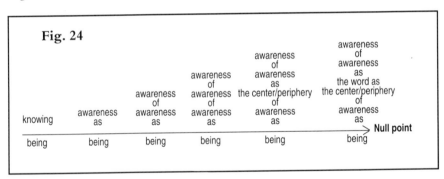

The creation of the word was a religious act; in fact, it was the first religious act, and much of religion since has been devoted to the maintenance of the center as well as safeguarding of the word. In this way it could be said that the main burden of religion has been the protection and development of consciousness. The fact that religion is now giving way to psychology only adds weight to this contention.

In a later chapters I will explore this contention further. But before I can do this, I must explain what exactly I mean by the word and how it forms the foundation of consciousness.

Notes

1. Cited in Thorlief Borman, *Hebrew Thought Compared With Greek* (New York: Norton, 1960), p. 58.
2. M. R. Vincent, *Word Studies in the New Testament* (McLean, VA: MacDonald Publishing, 1988).
3. "Pythagoras thought that he, who gave things their names, ought to be regarded as not only the most intelligent, but the oldest of the wise men" (*Selections from the Prophetic Scriptures* (Grand Rapids, Mich.: Wm. B. Eerdmans: Ante Nicene Library, 1975), vol. xxiv, p. 127).
4. Douglas firs, for example, exude an antifeedant chemical when they are attacked by beetles, and other fir trees in distant parts of the forest do likewise in response to a warning alleochemical secreted by the trees under attack.
5. "For all its crudities behaviorism, conceived as a methodology rather than a psychological system, taught psychology with brutal emphasis that 'The dog is whining' and 'The dog is sad' are statements of altogether different empirical standing, and heaven help psychology if it ever again overlooks the distinction" (Peter Medawar, *Pluto's RepublicIncorporating the Art of the Soluble and Induction and Intutition* [Oxford: Oxford University Press, 1984], p. 256). Apart from doubting that brutality could ever teach anything sophisticated, one can only want to remind the behaviorists that values—freedom and dignity, for example—do not have, nor are they reliant upon, empiricism for their support—that "the dog is whining" means, to most people, "I must try to do something about it."
6. Noam Chomsky, *Reflections on Language* (New York: Pantheon Books, 1975).
7. Martin Heidegger, *Existence and Being* (Chicago: Henry Regnery, 1949), p. 276. Italics are mine.
8. According to M.R. Vincent (1888, p. 384), "The preposition 'with' . . . denotes motion towards not merely as being near or alongside, but as a living union and communion; implying the active notion of intercourse." In other words, "with" is equivalent to the **(/)** I have been using to denote ambiguity.
9. Heidegger (1949, p. 281).
10. Heidegger (1949, p. 280).
11. Irving Stone (Ed.), *Dear Theo: Autobiography of Vincent van Gogh* (New York: Signet, 1937), p. 382.
12. Lama Govinda, *Creative Meditation and Multi-Dimensional Consciousness* (Wheaton, IL: Quest, 1976), p. 73,
13. My emphasis.
14. Lama Govinda (1976, p. 46).
15. Lama Govinda (1976, p. 27).
16. Henri Corbin, *Creative Imagination in the Sufism of Ibn 'Arabi* (Princeton, NJ: Princeton University Press, 1969; Ralph Manheim, Trans.).
17. Corbin (1969, p. 114).
18. Grace Rubin Rabson (Trans.), *The Autobiography of a Schizophrenic Girl* (New York: New American Library, 1951), p. 40.

Chapter 18

The Word as Metaphor

The drive toward the formation of metaphor is the fundamental human drive, which one cannot for a single moment dispense with in thought, for one would thereby dispense with man himself.[1]

NIETZSCHE

ACCORDING TO DE NICHOLAS, the wild bull used in the Spanish bull fighting (the *toro de lidia*) has two weaknesses: First he is an animal "on the spot" because he has only one spot, *la querencia*; and, second, his fury can be enticed away from his spot simply by moving the flaming cape in front of his horns.

Away from his one spot, the wild bull is lost, his fury is controlled, his power reduced, his death imminent. The first thing the bull does when charging into the ring is to give away his spot to the bullfighter by returning to it again and again.[2]

As I have said, the creation of a center is the basic creation of life, and it is the center that makes life possible. The bull, like all animate beings, is the center of being. But his querencia is also the center. When the bull is "on the spot," these two become one center and the bull acquires power correspondingly. The inner split, me-as-center/me-as-periphery is healed. But when he is away from the spot, the bull is divided against himself, the center is both here and there simultaneously, and so he is lost and powerless. This split is magnified a hundred-fold if the toreador stands "on the spot."

The word has the supreme value of being the spot from which one cannot be separated; from now on we can carry our querencia with us, create our own world by creating the word. The center can be intuited even though it cannot be known, it can be sensed although not seen; so, around that which is intuited and sensed, experience is gathered like iron filings around a magnet. How charismatic, how powerful, how immovable would be the one who spoke the first word! With what godlike mien would he, or she, have stood or walked! For a long time rulers were seen as semi-divine, as were the kings of Europe; they were even descendants of God, as were the emperors of Japan and China.[3] The divine right of kings came from their divinity as part man, part God. Myths and legends abound telling of the days when the gods walked the earth, and the gods were those who could speak the liberating word. But at source and origin was God: The word was God.

The Power of the Word

From where does the word get this power—the power to bring light into the world, to set the world free? Before the word is spoken, all is lost in twilight. Awareness and even consciousness of a kind are present, but a consciousness without clarity and stability, lacking (as Heidegger said) permanence, simplicity, and proportion. In this twilight, awareness is bound to what is perceived. The present is all. Memory exists, but no past; anticipation, but no future. With the word, with language, one can remember, relive, even recreate the past; one can plan, bring the future into, and so become part of the present.

We tend to forget that if words are to be words they must be spoken,[4] even if only subvocally as the inner monologue. That this is so means words are *something that is happening*. This something that is happening comes out of the one striving to reabsorb the center. The function of speaking is to provide a vehicle for the center and so make it articulate. But alas, words lose their containing power, and so the need to find new words goes on endlessly. We love stories and plays because they marshal and give more substance still to this something that is going on. This, too, is why people chatter endlessly. In this constant search to pin down the center in words, to make it absolutely permanent, stable, and unambiguous, to make it completely articulate, we invent myths, theologies, philosophies, sciences, ideologies, psychologies, and literature.

The Structure and Function of Words

The word is the embodiment of the idea. Idea reveals relations between phenomena, word expresses these relations. The structure of a word is the same as that of the idea it embodies. The word *logos* originally signified "both the *outward form* by which the inner thought is expressed and the inward thought itself."[5] This means the word is not merely a name for the idea, "but the idea itself expressed."[6] All that I have said about idea—the discovery of its structure as a dynamic field with core and halo—is therefore true of the word as well. The core of the word provides a vehicle for the null point as center; the null point gives the word permanence and simplicity. From the halo comes the life and scope of the word. The core gives the dictionary meaning, the halo gives meaning derived from metaphor and simile. Because this meaning shifts ceaselessly, ambiguity and tension pervade the word.

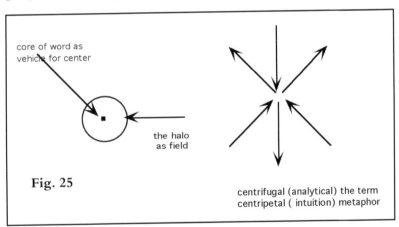

core of word as vehicle for center

the halo as field

Fig. 25

centrifugal (analytical) the term
centripetal (intuition) metaphor

That this is so, that the dictionary meaning of a word resides in the core and the metaphorical meaning in the halo, can be illustrated by considering the meaning of the word *meaning* itself. Meaning is derived from two contradictory tendencies: a tendency toward the center, which I have called the core and which could be called *intrinsic* meaning, and another tendency toward the periphery, which is *extrinsic* meaning. This

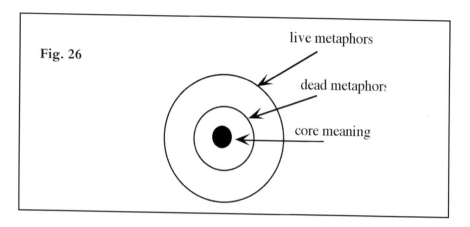

Fig. 26

live metaphors

dead metaphors

core meaning

periphery is what I have called the halo. The intrinsic meaning has its origin in the etymological root of the word. As words are something happening, it is significant that the roots of all Sanskrit words are verbs.

If I say the word tree, for example, most people conjure up an idea of something having a trunk, branches, and leaves. This is its *core* meaning. But what if I say, "The tree doesn't contain all the names because the family, like all families, has one or two skeletons in the closet"? Now I am talking about a family tree, recorded in some book or another. And if I talk about the number of presents under the tree, it's obvious I'm talking about a Christmas tree. These are dead metaphors. But a third level emerges, an essentially creative level, which keeps the word alive. This is the level of novel metaphor. Thus, the word tree looks inward to it roots and outward to its context in order to have meaning, and the tension between these two keeps a word alive.

So, the word is a *container* for the basic ambiguity. Metaphors capture the tension of opposing forces. To read poetry the reader must be actively involved in the creative process; because of this involvement, something new, inexpressible in words, is passed from the poet to the reader. In other words, both poet and reader invoke unity, the poet in creative expression and the reader in creative appreciation. The frog voice is the call for containment of the raw forces of ambiguity, each force struggling for supremacy. This struggle is focused by the idea and finds expression in the poetic word.

Words as Containers

The word is created to contain and give expression to ambiguity. Note that I use the word contain for two reasons. The etymology of contain is *con* and *tenir*. *Con* means "with" or "together," as in connect. *Tenir* means "to hold." Thus *contain* means "to hold together." To contain the ambiguity therefore is to hold the conflicting elements of the ambiguity together. With the living word as action, containment is an ongoing process. In addition, to say that a word contains the ambiguity also means that ambiguity is an inherent quality of the word itself. An obvious example is the word "cleave," which means both to unite and to separate. The extent to which language contains ambiguity is brought out well in William Empson's *Seven Types of Ambiguity*.[7]

The ambiguity contained by the word is, of course, the fundamental ambiguity, to which I have referred repeatedly throughout this book. It is the ambiguity at the source or origin, the source which is not past but now; the ambiguity inherent in One/knowing/being. This ambiguity is endless and can never be resolved; in the same way, the creativity out of which the word arises can never be exhausted. It is always reappearing in new guises—provided, that is, one can return to the source, past the demons of Eliot to the frog voice of Herr Benn. To understand this constant creative resurrection of the Word, and to understand how, the word 'contains' the ambiguity, we need to understand metaphor.

Metaphor

One of the great debates among scholars involves the question, what is a metaphor? In September 1977, a group of leading philosophers, psychologists, linguists, and educators arrived at the University of Illinois to join in a multidisciplinary conference on metaphor and thought. This conference drew nearly a thousand people.[8] In 1978, a symposium on the same subject was held at the University of Chicago.[9] Max Black, professor of philosophy at Cornell University, wrote in his paper *More About Metaphor*, "The extraordinary volume of papers and books on the subject produced during the past forty years might suggest that the subject is inexhaustible."[10] One bibliography has nearly three hundred pages of entries and contains perhaps as many as four thousand titles. Is it possible the subject is inexhaustible because the wrong kind of assumptions are being made, and the wrong kind of questions are being asked about metaphor—that the cart is pointing north while the light is in the south?

In the Harvard Eliot Norton lectures on the nature of music, Leonard Bernstein suggested that a metaphor is a statement saying, "This equals that, where this and that belong to two completely different and incompatible orders."[11] And Black says, "the 'mystery' of metaphor is that, taken as literal, a metaphorical statement appears to be perversely asserting something to be what it is plainly known not to be."[12]

In other words, according to Bernstein and Max Black, this is that but, at the same time, this is not that. In their book *Science, Order, and Creativity*, Bohm and Peat come to the same conclusion.[13] Using Shakespeare's metaphor, "All the world's a stage," they point out that, assuming that world = A and stage = B, then this is that, A = B. But, as they also point out, the world is patently not a stage; therefore A is not B. This is that and this is not that are incompatible, yet they are contained as unity by the metaphor. This is a direct echo of Arthur Koestler's definition of creativity quoted in Chapter 1. Thus a metaphor calls upon the creativity of the reader as well as of the poet to contain the ambiguity. It is this *mutual call to create,* essentially, that true art communicates.

Modern criticism has begun to take note that metaphor has much more than mere decoration to offer. Indeed, Wicker says that for some time now, "the truth has been emerging that metaphor is not just a way of describing things, but is a way of experiencing them."[14] Norman Mailer is equally bold in his assertion: "If the universe was a lock, its key was a metaphor rather than a measure."[15] And Ortony proclaims:

> Current criticism often takes metaphor *au grand serieux,* as a peephole on the nature of transcendental reality, a prime means by which the imagination can see into the life of things . . . [some] metaphors . . . deliberately emphasize the frame, as a prime means of seeing into the life, not of things, but of the creative human consciousness, framer of its own world.[16]

Irony

Irony is also indigenous to the human being; but once again the critics can no more account for the power of irony than they can for the power of metaphor. To appreciate irony one must not be taken in by it. Irony says something is the case which is obviously not the case, or vice versa.

One frequently encounters irony in the locker room when two men call one another names and insult one another, not, as it might appear, as an expression of aggression but as an expression of friendship. Although the ironical statement means what it says, what it says is not what it means; on the contrary, what it means is the very opposite of what it says. Thus irony, too, contains opposing forces, but in a way that is quite different to the way of the metaphor. What is more, some modern critics—for example I. A. Richards, Cleanth Brooks, and Kenneth Burke—have suggested that *every* literary context is ironic because it provides a weighting or qualification on every word, thus requiring the reader to infer meanings that are in a sense not in the words themselves. Thus every word has built into it a conflict of forces requiring a creative insight on the part of the reader or hearer to resolve it.

Nonverbal Metaphors

Bernstein's lectures were on the nature of music, and his talks had two main themes: Music is a language of ambiguity, and a prime ingredient of this language is metaphor. By musical metaphors Bernstein did not mean program music. When talking about musical semantics he used Beethoven's Pastoral Symphony as an illustration, but he dismissed the simulation of bird calls and the thunderstorm as superficial metaphors of relatively little importance in the face of intrinsic musical metaphors. Thus it is not only in *spoken* language that "metaphor is the omnipresent principle of language." Even so, nonverbal metaphors seem to have escaped the notice of those attending the seminars in Chicago and Illinois; among all the papers in the two collections published, only one strayed from a completely literary understanding of metaphor. Yet if, as Bernstein said, metaphor is intrinsic to musical semantics and not something acquired through association with literature, we cannot look simply to speech to understand it.

In physics, that bastion of the scientific method, Roger S. Jones says this about metaphor:

> It is generally acknowledged that scientists often use creative analogies and comparisons to extend theories and even to make new ones. Modern elementary particles are extensions of the Greek *atomos*, and William Harvey found the centralized sun of Copernicus a model for the heart

as center of the circulation of the blood. But I go beyond these relations that inform alone and suggest that scientists (and indeed all who possess creative consciousness) conjure like the poet and the shaman, that their theories are metaphors which ultimately are inseparable from physical reality, and that consciousness is so integral to the cosmos that the creative idea and the thing are one and the same thing.[17]

The part metaphor plays in the discoveries of science was a theme of Bohm and Peat's, as well. They discus at one point the Hamilton Jacobi theory of motion and talked about a metaphorical leap: "A particle *is* a wave," that could have been made. This, in turn, could have led to the development of quantum theory in the nineteenth century "almost without any further experimental clues at all."[18]

A few years ago Dustin Hoffman starred as an autistic man in the film *Rainman*. Hoffman's acting was a wonderful representation of autism, and most people who saw the film thoroughly enjoyed it. Yet, if one had asked those same audience members to spend a day with an autistic person, or a couple of hours watching a film featuring autistic people, they probably would have declined. So why would we enjoy watching Dustin Hoffman realistically portray an autistic person, but not enjoy spending time with an autistic person? It is because Dustin Hoffman is *acting*. Our pleasure comes from seeing him as the autistic person while knowing *he is not an autistic person*.

A story about Hoffman has some bearing on what I am saying. When he was acting in the film *Marathon Man*, he played the part of an itinerant. In some scenes this itinerant traveled by bus for several days and so had to go without sleep. In order to play the part as well as possible, Hoffman stayed up for that period of time without washing or shaving. Sir Lawrence Olivier is reputed to have heard about this and said, somewhat indignantly, "Good God, has the man not heard of acting?" How many in the audience would have found the scenes far less enjoyable, even repulsive, if they had known they were not being acted?

Dustin Hoffman playing the role of an autistic man and a child playing the role of parent with a doll or a hunter with a gun share something in common. The child knows the doll is not a baby and the stick is not a gun. Yet, at the same time for the child the doll *is* a baby and the stick *is* a gun.[19] The essence of the child's play is this pretense, and the pleasure comes not from the doll nor the stick but from the pretense.

This same pretense underlies the rituals, ceremonies, and parables of magic and religion.[20] In the Christian tradition, parables are frequently used in teaching. Sufi stories, metaphors of the human condition, are also full of irony. In Zen Buddhism, *koans*, which portray a kind of spiritual irony, are used as meditation aids.[21] Furthermore, as we will see in Chapter 20, this same pretense underlies ritual slaughter and human sacrifice. Understanding this, we have a key to understanding the ritual of the Mass, which is central to the Catholic faith.

What are we to make of this? How are we to understand it? Why this insistence upon this is that, knowing full well this is not that? If it is true that "to tolerate contradiction is to be indifferent to the truth," if the "person who, directly or by implication, knowingly both asserts and denies one and the same proposition, shows by that behavior that he does not care whether he asserts what is false and not true, or whether he denies what is true and not false,"[22] then all people are liars seeking to deceive themselves. Or perhaps the logical principle A = A, which the logician uses as a launching pad against ambiguity, is itself a metaphor, replete with irony! A is a *term*, a word stripped of its halo, the ultimate abstraction and the perfect metaphor for the null point. The irony is that the null point, as ultimate negation, cannot equal anything, not even itself.

An Example of Metaphor and Irony

To get a handle on metaphor and irony, consider the following poem, which has both. Written by Wilfred Owen, it is titled "Anthem for Doomed Youth": [23]

> What passing bells for these who die like cattle?
> Only the monstrous anger of the guns.
> Only the stuttering rifles rapid rattle
> Can patter out their hasty orisons.
> No mockeries now for them; no prayers nor bells,
> Nor any voice of mourning save the choirs,-
> The shrill, demented choirs of wailing shells;
> And bugles calling for them from sad shires.
>
> What candles may be held to speed them all?
> Not in the hands of boys, but in their eyes

Shall shine the holy glimmers of goodbyes.
The pallor of girls' brows shall be their pall;
Their flowers the tenderness of patient minds,
And each slow dusk a drawing down of blinds.[24]

Central to the poem is the absence of mourning, "no prayers nor bells, nor any voice of mourning," and in this lies the irony. On the one hand they (soldiers massacred in the First World War at Ypres, the Somme and Passchendale) die like cattle, so why should we mourn them? We do not mourn the death of cattle. On the other hand, we do not mourn them because there should be "No mockeries" now for those whose pall is the "pallor of girls brows" and whose wreaths are "the tenderness of patient minds." They are so far above and beyond our mourning that to mourn them, in the circumstances, would be to mock them. They are too unworthy to be mourned and at the same time their worth is beyond our mourning.

But there is irony within this irony because, after all, a mourning does occur and a funeral service as well, a passing bell and prayers, and also a choir—two choirs in fact. There are candles and wreaths and a memorial service, because at "each slow dusk a drawing down of blinds."

But, irony of ironies, what are these passing bells? "The monstrous anger of the guns." And the prayers? "The stuttering rifles' rapid rattle." And the choirs? "The shrill, demented choirs of wailing shells" on the one hand and, "bugles calling for them from sad shires" on the other. But even here, even with the bugle call, irony is not absent. The "bugles calling 'for' them from sad shires": does this mean the bugles are calling on their behalf, or are the bugles calling them home. If they are calling on their behalf, who will hear? If they are calling them home, yet again, for a more tragic reason, who will hear?

Is there or isn't there? Irony within irony, ambiguity within ambiguity. The ambiguity is forced upon us; we cannot turn away from it. These are men, but they are dying like cattle. What mourning can there be? Anger, despair, horror, desolation, pity, beauty, and tenderness all are contained here. But not in an overt way. Just, "no prayers nor bells, nor any voice of mourning." The wrenching, but binding, quality of irony in "And bugles calling for them from sad shires."

But the guns are *angry*! Can guns be angry, they are dead metal, machines, inert, lifeless. But the gun barks in anger, it explodes with anger, it jumps in anger, fire pours out of its mouth in anger. And to whom is the anger addressed? Is it addressed to those who die like cattle, or to those who sent them to die? And, in any case, whose anger is it? The poet's, the dying men's or is it just anger, disincarnate anger and all the more dreadful because it has neither host nor guest? Does it come from the same place as "no prayers nor bells, nor any voice of mourning"? Everything is compressed within the "monstrous anger of the guns." *Monstrous,* what an onomatopoeia.[25]

The feeling of Owen's poem of is of *outrage*—barely contained outrage. But, nevertheless, the outrage *is* contained, and therein lies the enormous power of the poem.

But what happens when words fail? What happens when rage has no words, when one is speechless, dumbfounded, overcome, beside oneself with rage? Consider the following observation of violence, which I quoted in Chapter 15:

> She pushes him, he pushes her, only she's doing all the talking. *He isn't saying a word....* Then *all of a sudden* she must have triggered off the right nerve because he lets fly with a right cross that I mean stuns. I mean she goes down like a rock!

Violence comes when words fail.

Cursing as Verbal Violence

Between words and violence lies an intermediate state, which is neither words nor violence, or perhaps, better still, is both words and violence. A discussion of this state will help us better understand a the power of words. I am referring to swearing or cursing the other.

"You fucking bastard! You shit-head!" For an English-speaking person these words are dynamite. When said by one person to another they can unleash murder; they can release angry power enough to kill an army. But why? It might well be that anything said in anger will catch fire in the other person, anger is so contagious. But even so, all languages have a repertoire of words that are used for wreaking nonphysical violence. They are always taboo words, words that are forbidden, and for this reason *profanity* is a form of abuse. The English swear word *bloody* once meant "by our Lady" and was a profanity. It has lost its power as a curse to the extent it has lost its profaning power.

Words are taboo because they come from sources of power, and the one who uses the taboo word usurps its power unless he uses it in its correct and limited context. Swear words are taboo words torn out of context and so have power but *no meaning*. The power comes from ambiguity which, no longer contained, releases the power and pain inherent in the underlying conflict. Swear words have neither metaphorical nor literal value; instead of being like a cylinder containing the thrust and recoil of the piston, they are like a bullet from a gun. The receiver of a curse can neither accept nor reject it. It is something like the old court room dilemma, "Are you still beating your wife. Answer yes or no!" The curse has no context, it makes one speechless and opens the primordial pain of unreconciled ambiguity. Pain has no words.

The Word Contains Violence

The German Military genius, Clauswitsch, once said, "War is diplomacy carried on by other means." But this is the cynic talking. He is saying diplomacy is concealed war. But the art of diplomacy both is and is not concealed war. The art of diplomacy is to be able to say something positive and something negative simultaneously. Diplomatic language walks the razor's edge. When it breaks down the alternatives are bargaining on the one hand or war on the other.

War is an appetite that grows by what it is fed on; I believe it is a way of seeking the One by inappropriate means. Like the two cats who are equally powerful, neither can give way; each claims to be the One, each claims to be the center. The function of the word is both to contain the violence and to provide a center. If the containing power of words breaks down, a vicious cycle is established from which violence sooner or later will erupt. In his book *Violence and the Sacred*, René Girard points out, "It is more difficult to quell an impulse toward violence than to arouse it."[26] The inertia built into words by their invoking unity makes violence difficult to arouse. But, once aroused, violence is like a flood breaking through the dam; the more the water pours through, the more the dam crumbles and falls before its onrush. Words as curses aid and abet the onrush. As Girard noted, "The more men strive to curb their violent impulses the more these impulses seem to prosper. The very weapons used to combat violence are turned against their users. Violence is like a raging fire that feeds upon the very objects intended to smother its flames."[27]

We who have a well-established language and subtle speech that has given us a legal structure of government and courts to which we can appeal, we who have an army and a police force to protect us and a long tradition of using diplomacy with our neighbors and other nations, we find the outbreak of violence shocking and incomprehensible. The average person sees his own violence as a personal failure. But it has not always been like this; indeed, even today it is like this in only a small part of the world. And even here it is precarious and always threatened from within and from without.

Primitive man was much more likely to be at loss for words, to be speechless with rage and its inversion, anxiety. For primitive man, Girard noted, violence was transformed into a sort of seminal fluid that impregnated objects on contact and whose diffusion, like electricity, is determined by physical laws. Contamination was a terrible thing, and only those who were already contaminated willfully exposed themselves to it. These exposed ones were the priests and warriors. Violence became the means by which violence was combated. In the Aztec civilization, for example, people engaged in what were called "wars of the flowers" and in ritual slaughter. Indeed, these practices were but two sides of one long ritual of slaughter. The war of the flowers was the means by which warriors were captured for use in ritual slaughter, a ritual used to quell violence.

For us today, this is horrifying, and many people would condemn these rituals without question. Indeed, there are some today who condemn even those trying to look at the question in a detached manner and see it as a creative process, even if a failed creative process. But there have been societies of people who not only thought differently from the way we do but whose whole conscious structures were different from ours. It may be that the Aztecs had a civilization which failed to evolve beyond a certain primitive means for establishing and preserving a center. Because we have the center well-established—buttressed by laws, reinforced by traditions, and held in place by public opinion—we can afford to forget it. Yet it is there. We call it the central government and it rules our lives. But what happens if the freedom to forget it is not there? What happens if society's whole preoccupation is to maintain and preserve the center?

Occasionally we see triumvirates, but they do not last long, and eventually the central role of leader falls to one person. He or she is the center, although the center is not him or her. In democratic societies the leader is elected and can be dismissed; but the center role is always there. The president is always the president, but Peter Jones or Mary Smith is not always the president. Invariably when a person has occupied the role for a sufficiently long time, the acrimony of the governed becomes so evident that the person must be replaced. We say that he or she loses authority, but the ancients would say that he had lost *mana* or *baraka*—that is, charisma. He had lost the power of the center and had to be replaced. When there was no election process, the way of replacement was to kill him or, rather, to sacrifice him. He was sacrificed because he was the center and the center could not die. The ancient cry, "The king is dead, long live the king!" attests to this. Indeed, if the god/man were to be killed but not sacrificed, the tribe would be lost.

An example of what happens when the center is lost is given by the fate of the Mayans at the hands of Francis Pizzaro. Mario Vargas Llosa once remarked on how strange it is that a culture as powerful and sophisticated as the ancient Mexican and Peruvian should have crumbled in the face of a small band of marauders, saying, "This question itself is centuries old, but not academic." Later, he answered that question:

> At the precise moment the Inca emperor is captured, before the battle begins, his armies give up the fight as if manacled by a magic force. The slaughter is indescribable, but only from one of the two sides. The Spaniards discharged their harquebuses, thrust their spears and swords, and charged their horses against a bewildered mass, which, having witnessed the capture of their God and master, seemed unable to defend itself or even run away.[28]

In the death of the god/man, the center is no more and the word loses its power to contain the conflict. In later times, when no longer incarnated in the god/man, the word was incarnated in the idol or totem. Then, instead of sacrificing the king, it was possible to sacrifice the totem or some substitute, the metaphor for the totem. The first totems were effigies of god/men, so human beings were still sacrificed. In ancient Greece it was the custom to keep slaves called *pharmakons* especially for the purpose of sacrifice. In classical Greek, the word *pharmakon* means both "poison" and "antidote to poison," both sickness and cure.[29]

In the Aztec civilization, humans were sacrificed as surrogate gods in the most violent way to restore the power of the center. In the next chapter we will look at this ritual of sacrifice to help us understand both the power and the importance of the center, and what happens when the word fails.

Notes

1. Daniel Breazeale (Ed. and Trans.), *Philosophy and Truth: Selections from Nietzsche's Notebooks of the Early 1870s* (Atlantic Highlands, NJ: Humanities Press, 1979), pp. 88–89.
2. Antonio T. de Nicolas, *Meditations Through the Rig Veda Four Dimensional Man* (New York: Hays Ltd., 1976), p. 2.
3. "Any disturbance in the sun accuses the emperor. Any disturbance around the sun accuses the court and ministers. A disturbance in the moon accuses the queen and harem. Good weather lasts too long shows the emperor is inactive. Days which continue to be cloudy show the emperor lacks understanding. Too much rain-fall shows that he is unjust. Lack of rain shows that he is careless. Excessive cold shows that he is inconsiderate of others, stormy winds show that he is lazy" (John Michell, *City of Revelation* [London: Garnstone Press, 1972], pp. 16–17).
4. Some say the word is sung or even danced, but for our purposes and for the time being, "spoken" is enough.
5. Vincent (1998).
6. Vincent (1998).
7. William Empson, *Seven Types of Ambiguity* (New York: W. W. Norton, 1977).
8. Ortony (1979).
9. Sheldon Sacks (Ed.), *On Metaphor* (Chicago: University of Chicago, 1978).
10. Ortony (1979, p. 19)
11. Leonard Bernstein, *Six Talks at Harvard* (Cambridge, MA: Harvard University Press, 1976), p. 123.
12. Ortony (1979, pp. 19–32).
13. David Bohm and F. David Peat, *Science, Order, and Creativity* (London: Routledge, 2000), p. 32.
14. Wicker (1975 p. 11).
15. Wicker (1975, p. 2).
16. Ortony (1979, p. 20).
17. Roger S. Jones, *Physics as Metaphor* (New York: New American Library, 1982), p. 5.
18. Bohm and Peat (2000, p. 40).
19. If anyone doubts this, let them read the *Calvin and Hobbs* comic strip in the newspaper.

20. We must not forget that the word *religion* (as with the word *yoga*) means to "tie back together, to yoke"; nor must we forget that the word *pretense* has strong affinities with the French word *pretender*, meaning "to claim." Metaphor and irony tie or yoke "this is that" to "this is not that."

21. Albert Low, *Return to the One* (Montreal: Montreal Zen Center, 1992).

22. Anthony Flew, *Thinking About Thinking* (Glasgow: Fontana, 1977), p. 15.

23. Wilfred Owen, *Anthem for Doomed Youth: The Collected Poems of Wilfred Owen*. (London: Chatto & Windus, 1963; C. Day Lewis, Ed.).

24. In England at this time it was customary to draw the blinds when a death had occurred in the family.

25. Onomatopoeia is its own kind of metaphor, its own kind of awareness as being.

26. René Girard, *Violence and the Sacred* (Baltimore: Johns Hopkins University Press, 1977), p. 2.

27. Girard (1977, p. 31)

28. Mario Vargas Llosa, "Questions of Conquest: What Columbus Wrought and What He Did Not." *"Questions of Conquest: What Columbus Wrought and What He Did Not." American Educator* (Spring 1992), pp. 47-48.

29. Girard (1977, p. 95).

Chapter 19

Violence and Creativity

Our only hope, or else despair
Lies in the choice of pyre or pyre
To be redeemed from fire by fire.
T. S. ELIOT[1]

VIOLENCE IS THE OUTCOME OF INTOLERABLE PAIN or, perhaps more frequently, of the threat of intolerable pain. It is a bid to end this threat or end the pain itself. I said in Chapter 13 that self-generation comes from the need to resolve conflict, but sometimes such a creative resolution is not possible, or is incomplete, or fails. Then, in the place of construction, destruction takes over. When a creative resolution fails, the conflict creates pain, and this pain underlies all "negative emotions." If the pain is severe and threatens to be bottomless, then anxiety, fear, dread, and panic surge up or anger, rage, and ultimately violence erupt. This occurs when conflict can find no issue, when each side is so evenly matched that neither can (or will) give way to the other. Then the pain becomes intolerable. Then the threat of annihilation looms, a threat that is always, fundamentally, the threat of *self*-annihilation.

The Double Bind and Ambiguity

This notion of a conflict that has no issue is similar to, but also considerably different from, Bateson's idea of the *double bind*.[2] As Bateson's theory is comparatively well-known and might be more immediately accessible, let me use it as a bridge. Bateson says a particular "experiential component" (i.e., something that we can experience) is common to schizophrenia, humor, poetry, art, and so on. This component is the double bind, the principle feature of which is this: No matter what a person does, he or she cannot win. The effects of being caught in a double bind can be serious enough to bring on psychosis. The woman in Chapter 11, faced with self-annihilation or of having to rend herself in two, was in a double bind.

According to Bateson, the necessary ingredients for a double bind are these:

1. Two or more people are necessary, one of whom Bateson designates the victim.
2. The experience must be repeated, because the double bind is not a trauma but a habitual expectation.
3. A primary negative injunction is necessary: "If you do that, I will punish you." We could put this more simply as the injunction, "This is that (which you must do)!"
4. There must be a secondary injunction conflicting with the first at a more abstract level. "Do not see this as punishment." "Do not think of what you must not do." "Do not submit to my prohibitions." "Do not question my love for you, of which the primary prohibition is an example." "I punish you for your own sake." This *is not* that; punishment is not punishment, although everyone knows this *is* that, punishment is punishment.
5. An overall negative injunction is made which prohibits the victim from leaving the field.
6. Finally, the complete set of ingredients is not necessary once the victim has learned to perceive his universe in double-bind patterns. Then almost any part of the double-bind sequence may be sufficient to precipitate panic or rage.

Bateson uses a Zen Buddhist koan to summarize the double bind: A master holds up a stick and says, "If you say this is a stick, I will punish you; if you say it is not a stick, I will punish you!" In a later chapter, I will discuss the reason for a Zen master saying this. For now, let me simply stress that Zen teachers use koans to help bring their students to awakening, not to punish them. They use the koan to put the student into a double bind from which the only escape its awakening. The koan nevertheless can be looked upon as a paradigm for the double bind. This means that the context within which the double bind is embedded must also be taken into account as well as the double bind itself.

The Zen master's challenge can be reworded, using a formula I have already used: "This is that; this is not that! What is it? Speak or you will be punished!" This is that; this is not that underlies metaphor and irony. These in turn arise out of the basic ambiguity, which says, *This is One [it is not two]. This is not one [it is two]*. Even this, as we know, is not the full story because within "this two" is contained *another* ambiguity: *this is knowing* [it is not being]; *this is being* [it is not knowing]. Furthermore, the One also contains a latent ambiguity: This is not ambiguous [it is one]; this is ambiguous [because One is not unambiguous]. All this is implied in the Zen Master's challenge.[1] Bateson's double bind is what he called "an experiential component" and lies down-stream of the basic ambiguity but, nevertheless, is derived from it. Bateson's double bind, moreover, can only be resolved in a destructive way, destructive to oneself or to others; the original double bind, as exemplified in the Zen Master's challenge, can be creatively resolved. This is one [it is not two;] this is two [it is not one] is another way of formulating Koestler's definition of creativity.

Therefore, two people do not necessarily have to be involved in a double bind. All that is required are two complementary and conflicting "situations," plus the urgent need to resolve the conflict before dire consequences ensue. With the basic ambiguity, the dire consequences are engulfment and suffering. Moreover, since our very existence arises from this basic ambiguity, we can never leave the field, even in death. The threat of self-annihilation is ever present for all of us. We are all plagued by an incipient double bind, which I referred to earlier as "a bodiless childful of life in the gloom / Crying with frog voice, 'What shall I be?'" Bateson's double bind, which may be present in all psychological traumas, simply acts as a trigger.

The Threat of Self-Annihilation

Martin Heidegger was keenly aware of the threat of self-annihilation and called it "dread," which he distinguished from anxiety or fear. He dismissed anxiety as simply "a mood, common enough, that comes over us all too easily, and is akin to nervousness."[3] Furthermore, he added, "fear of" is generally "fear about" something, and we are always afraid "of" this or that. In dread, however, although it is "dread of" it is not dread "about" this or that. ""Dread of" is always a dreadful feeling "about" *but not about this or that.* In dread, Heidegger noted,

> [T]here is nothing to hold on to. . . . Dread reveals nothing. . . . Dread holds us in suspense because . . . we . . . [along with every thing else] slip away from ourselves. . . . For this reason it is not "you" or "I" who has the uncanny feeling but "one."[4]

Heidegger went on to say, "Dread strikes us dumb . . . all affirmation fails in the face of it. The fact that when we are caught in the uncanniness of dread we often try to break the empty silence by words spoken at random, only proves the presence of Nothing."[5]

These words, which Heidegger said are spoken at random, are uttered because language is the human response to negation. It was in the face of the original negation (the original double bind) and the threat of the primordial punishment of engulfment, that consciousness was called into existence; and it is on the uncertain raft of language that human nature drifts across the ocean of birth and death. Language contains this is that/ this is not that, and incarnates the center. By doing this it orientates us: I am somewhere and someone; someone, moreover, who is aware of himself and aware of his awareness as the world. Not only are we oriented, but the world is recovered; it too becomes something that is somewhere. But when ambiguity is no longer contained, the center slips; then dread arises because the possibility of oneness devouring itself is brought to the fore.

Falling into hell is not falling to a place, nor is it a state of mind; it is falling through the bottomless fissure of knowing/being, a total loss of center. Anxiety, therefore, is not a mere mood akin to nervousness but a premonition, as anyone who awakens in the night in a cold sweat well knows. But Heidegger is right when he says that fear and anxiety are always about something definite. We are anxious, for example, about what will happen if we lose our job, or about how we will live if we lose our lover, or whether a pain is cancer, or whether we can earn enough to pay the rent. Anxiety always involves an element of "What will happen if?" That question, however, is a desperate attempt to verbalize the slipping away of the center, driven by a nonverbal premonition of what will happen if it does slip away, a premonition of the yawning divide. We are not then truly worried about these specific somethings. These specifics give us the last desperate means to maintain a hold on the center and contain the yawning divide, which is why we return to worries again and again, even though we know "it is no use worrying." It is not unusual to find a person holding onto his neurosis or to a pain, because striving to get rid of the neurosis, hoping to be cured of the pain, *gives a point* to his life. Without this point, without this center, he would start the slide toward dread and horror.

As Bateson pointed out, anger and rage are also ways by which the hell of horror is forestalled. Whereas fear and anxiety are passive escape reactions, rage and anger are active. In anger one holds on. Both anger and fear create tension in the body. It is as though a giant were to seize his right hand by his left and push down with one hand while pushing up with the other, with ever increasing force, trying to make each hand yield to the other. Just as the body can become rigid with fear and panic, so it can become locked in anger. It becomes tense, and just as most people have a residual negative emotion, residual anxiety or anger, so the body has a residual tension, a tension not susceptible to the usual ways we seek relaxation. This tension is the physical, or being, counterpart to emotion and it can be readily observed that tension can be translated into emotion and emotion translated into tension. With people who meditate it is not unusual, when their practice begins to deepen, for them to feel restless and sometimes anxious, or, even extremely angry. As meditation deepens, tension is released and transformed into negative emotions. Within all tension, both physical and emotional, focussed awareness reflects back on to itself in a kind of push and pull, or simultaneously holding on and letting go.

Positive as well as negative emotions are dependent upon the primary schism; but in a positive emotion, the power of the center is reinforced not threatened. Enthusiasm, pride, excitement, feelings of success and achievement, the feeling of getting somewhere, all these arise through the promise that, in one form or another, the power of the center will be increased. These are the feelings on which we draw when we talk in a general way about happiness.

For the sake of completeness, I should also mention a third class of feelings that, strictly speaking, are neither positive nor negative: contentment and boredom. These emotions arise when the center is neither threatened nor augmented. However, we are primarily concerned at the moment with painful emotions, particularly those leading to violence.

The Control of Violence

For a society to develop, it must find a way to control violence. All emotions are contagious, and violent emotions, if left unchecked, can infect an entire society (as, for example, in Ireland and the former Yugoslavia). The mechanism of contagion in a group is the same one that governs the generation of emotion in an individual. The same feedback mechanism and the same loss of center occur. When you are anxious, I am aware-as you, and so I am aware-of "your" anxiety as my own. Panic sweeping through a crowd, an attack of giggles passing through a group, and the spread of suspicion in a community are extreme examples of ways by which emotions spread. In *Violence and the Sacred*, Girard wrote, "the mechanism of reciprocal violence can be described as a vicious circle. Once a community enters the circle, it is unable to extricate itself."[6] Later, he added, "The purpose of the sacrifice is to restore harmony to the community," and he quoted a Chinese sage, saying, "It is through the sacrifices that the unity of the people is strengthened."[7] This may well seem like fighting fire with fire, but I suggest this is not so.

Today harmony and unity are maintained by peacekeeping and law enforcement agencies, which, according to Girard, are systems by which revenge is institutionalized:

Instead of following the example of religion and attempting to forestall acts of revenge, to mitigate or sabotage their effects or to redirect them to secondary objects, our judicial system rationalizes revenge and succeeds in limiting and isolating its effects in accordance with social demands.[8]

But even so, Girard says, the judicial system and the institution of sacrifice share the same function.

If it is true that sacrifice mitigates violence—an outcome of the double bind of ambiguity inherent in our nature—then we would expect sacrifice to be based upon the same fundamental ambiguity. And just as the word gives form to and contains the basic ambiguity, so does sacrifice. So both, in this way, defuse potential violence. In the face of the impossible this is that/this is not that (or you must have both/you can only have one) sacrifice and the word say, in effect, this *is* that/this *is not* that; they are two/they are also one. Therefore, you have both because you have one. Let's see specifically how this is accomplished.

The Ambiguity of Sacrifice

According to Girard, "In many rituals the sacrificial act assumes two opposing aspects, appearing at times as a sacred obligation to be neglected at grave peril, at other times as a sort of criminal activity."[9] Quoting two other writers, Henri Hubert Hauberk and Marcel Mauss, he adds, "Because the victim is sacred it is criminal to kill him, but the victim is sacred only because he is to be killed."[10] However, Girard dismisses what he calls the *sonorous ambivalence*, a term given to this circular line of reasoning by way of explanation. He says, although this term is persuasive and authoritative, nevertheless it has been extraordinarily overworked and sheds very little light on the subject of sacrifice. Girard is talking from the standpoint of traditional logic in which A=A and cannot equal not-A. If one adheres to this logic of non-contradiction then one will never be able to fully understand sacrifice. From this standpoint ambivalence would at best be only acceptable as a special case; otherwise it would simply be an admission of failure in thinking. But the logic of ambiguity allows us to understand sacrifice because, according to this logic, ambivalence is the rule and not the exception.

"Sacrificial substitution," Girard says, "implies a degree of misunderstanding. Its vitality as an institution depends on its ability to conceal the displacement upon which the rite is based. It must never lose sight entirely, however, of the original object, or cease to be aware of the act of transference from that object to the surrogate victim."[11] This is the mechanism of the metaphor. When, for example, Wilfred Owen writes about, "the monstrous anger of the guns," we must not understand him to mean that the *guns are angry*, although at the same time we must realize the guns *are* angry. One could use Girard's expression and say, "believing the guns are angry" implies "a degree of misunderstanding" necessary for a metaphor to work. In drama this "degree of misunderstanding" is called the suspension of disbelief. This suspension of disbelief is possible only if we can say "this is that" knowing all the while that "this is not that." Furthermore, it is also true to say, with Girard, that the vitality of a play or a metaphor, as well as of the ritual of sacrifice, "depends on its ability to conceal the displacement upon which it is based." In other words, the vitality is dependent on our ability to say this is that, the guns are angry, but bearing in mind all the while Girard's admonition that we must not "cease to be aware of the act of transference from that object to the surrogate victim." That is, we must not cease to be aware the guns are not angry.

Girard quotes from the play *Ion* by Euripedes, and the quotation is so apt to what I am saying I will repeat it here.[12] Girard starts off by way of introduction saying,

> The-two-in-one nature of blood—that is, of violence—is strikingly illustrated in Euripedes' *Ion*. The Athenian queen, Creusa, plots to do away with the hero by means of an exotic talisman: two drops of blood from the deadly Gorgon. *One drop is a deadly poison, the other a miraculous healing agent* [author's italics]. The queen's old slave asks her the origin of this substance:
>
> **Creusa:** When the fatal blow was struck a drop spurted from the hollow vein. . . .
> **Slave:** How is it used? What are its properties?
> **Creusa:** It wards off all sickness and nourishes life.
> **Slave:** And the other drop?
> **Creusa:** It kills. It is made from the Gorgon's venomous serpents.
> **Slave:** Do you carry them mixed together or separate?
> **Creusa:** Are good and evil mixed together? Separate of course.

Girard, commenting, says, "Nothing could seem more alike than two drops of blood, yet in this case nothing could be more different." This is that/this is not that. We can say blood is a metaphor for blood, which means (sacred) violence is a metaphor for (criminal) violence. In this lies the origin of catharsis.

The Symmetry of Violence

To understand this further, let's follow Girard in his comments about sacrifice, particularly the passages in which he talks about the symmetry of the *tragic dialogue,* the dialogue of reciprocal violence, which may be verbal or physical. He uses Euripedes' play *Phoenician Women* as an example of the structural similarity between two manifestations of violence. In *Phoenician Women,* a duel is fought between two brothers, Eteocles and Polyneices. Girard says of them, "There is nothing in this account that does not apply equally to both brothers: their parries, their thrusts and feints, their postures and gestures are identical. 'If either saw the other's eyes appear over the rim of his shield, He raised his spear.'"[13] This symmetry continues throughout the battle and even into death itself. Quoting now from the *Phoenician Women,* "They hit the dust and lay together side by side; and their heritage was still unclaimed." Even their deaths do not end the matter, for their armies turn take up the struggle.[14] The tragic dialogue, says Girard, is a debate without resolution.

This debate without resolution is precisely the instigator of horror and dread we saw earlier in the double bind. Because the two sides are evenly matched, the two injunctions have equal force; therefore, ultimate disaster threatens. "Tragedy," says Girard, "is the balancing of the scale, not of justice but of violence." According to Girard, violence effaces the differences between the antagonists: "The more a tragic conflict is prolonged, the more likely it is to culminate in a violent mimesis; the resemblance between the combatants grows ever stronger until each presents a mirror image of the other."[15]

So why does Euripedes, by way of tragic dialogue, present the spectators with the dynamics of ultimate violence, the swallowing of the self by the self? The same question might be asked about the violence and horror that one sees on television and at the films. The same answer could be given in both cases. It is for purgation, purification, *catharsis.* However, the line between fact and fiction, particularly on TV, is so blurred that one cannot suspend disbelief because of the realism. In this case instead of acting as a catharsis is could act as a stimulant to violence. The word *catharsis* refers to "the mysterious benefits that accrue to the community upon the death of a human *katharma* or *pharmakos.* The process is generally seen as a religious purification and takes the form of cleansing or draining away impurities."[16] The spectators see ultimate violence, but they *also* see a play. The very stylization of the play, the dramatic verse, the stage, the actors, all this is a constant reminder *this is not that*. The play is therefore a metaphor for sacrifice. The Passion play is a metaphor for the Passion, and the Mass is its ultimate refinement (a refinement which, incidentally, is destroyed, along with the vitality of the Mass, when one asks such questions as "Is the host *really* the body of Christ?" or "Is this really that?").

Girard observes, "Men cannot confront the naked truth of their own violence without the risk of abandoning themselves to it entirely."[17] In the sacrificial act men *did* confront the naked truth of their own violence, 'this is that,' but at the same time, did not confront it (this is not that). In allowing this to be done, the sacrificial act *contained* the violence. We must emphasize that this containment is the same containment as the containment of conflict by the word, because in both cases it is the primordial ambiguity, the source of the creative power of the universe that is contained. By this containment those attending the ritual of sacrifice evoked the nouminous presence and power of the containing one, which they looked upon justifiably, as evoking the presence of God; not God as a symbol, idea, or belief, but God as the One living power of the world.

Death of the King

In ancient times a major force in the control of violence resided in the charisma of the leader whom I have called the god/man. The god/man incarnated and at the same time contained the One power. Yet evidence suggests that originally it was the leader who was sacrificed; only later were sacrificial substitutes made in the form of captives and slaves. Even then the surrogate victims were often dressed as and coached to mimic the god or god/man. In the Aztec religion, Broda, Carrasco, and Moctezuma tell us,

> [A] festival called Toxcatl was dedicated to the ferocious God Tezcatlipoca. Elaborate efforts were made to find the perfect deity impersonator for this festival. The captive warrior had to have a flawless body, musical talents, and rhetorical skills. For a year prior to his sacrifice he lived a privileged existence in the capital. We are told that just before the end of the sacrificial festival he arrived at a small temple called Tlacochalo . . . he ascended by himself, he went up of his own free will, to where

he was to die. As he was taken up a step, as he passed one step, there he broke . . . his flute, his whistle and was then swiftly sacrificed.[18]

How are we to understand this most violent of all violent behavior? Above all, how do we understand the violent destruction of the leader?

Let us put to one side any negative judgments we may have. To judge this violence as evil puts it outside our comprehension. To dismiss it as the raving activities of madmen silences any inquiry. A logic underlies all activity, even psychotic activity. The same logic underlies creativity and violence, love and hatred, spirituality and war. The agony of the captive warrior atoned [at-oned] the agony of those participating in the sacrificial rite, in the same way that the agony of the One in the garden of Gethsemane atones for the sins of the Christian and makes the Christian whole. God sacrificed Himself as Christ on the cross of contradiction, and in so doing atoned for the sins of humanity, sins that have their roots in the loss of fundamental unity in an act of disobedience and separation in the primordial garden of One called Eden.[19] One sacrifices the One to attain the One.

Restoring the Power of the Center

Let's return to the question, "Why was the leader sacrificed?" The Aztecs' sacrifice not only reconciled the implacable this is that/this is not that, but had the equally important task of restoring power to the center. These two functions of the sacrifice are not separate but complements of each other. The Aztecs had a fascination with (one might be tempted to say, an obsession with) the center. The heart of the sacrificial victim is itself a center. The fifth sun—the sun to which the offering of the warrior's beating heart was made, the sun that was the incarnation of Oneness for the Aztecs—is also the center, the central sun in the Aztec calendar. In a magnificent stele of this calendar, the fifth sun is carved at the center of a huge circle. Four other suns, each representing one of the four cardinal points of the compass, occupy an inner zone of the same circle; but central to them is the fifth sun, and the whole therefore has the form of a mandala. The center of power, the human heart, is offered as a metaphor of the heart of the god, the sacrificial victim being a metaphor for the god. The conflict inherent in the center—this is that/this is not that—is neutralized and stability is restored.

But establishing and maintaining the center required immense labor and the investment of great wealth. As Joanna Broda, David Carrasco, and Eduardo Matos Moctezuma point out, human sacrifice was carried out "within a larger, more complex ceremonial system in which a tremendous amount of energy, wealth, and time was spent in a variety of ritual festivals dedicated to a crowded and hungry pantheon."[20] There was a preparatory period, which he describes as follows:

> They began with fasts and nocturnal vigil offerings of flowers, food, rubber, paper, poles with streamers, as well as incenses; the pouring of libations; and the empowering of temples, statues and ritual, participants, moving to music ensembles playing sacred songs, passed through the ceremonial precinct before arriving at the specific temple of sacrifice.[21]

The major ritual participants to be sacrificed were called *in ixiptla in teteo* (deity impersonators). The authors further tell us:

> The human victims were ritually bathed, carefully costumed, taught to dance special dances, and either fattened or slimmed down during the preparation period. They were elaborately dressed to impersonate specific deities to whom they were sacrificed. . . . Usually the ceremony peaked when splendidly attired captors and captives sang and danced in procession to the temple, where they were escorted (sometimes unwillingly) up the stairways to the sacrificial stone.[22]

Apart from the expenditure of great wealth and time in elaborate ceremonies and sacrifices addressed to maintaining the power of the center, this obsession with the center is also illustrated by the layout of the Aztec cities and temples. They believed their world was a land surrounded by water. At the center, or what they called the *tlalxico* (which we could translate as the navel) of this world stood their capital city *Tenochtitlan*. At the center of the city was the temple and at the center of the temple was the sacrificial altar and the fifth sun. Through this center flowed the horizontal as well as the vertical cosmos.

That these sacrifices, rituals, and ceremonies were addressed to restoring the power of the center is borne out by Broda, Carrasco, and Matos Moctezuma, who tell us:

The Aztecs seek a vital sense of power at their Great temple. They act against the growing disequilibrium in their world through aggressive ritual activity at their sacred center. They attempted to revitalize themselves at a time of deep crisis by climbing their temple with captive warriors and, after ceremonial dancing and singing, killing them on an 'altar.' Aztec history and myth tell us that the practice of temple and mountain ascent to revitalize the world through ritual killing was a time-honored tradition.[23]

Thus the center was a source of power and the sacrificial rites were a means of revitalizing that power, a power that, through its loss, brought about a deep crisis and suffering.

The God/Man as Center

But what happens when we lose the power to reach the center? Or, to ask the same question in the way the Aztecs might have asked it: "What happens if the Center loses its power?"

The god/man spoke the first word, the word that was with God, the Word that *was* God. In other words, originally the word was not separate from the One who speaks. As the Monad, the Word is the One as well as the center, or better still the Word is the One and the *One as center*. That One who spoke or sang the original word was the center of all and as such would have incarnated enormous power, radiance, and charisma. Others encountering him or her would be naturally enthused and raised to a higher level of hope and joy. In such an encounter they would be able to release their own burden of unresolved conflict and anxiety or rage. Leaders throughout time have been accredited with healing power, the most striking example of which were the miracle cures of Christ. In the Middle Ages kings were expected to lay their hands on the heads of their subjects and cure them of a variety of ills. Even today leaders have been reputed to have this capability. People were known to have had "spiritual" experiences and spontaneous healing in the presence of Hitler. During the fall of the Romanov dynasty, a monk, Rasputin, dominated the ruling class of Russia, principally through his reputed power to be able to bring relief to the sufferings to the young Romanov. Today's televangelists claim cures and so command immense wealth, donated by the faithful who see in them the power of God. Leaders of some modern cults inspire profound loyalty and great energy and enthusiasm in their followers.[24] But this power—dissipated as it is through the veil of culture and the hard crust of dead words—is but a pale shadow of that former glory. The power of charisma diminishes in proportion to the rise of the rational net of logic and technology. The original god/man was a sun; his descendants are but candles.

But charisma, like the dust on the wings of a butterfly, has a tendency to wear off. Ramana Maharshi, the great Indian sage, said that one should not stay with one's teacher for more than three months, after that one begins to notice his warts. One falls in love and one falls out just as easily. Charisma blooms as power, but is nourished by yearning,[25] the yearning of the followers of the great makes the potential of the great shine forth. How many idols have discovered their own feet of clay in the darkness after the light of adoration has faded? Another great teacher, Nisargadatta, said teachers are made by their followers, something of which politicians and rock idols, no less than prophets and messiahs, are only too keenly aware. The confusion between spirituality and charisma, mistaking the one for the other, is the same mistake as confusing the One with the incarnation of the One: they are not the same although they are not separate.

God/men are first of all men and only then the mouthpieces of God. It's hard to understand how people could be taken in by some of the Rasputin rogues who have stalked humankind, until we realize that the power of the center and giving voice to the center are not separate, but are not the same. The power of the center is not illicit, nor can it fade; but the power of the humans to incarnate that center can fade with old age, injury, or illness. This power can also founder in the sea of conflicting forces too powerful for it to reconcile. Early human beings were exposed to dark forces beyond our ken. The world was still twilight, made more mysterious, dark, and magical by the approaching dawn. Even the effulgence of the god/man would not have been bright enough to dispel the gloom. Storms, plagues, eclipses, eruptions, and strange psychic fevers would have aroused fogs of doubt, despair, fear, and dread.

And so the ailing or failing god/man would be killed, in order that, resurrected, he could regain his power as the center. "The king is dead! Long live the king!"

"Every God, hero, Mythic creature ...embodies the interplay of violence projected by generative unanimity,"[26] writes Girard. To these early people, only acts of unanimity, acts of One mind were possible. When disasters struck, the Gods were angry; when the sun shone and peace reigned, the Gods were pleased. If the Godman could raise hopes, enthuse, radiate energy, He could also bring down the wrath of the heavens. The Godman was this "contradictory, ambiguous interplay of violence projected by acts of generative unanimity." "Dionysius," says Girard, "is at one and the same time the most terrible and the most gentle of the gods. Zeus hurls thunderbolts but is as sweet as honey." Christ calls on all to love, but He brings not peace but a sword. "Come unto me all ye who are heavy laden ," He said. But He also said, "Whoever is near me is near the fire!"[27]

This same contradiction is to be found in the sacred king. He, too, is a monster. "He is simultaneously god, man, and savage beast." He is the embodiment of the double bind. "I have used the phrase," says Girard, "'violence *and* the sacred; I might as well have said 'violence *or* the sacred'. For the operations of the violent and the sacred are ultimately the same process."[28] "I hit you because I love you." Basic to an understanding of the center is the classic double bind; the center separates, and it binds and this is so because underlying the center is the center/periphery ambiguity. Even in the word *sacred* lies the ambiguity whose etymology is in the Latin *sacer,* meaning both cursed and holy; and the word *heiros* (derived from the Vedic *isirah*) which means vital force, but also buried in it is the word *ire* with all its baleful meanings.[29] Death is the most violent of acts, above all when the means are violent. Hence the Christian crucifixion or tearing out the heart by the Aztecs. "To sacrifice is to make sacred, but the sacrifice of early man was to kill and kill in the most painful way, to kill in such a way that the victim knew his own death even while his heart is torn out and held high." This is the only way regeneration, resurrection, is possible.

Anthropologist Frances Huxley explains it this way:

> It is the fate of the prisoner to act out a number of contradictory roles and incarnate them in himself. He is an enemy who is adopted; he takes the place of the man in whose honor he will be killed; he is an in-law and an outcast; he is honored and reviled, a scapegoat and a hero; he is intimidated but if he shows fear, is thought unworthy of the death that awaits him. By acting out these primarily social roles he becomes a

complete human being, exemplifying the contradictions that society creates; an impossible situation, which can only end in his death. The impossibility is exaggerated when he is charged, by ritual, with the powers and attributes of the culture hero: he becomes the representative of the other world living in the center of this one, a Janus figure too sacred to live with.[30]

For Huxley, the double bind, this impossible situation, comes from "contradictions that society creates." We suggest its genesis is much more primordial. Furthermore, it has to be added that the very impossibility of the situation makes the ensuing violence sacred. The pain *in extremis* of the victim is the expression of this impossibility.

Girard claims that early human beings were trying to reproduce an original event that actually took place—to recover the unanimity that occurred and recurred around the surrogate victim. Let me now suggest that the original event is the birth of consciousness, by the containment of the original ambiguity through the word. Rebirth, or regeneration (which means reenactment of the original event) is necessary because the forces of conflict increase and the center can no longer hold. Anxiety, dread, panic, rage, and violence threaten. So violence must be acted out; in this way, the ambiguity of this is that/this is not that is reconciled, and with this reconciliation the center is restored and peace reigns once more. Thus the birth of consciousness is the primordial religious act, and the maintenance of consciousness the primary religious concern.

Notes

1. T.S. Eliot, *The Four Quartets* (New York: Harverst Books, 1974).
2. Gregory Bateson, *Ecology of Mind* (New York: Ballantine Books, 1972), p. 206.
3. Martin Heidegger, *Existence and Being* (Chicago: Henry Regnery, 1949), p. 305.
4. Heidegger (1949, p. 336).
5. The Nothing to which I am referring should be called negation because it is not the same, descriptively, as the Nothing of Heidegger, although we may well be using different words to describe something that is common to both of us. Heidegger's Nothing is the source of being and therefore would be closer to what I have been calling Oneness. We encountered a harmonic of this negation when we talked about the generation of the null point in Chapter 16.
6. René Girard, *Violence and the Sacred*, (Baltimore: Johns Hopkins University Press, 1977), p. 81.

7. Classic literature of China CH'U YU ll. 2 8, cited in Girard (1977).

8. Girard (1977, p. 23).

9. Girard (1977, p. 1).

10. Girard (1977, p. 1).

11. Girard (1977, p. 5).

12. Girard (1977, p. 38).

13. Girard (1977, p. 44).

14. Girard (1977, p. 45).

15. Girard (1977, p. 47).

16. Girard (1977, p. 287).

17. Girard (1977, p. 82).

18. Joanna Broda, David Carrasco, and Eduardo Matos Moctezuma, *Myth, Cosmic Terror, and the Templo Mayor: From the Great Temple of Tenochtitlan* (Berkeley: University of California Press, 1987), p. 153.

19. See, Albert Low, *The Butterfly's Dream: In Search of the Roots of Zen* (Boston: Charles E. Tuttle Publishing, 1993).

20. Broda et al. (1987).

21. Broda et al. (1987, p. 152).

22. Broda et al. (1987, p. 151).

23. Broda et al. (1987, p. 152).18. Carrasco and Moctezuma p 153 1987

24. The etymology of the word *enthusiasm* is *entheos*: *en* meaning "in or within"; *theos* meaning "God."

25. The etymology of the word *charisma* is from the Greek *charien,* which also means "to yearn."

26. The etymology of *unanimity* is *unus* "one" and *animus* "mind."

28. Girard (1977, p. 258).

29. Girard says the following about the etymology of the Greek word *thysias.* "[It] signifies priestess of Bacchus or one of the Bacchantes. The word is derived from *thyiein,* or . . . *thymos.*" Then he quotes from Henri Jeanmaire:

    The probable etymology of the word suggests that it is connected with a verb whose sense remains somewhat ambiguous; it signifies to make a sacrifice, on the one hand, and on the other to hurl oneself impetuously or to whirl around like something caught up in a tempest, or to swirl about like the waters of a river or sea, or bubble up like spilled blood, like anger, like mad rage.

    Girard continues, "Jeanmaire goes on to say that these two apparently vastly different usages of sacrifice and violent energy need not be separated."

    Some modern observers have remarked that the death throes of the sacrificial victim and the convulsive gestures of the possessed person are both seen as manifestation s of divine intervention and that the analogy between them is appreciated and explicitly expressed (in Girard, 1977, p. 265).

30. Quoted by Girard (1977, p. 27).

Chapter 20

The Temple and the Word

Man, temple and cosmos were ... identical.[1]
JOHN MICHELL

I HAVE DWELT AT LENGTH on the torment that must have preceded the creation of the first word, a torment that came from a center that was simultaneously the observer and the observed. To give a sense of the kind of pain this must have caused, I quoted a man who told of his manic experience, which is accompanied by a loss of the *I*—that articulation which bridges the gap at the center. He said that in the manic state you lose all sense of yourself as a person among other persons. "You feel yourself dissipating; your distinctiveness vanishes," any sense of the I, he says, is blotted out. Martin Heidegger pointed out that when we are caught in the uncanniness of dread caused by the encounter with nothing, the loss of I, we often try to break the empty silence by words spoken at random.[2]

The first human beings, still without language, must have been prey to frequent and devastating attacks of this kind and, because the stress involved in containing the ambiguity would have been so great, one of the most important concerns for them would have been to find ways by which this containment could be enhanced. This would have continued to be necessary even after the creation of the word, because, like all created things, the word would have been subject to decay, and so new words would have had to be continually created. A rabbi summed up the effort that was necessary saying, "The universe is always in an uncompleted state, in the form of its beginning . . . it requires continuous labor and unceasing renewal by creative forces. Were there a second's pause by these forces the world would return to primeval chaos."[3] Additional ways and means had to be developed to shore up the word and so help contain the forces involved. These ways and means developed into what we know as culture and civilization.

The Role of Religion

As noted at the end of the last chapter, these ways and means originally came from what we call religion; indeed, in the beginning the religious and the secular were one whole. When we think of religion, we tend to regard it is an homogenous activity that is clear in its intent and methods. We think religion has simply to do with the relation of God and the human being, with a set of beliefs surrounding that relation. There are not many people who would be willing to consider, as Eric Hoffer suggested, that nazism, fascism, and communism are religions. Similarly, the tribal rituals of the American Indian, Australian aborignes, and Africans have, until recently, been viewed as primitive practices of inferior races. But in the course of this investigation, I have demonstrated that human beings are subject to forces that are neither in the realm of knowing nor being, matter nor mind, but instead come out of, so to speak, an *intermediate* zone between the two. Dynamic energy and the power of the center are forces of this kind, and so is the tension in the relationship of you-me. These forces are neither from knowing nor being, but all have their source in the intermediate zone. This means that they have their origin upstream of consciousness and experience, and a major concern has thereby been to find ways by which these forces can be made accessible to knowing and so contained, controlled, placated, or obeyed. These ways are essentially *religious* ways.

A major religious concern is the articulation of the center, its maintenance and, where necessary, its restoration. Another related task of religion has been to find ways by which the power of the center, and the energy of the basic ambiguity from which the center emerges, can be grounded, so that this energy is put to the use by the tribe. These included the use of taboos, ceremonies, and rituals devoted to the center, with which much of the lives of our forebears were occupied with. Another major concern of religion was to find ways by which the I-Thou relation could be relieved of its mental and physical trappings, as well as the stress these involve, and so be known in its purity.

These two concerns—the practical and the devotional—were supplemented at times by a third concern, the *spiritual*, through which the ambiguity, instead of being contained, was transcended. In this and the next two chapters, I will review briefly these three ways, using as examples the temple as the religious and magical, Sufism as the devotional, and Zen Buddhism as the transcendental. In reviewing these three ways I will show how each, in its own way, came out of the basic ambiguity. Let it be said that one rarely encounters any of these ways in its purity and the more "primitive" the religion the more likely it is that all three will be found inextricably woven together. Furthermore this study is intended to be suggestive only and by no means exhaustive. After reviewing the religious ways, I will explore music, that strange phenomenon that has accompanied human beings in all their endeavors, and for which no real understanding of its place has been found. By studying music I will have the opportunity to make a review of all that we have said in this book.

In this chapter let's concentrate upon the role of the temple and see it as the means *par excellence* for articulating and grounding the center, and for containing the forces generated by the basic ambiguity.

The Temple as Repository of Vital Force

I have suggested that, most likely, the first word was uttered not as speech but as song. It is also likely that the song was accompanied by dancing. Dancing, as well as uttering the creative word, has often been associated with the primordial creative act. In her book on the sacred dance, Maria-Gabrielle Wosien said,

> Shiva Nataja, Lord of the Dance, sends pulsating waves of awakening sound through matter, thereby seducing it to life from lethargy.[4]

> With the creation of the universe the dance too came into being, which signifies the union of the elements.[5]

The continuous coming face-to-face with the divine center was celebrated in the ritual encircling of sacred sites objects or persons, as well
as in round dances around a holy center. To circumscribe the center was
to be in constant relationship with the source of being.[6]

In other words, dancing was a way by which sacred space was created and later this space would have been enhanced in such a way that
shrines, sanctuaries, and temples would have developed.

For the postmodern person, whose interest in religion is likely to be
intellectual at best, and who uses religion as but an adjunct to birth, death,
and marriage, the central importance of the temple in earlier societies is
but another example of their extravagant superstition. The belief that
temples were the center of the world, and that they contained the
conflicting cosmic forces from which the vital powers necessary to sustain life are generated, are viewed today as oddities that only pre-scientific,
unenlightened, human beings could entertain. Such primitive ideas, it is
believed can now be shown to have been but idle superstition.

Sir James Frazer, for example, was of the opinion that magic arose out
of two different misapplications of the association of ideas.[7] "Magic," he
says, "is a spurious system of natural law as well as a fallacious guide to
conduct; it is a false science and an abortive art."[8] Later he opines that
"It is a truism, almost a tautology, to say that all magic is necessarily false
and barren; for were it ever to become true and fruitful, it would no
longer be magic but science."[9]

This is somewhat like saying that if poetry were to become true and
fruitful it would become prose. Magic is a vast subject and cannot be
dismissed so lightly, even though, just as there are many spurious scientists, so there would have been many spurious magicians. It is obvious,
however that one aspect of magic had to do with acting out metaphors.
The "false association" Frazer speaks of is the same false association that
Wilfred Owen makes when he says that the guns are angry. Through
magical ritual the magician was able to bring into play the force of unity
that lies upstream of "This is that; this is not that." The same force of unity
that is invoked by the poet.

The belief that the temple was the source of vital power has some
minor reverberations in our society. Underlying the structure of the temple
was the "Temple Idea" or *imago templi*, and this has carried some of its
fascination into the modern era through the rituals of the Freemasons. The

imago templi emerges in what a Sufi master called *"the meeting place of the two seas"*[10]—the name given to the intermediary realm "where," as Henry Corbin says, "everything that appeared inanimate in the world of sense perceptions comes alive."[11] It is from within this intermediate zone that the drive emerges that we know as religion. Corbin says that "Each manifestation of the Imago constitutes a unity in itself, without requiring a transfer of power. It is itself its own time."[12] In other words, each temple is a whole, a monad, and the history of the temple is not part of secular, successive history. Corbin goes on to say, "These unities of discontinuous time are the times of the Imago templi: they erupt into our own time and confer the dimension of eternity upon the scissions they produce."[13] This is true of all creativity and each monad or organism is an eruption and each is out of time. Put differently, each is its own time. This eruption that confers the dimension of eternity also gives the suddenness, the explosive quality, that we referred to when we discussing creativity in Chapter 14.

It could be said that all sacred constructions represent the universe in symbolic form. Wosen pointed out that the closing of the sacred precincts with gates was essential if the rite was to be effective, safe guarding and concentrating the influence issuing from the sacred object, animal or person within the confined area. Sacred paths led to this object along which the pilgrimages were, and still are, made for renewed contact with the power. Circumambulation of sacred mountains, trees, temples, and shrines is one of the oldest of religious activities and has been practiced universally since megalithic times. It is the age-old method by which the center is affirmed.

Wosien noted that the sanctuary's holy of holies is often wholly or partly below ground and therefore not visible or directly accessible to the worshiper. The faithful walk or dance round the sanctuary and in this way become connected with the center. If the sanctuary were built on high ground, or if itself were a holy mountain, he would likely ascend it.[14]

Out of the "meeting place of the two seas" of knowing being, I have said the null point, the origin and cause of all creativity, arises.[15] The articulation of this point is a pre-occupation of life. Roger Cook describes this process:

> The Center is first and foremost the point of absolute beginning where the latent energies of the sacred first broke through, where the super-

natural beings of myth, of the gods or God of religion, first created man and the world. Ultimately all creation takes place at this point, which represents the ultimate source of reality. In the symbolic language of myth and religion it is often referred to as the "navel of the earth," "Divine egg," "hidden seed" or "root of roots."[16]

This center finds form in the cosmic tree, the sacred mountain, the megalith, and eventually the idol. The totem pole, the maypole, the stupas of Buddhism, the cross at the crossroads throughout Europe, and the altars of the church, all articulate the sacred center.

The power of the Temple comes, in part, from its articulation of the center, sometimes referred to as the *Omphalus*, world navel. At the center of the Temple of Jerusalem was a huge native rock which Jewish legends looked upon as an Omphalo. Called in Hebrew *Ebhen Shetiyyah,* the Stone of Foundation, this rock was the first of God's creations and placed by Him amidst the as yet boundless fluid of the primeval waters. According to legend "just as the body of an embryo is built up in its mother's womb from its navel, so God built up the earth concentrically around this stone, the Navel of the Earth. And just as the body of the embryo receives its nourishment from the navel, so the whole earth too receives the waters that nourish it from this navel."[17] This nourishment is the power that is generated by the power of the center.

John Michell, who did considerable research into the symbolism of the Temple, also said that the temple is at the center. Mitchell went on to say "within it is the King's chamber, and the King on his throne at the heart of all. Not only did he symbolize the sun, he actually was the sun of the social order as the proton is of the atom. From him emanated the solar radiance by which the kingdom was made prosperous and fertile." Thus the temple was his instrument, but this instrument "not only acted as a transmitter of his power, but as an accumulator of the cosmic forces by which he was charged."[18] In other words, the temple was both center and periphery at the same time: as center it emanated power, as periphery it received and accumulated power.

Powerful supporting evidence for the view that the temple was simultaneously the accumulator and transmitter of power, center and periphery, comes from the fact that *eyes* became a prominent feature of most statuary in temples during what Julian Jaynes calls the *Bicameral* era (circa

3000 BCE). Bicameral means "having two legislative chambers," which Jaynes theorizes are the two halves of the brain, but which with equal justification could be thought of as the two irreconcilable, but complementary, centers: me-as center and me-as-periphery.

I have written at length in other books about the importance of understanding the "look" if we are to understand the basic ambiguity.§ To look into the eyes of another is to see and be seen simultaneously. This can trigger the basic schism generating intense love or it can throw one into the vortex of hell. Jaynes points out that eyes became a prominent feature of most temple statuary throughout the bicameral period, and he established what he called the "eye index" of an idol using the diameter of the human eye, which is about 10% of the height of the head, as a basis.[19] He said one famous group of statues has "eye indices of as high as 18% — huge globular eyes hypnotically staring out of the unrecorded past of 5000 years ago with defiant authority." Even to see these eyes reproduced in print stirs some deep and primeval awe. (Figure 26)

Fig. 27

The eyes of the god of the temple, who was already at the center of the "meeting place of the two seas," would generate enormous power which would then have to be grounded by the center. The more powerful the grounding, the greater the forces contained, and the more nouminous and life giving would be the temple.

§   See Albert Low, *The Iron Cow of Zen* (1991, pp. 81-95 and *The Butterfly's Dream* (1993, pp. 123-127).

Astronomy and the World Center

Prehistoric people carefully observed the heavens, and archaeologists believe the large stone monuments built across Northern Europe about 3,500 years ago, of which Stonehenge was one, served as giant compasses, calendars, and computers of seasonal patterns. They were also sacred precincts for religious rituals. Some, for example the Great Pyramids, were also reliquaries of relics, being the burial places of the pharaohs. Astronomer Richard Proctor estimated the sun's height at the equinoxes, as well as certain key stars and constellations, could be sited and aligned very accurately through the huge, graduated slots built into the very body of the Great Pyramid. Proctor believes the truncated top surface of the pyramid before its completion could have been used as an astronomical and astrological observation platform high over the Gizeh plateau, with a view commanding the entire compass.

Today's stronomers see kindred spirits in the ancient builders, and, because of the accuracy of measurement with which so many of these constructions were built, modern astronomers naturally believe that ancient people had aspirations and aims similar to their own. However, if consciousness has evolved, the idea of a people, still struggling with the elementary aspects of stabilizing consciousness, which must have been a very slow process for centuries, having also been able to afford the luxury of contemplating the heavens in a detached and objective way, seems very improbable. It has been estimated it would have cost the society that built Stonehenge, relatively speaking, the same amount that it cost the United States to get to the moon. It would make much more sense if we turn it all around and say these sites were not used to survey the heavens in a detached scientific way, but, on the contrary, to have the heavens confirm and support human beings, and above all human consciousness. This was done by having the constellations confirm, and so "ground," the center, and in this way bring the vast power of the heavens into play to contain ambiguity, thereby participating in stabilizing consciousness.

Additional support for this view is that the Notre Dame cathedrals built in France were all designed according to an alignment with the constellation The Virgin.[20] The sun was employed as the means by which the proportions of a cathedral were determined. In his book, *The Mysteries Of Chartres Cathedral*, Louis Charpentier writes that the first step taken in the construction of a temple was to erect a pillar at the sacred center.[21]

It is around this center that the cathedral will be built. Charpentier goes on to say "the height of the basic pillar had capital importance in the sense that through the play of solar shadows it indicated the dimensions whose relationships were a projection of those obtaining between celestial bodies."[22] He says that the pillar gave the cathedral its position, not only on earth, but also in relation to the planet and fixed stars. If the temple were in fact the cosmic center, and the evidence is overwhelming that it was so, and if, as I have said, it be imperative for the One to reabsorb the center (another important theme of all religious ceremonies), then the temple would need be designed with this primarily in mind. Having the whole firmament confirm the centrality of the temple added immeasurably to its power to accomplish this.

The power of the temple is enhanced by the relics of saints and holy men who were themselves repositories of this same power of the center. This is why the temple became the tomb of the Godman—for the Buddhist stupas as well as Christian cathedrals and churches.

Squaring the Circle: Union of the Opposites

The temple was the center because it was also the place of union between cosmic and terrestrial forces, the place where the tension between knowing/being was contained. This union added to the power of the temple although these two—the power coming from containing of the tension and the power of the center—are but two aspects of one power. The circle squared, a basic problem in the construction of ancient temples, is a symbol of this union of two incommensurable elements and thus an image of both micro- and macrocosmos. Mind and matter each belong to a different order and cannot be described in the same terms, anymore than linear measurements can be expressed in terms of weight. The square symbolizes within the microcosmos the body; and within the macrocosmos it symbolizes solid matter. The circle symbolizes the soul in the microcosmos and spirit in the macrocosmos:

> In Plutarch's account of the founding of Rome the outline of the city is described as a circle drawn from a fixed center and also as a square with four corners. This plan of the circle squared is preserved in the architecture of Stonehenge, in St. John's description of the holy city and in other examples that remain of the cosmic temple, of which the most impressive is the Egyptian Great Pyramid."[23]

John Michell called the temple an *equilibrato* whose function was to express in harmony all the diverse and contradictory aspects of nature.[24] This means, in our terms, that it expressed *all* of the basic ambiguity, including the ambiguity of me-as-center/me-as-periphery, and not just the ambiguity of knowing/being. In so far as the ambiguity of me-as-center/me-as-periphery is so fundamental, it is natural that it was a key element in the construction of sacred sites. Because the temple is simultaneosuly a transmitter and receiver of cosmic forces, it is not surprising to find this ambiguity expressed not only in the eyes of the gods but even in the very ground plan of the site. Two very important schemata came into being on which such ground plans of temples were based: the first was called the *vesica pisces* (the vessel of the fish), and the second *the golden section,* usually either *the Golden rectangle,* or its companion *the Golden triangle,* often found in the form of the pentagon.

Vesica Pisces

Vesica pisces means the "vessel of the fish," and a glance below at Figure 27 shows why it is called a fish. The vesica is created by having two circles intersect so that the *center of one circle is at the periphery of the other,* and vice versa. This is just the same situation as can be found with the look. Two

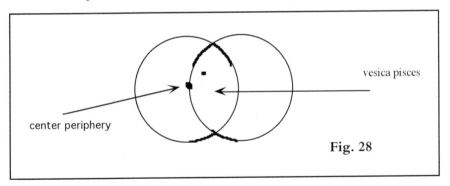

vesica pisces

center periphery

Fig. 28

centers therefore emerge, each of which is simultaneously at its own periphery and at the center and periphery of the other. Between these two centers, in a situation where only one center is possible, enormous tension is generated. It is in this field of force that a sacred space is created.

Some social commentators have pointed out that sport has become a religion of our age, and it is interesting to see that this same vesica pisces is at work in the space in which a game of football, soccer, or ice hockey is played. In Appendix 4 we have shown what we mean by saying a field of force is generated, using a soccer pitch as an illustration.[25]

Although vesica pisces is associated with the architects who constructed the medieval cathedrals and the creation of some of the paraphernalia associated with Christian ritual, it is not simply a Christian symbol. According to one authority, it makes its appearance at the beginning of a new era, when tension is at its greatest. The Greek name for the vesica is *the holy of holies* and it has been respected from the earliest times as a symbol of the sacred marriage.[26]

William Stirling says,

> This mysterious figure, Vesica Pisces, possessed an unbounded influence on the details of sacred architecture; and it constituted the great and enduring secret of our ancient brethren. The plans of religious buildings were determined by its use; and the proportions of length and height were dependent upon it alone."[27]

The vesica is said to be the "the womb from which are generated all the numbers and ratios of the Temple."[28] It was an attribute of the virgin and the feminine aspect of the Savior as symbolized by the wound. To the old builders it was "an archetype of ideal beauty," but it was also regarded by others "as a baneful object under the name of the Evil Eye, and the charm most generally used to avert the dread effects of its fascination was the Phallus."[29]

This ambivalence towards the vesica pisces is the same ambivalence generated by me-as-center/me-as-periphery, from which comes both joy and anxiety, both creativity and violence. The Evil Eye creates intense anxiety and horror and at its worst causes a collapse into panic and terror. The look, a fixed unwavering stare, gives concrete form to me-as-center/me-as-periphery, bringing to the surface the schism, or wound, in being. This very same look, however, can be the expression of deep love as well. This is why both the vesica pisces and me-as-center/me-as-periphery would be seen both as the wound on the one hand, and, in view of its creative, generative capabilities, as the womb on the other.

The Golden Rectangle as a Container of Forces

The golden rectangle is well known. It has sides whose proportions are 1:1.618. By cutting off a square from the rectangle, a new rectangle is formed isomorphic with the first and therefore also having sides whose proportions are 1:.618. This in turn can be reduced by cutting off a square and a further rectangle, isomorphic with the others, is formed and so on. (Figure 28).

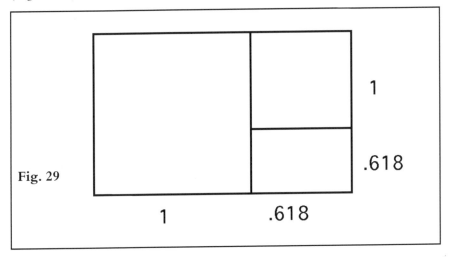

Fig. 29

The golden rectangle was used as ground plan in Greek as well as Indian architecture. Buddhist statues, Zen Buddhist gardens, Japanese shrines, and even the tatami mats found in Zen meditation halls. All have proportions based on the golden rectangle. Not only does human architecture conform to the golden rectangle, but nature also conforms to it: flowers, frogs, butterflies, trees and so much else in nature grow within the limits established by the golden rectangle. This is possible because the golden rectangle is able to contain the impossible contradiction of me-as center/me-as -periphery. To better understand what is meant by this let us refer to Gyorgy Doczi's book *The Power of Limits.*

Doczi makes a thorough study of the golden rectangle and its influence in life and art. He starts his book by pointing out that the florets of a daisy "grow at the meeting point of two sets of spirals, which move in opposite directions, one clockwise, the other counterclockwise."[29] These spirals, he says, unfold from the center of the daisy. Now this means that *at the very centre are two centers*, one evolving clockwise the other anti-clockwise and yet these two centers are one. A formula which could describe the growth of the spirals conforms to the formula for the golden rectangle in which, to quote Doczi, "the small part (Minor) stands in the same proportion to the larger (major) as the large part stands to the whole."[30] The process by which the daisy's harmonious pattern grows is, in Doczi's words, "a joining of complementary opposites." This is striking similar to Corbin's more picturesque words, "the meeting place of the two seas," and is in agreement with what we have been saying about ambiguity. The center out of which the daisy grows is the growing tip of the organism and therefore it is a vital, alive center, not simply an abstract or hypothetical one.

Doczi coined a new word *dinergy*. He did this because he felt that although there are a number of different words associated with aspects of the pattern forming process that comes from the union of opposites, none of these words express the generative power of this union. The word *polarity,* for example, refers to opposites but does not indicate that something new comes into being. *Duality* and *dichotomy* imply division, but do not mean joining. *Synergy,* he says, indicates joining and cooperation but does not refer specifically to opposites. He gives the etymology of dinergy as dia, "across, through, opposite" and "energy." Dinergy, he says, is the creative energy of organic growth, it is what gives power to the growing tip. It is what we have been calling dynamic unity, and the golden rectangle can be seen to be the sacred space within which dinergy is generated.

Dinergy, Doczi observes, is one of nature's most basic pattern forming processes. The golden rectangle can be seen as the visual representation of dinergy (or dynamic unity) whose structure is the basic ambigu-

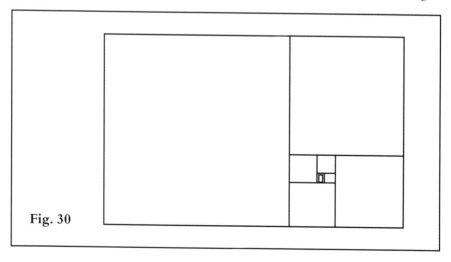

Fig. 30

ity. One of the ways that the golden rectangle can be created is by adding squares that diminish in size according to the number of the golden mean.

The proportions of the squares are therefore 1:.618 but each square in its turn will be a representative of Unity. This diagram is often called the *whirling squares*. As squares are added, a spiral is generated which begins and ends in infinity, or, better still, in unity. Throughout the spiral the same tension that we showed to exist between the two unities, inclusive and exclusive, is to be found. Each square includes the succeeding one and excludes the preceding square. The spiral could thus be envisioned as a force seeking resolution in a point of rest which, however much it is sought, can never be found. It thus illustrates unity seeking an ultimate unity, or unity seeking to re-absorb the null point. This force is not just a centripetal force going towards a center, it is also, at the same time, a centrifugal force seeking totality or wholeness.

Spirals have often been associated with ancient architecture. "Intertwined spiral mazes from Neolithic times, identical with the Cretan laby-

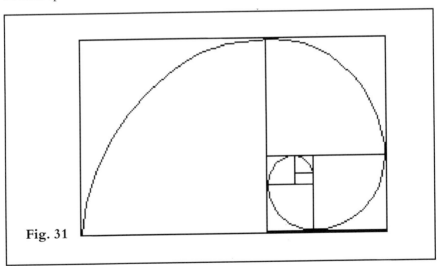

Fig. 31

rinth, the Maori tattoo and the American Indian Tapu'at, are carved into the rocks of barrow tombs in New Grange, Ireland. These double spirals have been interpreted as symbols of death and rebirth, because as one follows the line coiling inwards, one finds another line coming out in the opposite direction."[31] These spirals are often found in the form of labyrinths. One of the most famous of these is the labyrinth of Chartres, an elaborate spiral leading to, and away from, a center. Charpentier suggests a labyrinth is a dance pattern written in the ground, which might well give support to the idea that the earliest ground plan for temples were traced by dancing and not by surveying. Another commentator on the spiral and dance says that spiral dances were often healing and regeneration dances "to enable man to escape from the materialized world and to enter the beyond, through the 'hole' symbolized by the center."[32]

Other forms hold special meaning. A golden triangle is also derived from the sacred mean. The pentagon, which is derived form the golden triangle, has always been considered the symbol of man. "The golden section is the most distinctive shape we derive from the architecture of the plant and the human figure"[33] It is even possible that a temple covering hundreds of square miles may well have been "built" on the basis of the golden triangle and the pentagon derived from it. In *The Holy Place*, Henry Lincoln tells of Rennes-le Chateau and its relation to what Lincoln calls "the eighth wonder of the world": a temple whose boundaries are established by five mountains, each ten miles from the other. These five mountains lie precisely at an angle of a gigantic pentagon. At the center of the pentagon is a treasure and many people have speculated and sought this treasure, wondering what it can be. The treasure is undoubtedly the center itself.[34]

Sacred geometry continues to fascinate many even in these postmodern times. From my point of view their main interest is that they are a basis for generating sacred space and so containing the basic ambiguity, a containment basic to the generation and maintenance of human consciousness.

Notes

1. John Michell, *City of Revelation* (London: Garnstone Press, 1972), p. 19.
2. Martin Heidegger, *Existence and Being,* p. 336.
3. David Maclagen, *Creation Myths* (London: Thames and Hudson, 1977), p. 14.
4. Maria-Gabrielle Wosien, *Sacred Dance* (London: Thames and Hudson: London, 1974), p. 7.
5. Wosen (1974, p. 7).
6. Wosen (1974, p. 21).

7. James G. Frazer, *The Golden Bough* (London: St. Martins Library, 19??), p.15.
8. Frazer (19??, p. 15).
9. Frazer (19??, p. 65).
10. Corbin *Temple and Contemplation* (London: Institute of Ismaili Studies Ltd., 1986), p. 266.
11. Corbin (1986, p. 266).
12. Corbin (1986, p. 268).
13. Corbin (1986, p. 268).
14. Wosien (1974, p. 24).
15. Roger Cook, *Tree of Life: Image for the Cosmos* (London: Thames and Hudson, 1974), p.9. The Cabalistic text says, "When the Concealed of the Concealed wished to reveal himself, he first made a single point: the Infinite was entirely unknown, and diffused no light before this luminous point broke through into vision. Beyond this point nothing is knowable. and that is why it is called *reshith*, beginning, the first of those creative words by which the universe was created." Paul Klee echoes this when speaking of the "irritated point as latent energy." Klee also observed that "At the slightest impetus the point is about to emerge from a state in which its mobility is concealed, to move on upwards to take on one or more directions."
16. Cook (1974, p. 9).
17. Michell (1972, p. 27).
18. Michell (1972, p. 20).
19. Julian Jaynes, *The Origin of Consciousness in the Breakdown of the Bicameral Mind* (New York: Houghton Mifflin, 2000), p. 169.
20. The arrangement of the three Great Pyramids reflects the arrangement of the stars in Orion's belt and numerous correspondences can be found between the architecture of pyramids and the heavens, particularly the constellation of Orion. See Robert Bauval and Adrian Gilbert, *The Orion Mystery: Unlocking the Secrets of the Pyramids* (Toronto: Doubleday Canada, 1994). Furthermore, intricate and minute lunar, solar, and stellar correspondences exist between the various parts of the Angkor Wat temple complex in Cambodia and the heavens. See Eleanor Mannikka, *Angkor Wat: Time, Space, and Kingship* (Honolulu: University of Hawaii Press, 1996).
21. Louis Charpentier, *The Mysteries Of Chartres Cathedral* (London: RILKO, 1966) p. 83.
22. Charpentier (1966, p. 85).
23. Michell (1972, p. 57).
24. Michell (1972, p. 59).
25. See Appendix 4.
26. Michell (1972, p. 72).
27. Michell (1972, p. 72).
28. William Stirling, *The Canon* (London: Garnstone Press, 1974), p. 12.
29. Stirling (1974, pp. 12-13).
30. Gyorgy Doczi, *The Power of Limits* (Boulder: Shambhala Publications). 1981).

31. Doczi, (1981, p. 27).
32. J. E. Cirlot, *A Dictionary of Symbols*, transl. by Jack Sage (London: Routledge & Kegan Paul, 1962), p. 292.
33. Doczi, (1981, p. i).
33. Doczi, (1981, p. 85).
34. Henry Lincoln, *The Holy Place* (London: Corgi Books, 1992), p. i.

Chapter 21

Sufism and the Ambiguity of You and Me

If then you perceive me, you perceive yourself.
But, you cannot perceive me through yourself.
It is through my eyes that you see me
and see your self,
Through your eyes you cannot see me.
A SUFI POEM[1]

ESIDES THE magical (yet highly practical) way by which ambiguity is contained, we must take note of the way of devotion, of longing, and yearning. I have chosen the Sufi teachings as most representative of this way and will make brief reference to the work of Ibn 'Arabi to illuminate this approach to our subject. Preserving the center plays an important part in the Sufi tradition, but yearning for, and entering, a pure relation of I-Thou is its heart.

Awareness-of, what I have also called "focussed' awareness," is upstream of consciousness and this is why we cannot grasp the Other as a form in consciousness. I indicated earlier that *you* are, as it were, a hole in existence through which I can fall into heaven or damnation. One of the functions of consciousness is to provide ways by which a direct encounter with you can be avoided. I said earlier in the book, that I take ready made words and names, stereotypes, phrases, ways of acting and reacting as buffers against reality, veils to hide you in. But these buffers sometimes collapse, the veils tear, and I stand outside myself in ecstasy or horror. You and I together reflect each other as a mirror and image, a perfect unus-ambo, but, who is the mirror and whom the image cannot be determined. Love, human love, the love of a man for a woman, releases me into moments of standing outside, of ecstasy, when you and I are two but one. But, this love is the echo of another, divine love, the love of God, the Love of I for Thee.

I-thou, this unus-ambo, the source of mystical delight, also looms as the source of endless torments of hell. We have generated consciousness from the Word to ward off hell and so we have denied ourselves heaven. But some people, because of the creative power of unity, can rise above the trammels of consciousness, escape its atmosphere of words, and can even describe, haltingly, what they find. For the last several centuries or so these people have been the artists, thinkers, and scientists who have, through their labor, enlarged and enriched consciousness. But before these the *nabiim*, the prophets of the Hebrew Bible, spread the word.

Consciousness can be likened to a tree. The esotericists of antiquity sometimes depicted this tree as inverted, with the roots in the air and branches below. The roots of consciousness are in ambiguity; the trunk is dynamic unity; the branches come from the dilemmas that have been presented, resolved, or ignored. With the passage of time the foliage gets ever more dense, ever more differentiated, blocking the light.

At the time of the gods, the tree was but a sapling and the nabiim, who have been called (wrongly according to Julian Jaynes) the "prophets" of the Bible, were the artists.[2] Jaynes describes how the word nabiim comes from a root word that has has nothing to do with foretelling the future, but rather with "flowing and becoming bright." The nabi, therefore, is "one who metaphorically was flowing forth or welling up with speech and visions." The nabiim were transitional men between the time of the gods and the time of Jehovah, and they were partly subjective and partly bicameral. The word bicameral, as discussed in Chapter 20, means two legislative chambers, and we can view it as a metaphor for the two centers, the schism: me-as-center/me-as-periphery. In the bicameral era, consciousness was not centered upon a stable *I*, as we know it today, and the center was still to be found in the idol held in place by the temple.

With the emergence of the self and the gradual integration around a new introjected center, the nabiim all but disappeared. Now and again someone similar to a nabi has appeared, perhaps as a throw back to the source—not necessarily a throw back to the source as *past,* but to the source as *origin.* One of these might have been the nineteenth century Indian saint Ramakrishna. Ibn 'Arabi is another such creative spiritual genius though from an earlier period.

Ibn 'Arabi is known to his modern disciples as *Muhyi'd-Din,* the Animator of Religion, and countless Sufis and spiritual seekers still regard his tomb in Damascus as a center of pilgrimage. He was born in 1165. He fell gravely ill as a child and it was during this illness at the tender age of 8 or 9 that he gained entrance into what Corbin calls the world of "real and subsistent images," known in Arabic as *"alám al -mithál,* the intermediate realm of Active Imagination. I have said that the Sufi way is the way of adoration and devotion. The connection between mystical and erotic love is brought out clearly in one of Ibn 'Arabi's mystical poems that he wrote and dedicated to a young and very beautiful young woman. He said, "Whatever [mystical] name I may mention in this work; it is to her that I am alluding. Whatever the house whose elegy I sing, it is of her house that I am thinking ."[4]

The term *imagination* as used by Corbin when discussing Ibn 'Arabi and other Sufis must not be confused with *fantasy.* Corbin says that imagination is "the magical intermediary between thought [knowing] and being." Specifically he said it was "an incarnation of thought [what we are calling 'knowing'] in an image, and the presence of this image in being."[5] In our secular age of clear and distinct concepts, imagination has taken on a connotation that means the opposite of reality. To imagine is to create an illusory, even delusory, world. We have completely degraded imagination, turning it to mere illusory fantasy. Artistic creations are, in our view, simply fragile and incidental when compared with the solidity of social, technological, or economic achievements. Corbin says, "All indemonstrable, invisible, inaudible things are classified as creations of the Imagination, that is, of the faculty whose function it is to secrete the *imaginary,* the unreal."[6]

However, as I have insisted, an intermediary realm of invisible and inaudible forces (what I have called the realm of dynamic unity) must not be ignored. In a study on music, Victor Zuckerkandl, says "music does not come out of the physical nor out of the psychic component but out of *a third, a purely dynamic, component.*"[7] Mathematics, to the extent that it is dependent upon number at least, also has its origin in this intermediary realm. Von Franz, a student of Jung, writing on the origin of number, said, "In analytical psychology it is said, 'In the *unus mundus* . . . there is no incommensurability between so-called matter and so-called psyche . . . number is a key to their [mystery] since *it is as much discovered as it is invented. It is quantity as well as meaning.*'"[8]

When discussing this intermediate realm earlier, I hesitated to call it a "creative" realm, for fear readers might construe it to mean a psychological realm only. In a similar way we must be careful how we interpret the imagination, and must not construe it to be simply in the realm of knowing. This would be a mistake because this realm is the realm both of ideas and of being, and is now all but ignored except by a few fringe parapsychologists. However, Corbin argues that "The cosmology of Sufism possesses a dimension . . . which takes account of such [paranormal] experience [which are] the effects of a spiritual energy whose source is the heart and whose organ is the active Imagination."[9]

The preservation of the center plays an important part in the Sufi tradition. Active Imagination is closely associated with the *heart*, the dynamic center. As noted at the beginning of this chapter, the center has an important place in the Sufi tradition. In his fascinating study *The Man of Light in Iranian Sufism*, Corbin says,

> Orientation is a primary phenomena of our presence in the world. A human presence has the property of spatializing a world around it, and this phenomenon implies a certain relationship of man with the world, *his* world, this relationship being determined by the very mode of his presence. The organization, the plan, of this network has depended since time immemorial on a single point: the point of orientation, the heavenly north, the pole star.[10]

This center provides both the inward dimension as well as the vertical dimension. To go to the center is to go up; to go up is to go to the center. A pyramid, as well as a holy mountain, symbolizes this correspondence, in so far as when one climbs it one goes up and to the center as well. Heaven is up because it is in the center, not because God lives in the sky beyond the clouds. In Sufism the concept of the North is of primary importance because, "It is in accordance with the way in which man inwardly experienced the 'vertical' dimension of his own presence that the horizontal dimensions acquire their sense."[11] This vertical dimension is the dimension of *value*. Values "come out of" the center. Corbin further notes that the orient sought by the mystic cannot be found on a map; it is in the direction of "the north, beyond the north." Only by going upward can one find this cosmic north. One must travel a straight path, which means not deviating to the east or west. The discovery of the inner world which shines by its own light, and is indeed the world of light, means climbing the peak that is being drawn toward the *center. This inner world is* an innerness of light as opposed to the spatiality of the outer world which, by contrast, will appear as darkness.[12]

The connection between the Active Imagination and the center is well illustrated by Ibn 'Arabi's own spiritual life which, Corbin says, was intensified by his stay in Mecca, the cosmic center for the Sufis. "His circumambulations, real or imagined, of the Ka'aba internalized as a 'cosmic center,' nourished a speculative effort to which inner visions and theophanic perceptions lent experimental confirmation."[13] Corbin says that decisive events in one's spiritual life occur only at the center of the world, "at the pole of the internal microcosm." It was at Mecca that the real and decisive event of Ibn 'Arabi's life occurred, and which was provoked by meditation "around the Ka'aba," the "center of the world."[14] This event was an encounter with his personal holy Spirit. Such an encounter with theophanic persons always signals a return to the center of the world, because communication with the *'alam al-mithal* is possible only at the center of the world. This holy Spirit, who was his companion and celestial guide, was called *Khidr*. This figure of Khidr is Thou, underlying all encounters with you. As we have said, I do not *encounter* Thee; both Thee and I arise simultaneously out of a common source.

When one encounters this kind of statement that Ibn 'Arabi met his celestial guide and companion, the distinction between Active Intelligence and fantasy becomes important. One naturally asks oneself "what kind of person is this holy Spirit, Khidr," who, according to the Koran, was also the spiritual guide of Moses? Is he just a fantasy, the perception of an archetypal image, or is he a real person. As Corbin says, either answer carries with it its own difficulties. If we adopt the Jungian point of view, then Khidr is an archetype, a product of the collective unconscious, which is

ultimately in the realm of knowing. As such he is a product which bor-
ders on being a figment of imagination, if not of the intellect, and anyhow loses his reality. And if we think of him as a real person, he is to be
found in the realm of being; and furthermore, it will be difficult to distinguish between Khidr's relation with his disciple and the relationship that
any other spiritual teacher can have with him. We must bear in mind that
the same question can even be asked about "you." Not you as a person-
ality, as a man or woman, as my boss or my friend, but you who sustains
all these. Are you a figment of my imagination, or do you exist apart from
me, over there — as a body or some soul inhabiting a body — or must
you be understood in some other way?

The cynic invariably claims "humans create God in their own image." To say God is the creation of active imagination seems to confirm
the cynic's point of view. However, Ibn 'Arabi would say humans do create
God in their image, but this is because God creates the human being in
His image. "The God whom [humans] 'create,' far from being an unreal
product of our fantasy, is also a theophany, for man's active Imagination
is merely the organ of the absolute theophanic imagination." For Corbin
prayer is the ultimate theophany, the ultimate appearance of God to the
human being, and in this way is creative; but the God to whom the prayer
is addressed, because it creates him, is precisely the God who reveals
Himself to prayer in this Creation.[15] This is why the imagination of the
human being is not simply fantasy. This same theophanic Imagination that
the human being uses in prayer, is the same power which created the
human being in the first place.

Human imagination is the Imagination of God continuing to reveal,
in its image of God, what this imagination first showed when first creating the human being. The forces that create a work of art are the same
forces as those that create the artist. When active imagination is true to
divine reality "it reveals, it liberates, provided we recognize the function
with which Ibn 'Arabi endowed it and which it alone can perform,
namely, the function of effecting a *coincidentia oppositorum.*" A Sufi was
asked, "Whereby do you know God?" And he replied "By the fact He is
the *coincidentia oppositorum.*"[16] One could look upon the ambiguity know-
ing/being as the *oppositorum*, in which case the *coincidentia oppositorum*
could perhaps be the basic ambiguity that is the very heart of creativity
both Divine and human.

er's bisociation is a kind of *coincidentia oppositorum* is. He said
·ises when a single situation or idea is perceived in "*two self-*
c   *abitually incompatible frames of reference.*" And so at the human
lev\   rundamental *coincidentia oppositorum* would be *me-as-center/me-as-
peripr.. /.* This is the source, as we have said, of the creative impulse. This
could well give us a way by which to understand Ibn 'Arabi's vision. Here,
Khidr would corresponded to what I have prosaically called the viewpoint,
the *me* in me-as-center/me-as-periphery. Khidr is the unity underlying
the conflict, an essentially personal unity. Let me quote Corbin at some
length to support what I have just said:

> The term self [me] refers neither to the impersonal Self, to the pure act
> of existing attainable through efforts comparable to the techniques of
> yoga, nor to the Self of psychologists. The word [is] employed solely in
> the sense given it by Ibn 'Arabi and numerous other Sufi theosophists
> when they repeat the famous sentence: He who knows himself knows
> *his* Lord. . . . This Lord is not the impersonal self, nor is it the God of
> dogmatic definitions, *self*-subsisting without relation to *me,* without be-
> ing experienced by *me.* He is the one who knows himself through my-
> self, that is, in the knowledge that I have of him, because it is the
> knowledge he has of me; it is with him alone, in this syzygic unity, that
> it is possible to say *thou.*[17]

The One as Monad

"He who knows himself knows his Lord" underlies the doctrine of the
monad and of the microcosm and the macrocosm. This lofty idea of the
macrocosm and the microcosm was once brought home to me in a
humble way when looking at the label on a bottle of OK sauce, a popular
table sauce in Canada and the British Isles. In the illustration on the label was included a picture of a bottle of OK sauce. Everything that is true
of the macrocosm, the label on the bottle, is true of the microcosm, the
label on the bottle in the label; as above so below. This has been a recur-
rent theme of this book: what is true of the cosmos is true of me and
conversely. This notion as above so below is gaining respectability in
scientific circles with the advent of fractals and holography.

"He who knows himself knows his Lord" is another way of saying
as above so below, but it also implies that the human being is a creator

because God is a creator. The evolution of the world is replayed in the evolution of consciousness. Corbin puts it this way "Each being is an epiphanic form of the Divine being, who in it is manifested as invested in one or more of his Names."[18]

The doctrine of Names is somewhat abstruse and difficult to reduce to a simple formula. A name is an emanation of the Godhead, but each emanation is a totality. The universe is a whole, One. Again let us quote Corbin who says, the universe is the,

> totality of the Names by which He is named when we name Him by His names. Each divine Name manifested is the lord of the being who manifests it. Each being is the epiphanic form of his own Lord, that is he manifests only that aspect of the divine Essence, which in each case is particularized and individualized in that Name. No determinate and individualized being can be the epiphanic form of the Divine in its totality.[19]

Of all the names or "Lords," Ibn 'Arabi says each being, "has as his God only his particular Lord, he cannot possibly have the Whole."[20] Yet he also says, "Here we have a kind of kathenotheism verified in the context of a mystic experience; the Divine Being is not fragmented, but wholly present in *each* instance, individualized in *each* theophany of His Names, and it is invested in *each* instance with one of these Names that He appears as Lord."[21] Each is not the whole, but the whole is in each. It is like a number of puddles reflecting the moon. Each puddle is not the whole, but the whole is reflected in each. Each is the monad and therefore, the whole, but the whole is more than any one monad. We will return to this again at the very end of the book.

Yearning And Dynamic Unity

According to the teachings of Ibn 'Arabi, the human being is a creator because God is a creator and "the Divine Being is a creator because he wished to know himself in beings who know Him." The word *Al -Lah* is derived from the root word *wlh* meaning "sad," "to be overwhelmed with sadness," "to sigh toward," "to flee fearfully toward." By another etymological root, Corbin also derives the meanings of to desire, to sigh, to feel compassion, from the word Allah.[22] Al-lah, then, expresses sadness, nostalgia, "aspiring eternally to know the principle which eternally initiates it." The same is true of what we have called unity. Unity cannot be known and, strictly speaking, should not be named, because to name is to contain, but unity cannot be contained, it is that which contains. I have also made the point that unity is sighing after, longing for unity. I referred to this in Chapter 13, discussing creativity when speaking of the frog voice and Van Gough's tragic cry, "Something is alive in me: what can it be!"

Allah is often thought to be the Arabic word for God, but unity or the Godhead in Islamic gnosis cannot be known or even named as "God." Corbin says that Allah is the nostalgia of the revealed God, and this means revealed to the human being, yearning to be once more *beyond* his revealed being. The yearning of Allah to be beyond his revealed being thus can be likened to the striving of unity to reabsorb the null point. This yearning manifests as dynamic unity and appears as "focussed awareness," "intentionality," the need for purpose and meaning, the search for perfection and the longing for the beloved. Corbin goes on to say, "Nevertheless the aspiration of the revealed God yearning to know the God he reveals, is, in the first and highest of creatures, identical with 'the sadness of the *Theos agnostos* [unknown God] yearning to be known by and in the same creature.'"[23]

The revealed God is man's creation; this creation comes out of man's yearning to know the God he reveals in this creation. But, this yearning is identical with the sadness of *Theos agnostos* yearning to be known by man. With this the circle is complete. God's yearning to be known is the human being's yearning to know God. The human being is a mirror by which God sees himself and, in this, God is both observer and participant. This is summed up in Corbin's saying "the gnostic's *heart* is 'the eye' by which God reveals himself to Himself," and the heart of the gnostic is like a mirror in which the microcosmic form of the Divine Being is reflected.[24] Dynamic unity is turned back on to itself in the purest form of I-Thou. Corbin says,

> When, in contemplating an image, an icon, others recognize and perceive as a divine image the vision beheld by the artist who created the image, it is because of the spiritual creativity, the *Himma*, which the artist put into his work. Here, we have a compelling term of comparison, by which to measure the decadence of our dreams and of our art.[25]

But even creating an image or icon already signals the decline from the creativity of Ibn 'Arabi, a decline brought about by the dispersal of dynamic unity, or to use Ibn 'Arabi's language, the dispersal of creative power of the heart (himma), a dispersal caused by the proliferating foliage of consciousness.

I coined the phrase *dynamic unity* to designate the power generated by the fundamental ambiguity, but the full meaning of what lies behind this expression can only come from the whole text of this book. In a similar way, Corbin says the word *himma* is a difficult word to translate into English. He says, "It is an extremely complicated notion which cannot perhaps be translated by any one word. Many equivalents have been suggested: meditation project, intention, desire, force of will."[26] However, he goes on to say that the definition of himma that encompasses the other definitions is "the creative power of the heart." Instead of using the expression "power of the heart," remembering heart means *center,* I say the aspect of himma encompassing all the others is "the creative power of the center." In seeking to elaborate upon the word himma, Corbin says its content is perhaps best suggested by the Greek word *enthymesis,* which signifies "the act of meditating, conceiving, projecting, ardently desiring—in other words, of having (something) present in the *thymos,* which is a vital force, soul, heart, intention, thought, desire."[27]

Himma is both the power and destiny of creativity and, because of the dispersal of consciousness, I indicated that this power declines. The force of an intention was so powerful in the *nabiim* and in Ibn 'Arabi, as to project and realize a being external to the being who conceives the intention, and this corresponds perfectly to the character of the mysterious power Ibn 'Arabi designates as *himma.*[28] As Corbin says, out of himma come a large group of phenomena many of which today are the concern of parapsychology, including extrasensory perception, telepathy, visions of synchronicity, etc. [29]

The human being emerges out of Creative imagination, and this Creative imagination is also the source of human creativity; the creativity which, while creating the bird, through the bird creates the nest. But as Corbin says, "As it is exercised by most men, its function is representational; it produces images which are merely part of conjoined Imagination inseparable from the subject." But even here, "pure representation does not, *eo ipso,* mean 'illusion'; these images really 'exist'; illusion occurs when we misunderstand their mode of being." The artist lies halfway between the nabiim and the average human being. Each of us is basically a nabiim whose most profound creation is that of I-Thou. It is only when we release ourselves from the containing power of the word that we can realize that this creativity comes from Thou seeking to know thyself.

Notes

1. Henry Corbin, *Creative Imagination in the Sufism of Ibn 'Arabi*. Trans. Ralph Manheim. (Princeton: Princeton University Press, 1969). Bollingen series). This is the main source for my discussion of Ibn 'Arabi. For additional information on Ibn 'Arabi, see Stephen Hirtenstein, *The Unlimited Mercifier: The Spiritual Life and Thought of Ibn 'Arabi* (Ashland: White Cloud Press, 1999).
2. Jaynes, (2000, pp. 299-300).
3. Corbin, (1969, p. 138).
4. Corbin, (1969, p. 179).
5. Corbin, (1969, p. 179).
6. Corbin, (1969, p. 181).
7. Victor Zuckerkandl, *Sound And Symbol: Music And The External World*. Trans. Willard Trask. (Princeton: Princeton University Press, 1956)
8. Marie-Louise Von Franz, *Number and Time* (Evanston: Northwestern University Press, 1974).
9. Corbin, (1969, p. 48).
10. Henry Corbin, *The Man Of Light In Iranian Sufism*. Trans. Nancy Pearson. (Boulder and London: Shambhala Publications, 1978), p.1.
11. Corbin, (1978, p. 1).
12. Corbin, (1978, p. 12.
13. Corbin, (1969, p. 52).
14. Corbin, (1969, p. 52).
15. Corbin, (1969, p. 188).
16. Corbin, (1969, p. 188).
17. Corbin, (1969, p. 95).
18. Corbin, (1969, p. 121).
19. Corbin, (1969, p. 121).
20. Corbin, (1969, p. 121).
21. Corbin, (1969, p. 121).
22. Corbin, (1969, p. 113).
23. Corbin, (1969, p. 113).
24. Corbin, (1969, p. 224).
25. Corbin, (1969, p. 224).
26. Corbin, (1969, p. 220).
27. Corbin, (1969, p. 222).
28. Corbin, (1969, p. 223).
29. Corbin, (1969, p. 224).

Chapter 22

The Zen Response

Take the Upanishads as the bow, the great weapon, and place upon it
the arrow sharpened by meditation. Then, having drawn it back with a
mind directed to the thought of Brahman, strike that mark, O my good
friend — that which is the Imperishable. Om is the bow; atman is the
arrow; Brahman is said to be the mark. It is to be struck by an
undistracted mind. Then the âtman becomes one with Brahman,
as the arrow with the target.
MUNDAKA UPANISHAD

LET'S NOW CONSIDER the third religion, the religion of transcendence. It might be protested that the way of devotion too is a way
of transcendence. A Zen teacher would undoubtedly agree, but would go
on to say that even that transcendence must be transcended. Let us see
what that might mean.

Eugen Herrigel in *Zen in the Art of Archery* recounts how his teacher
divided the process of learning archery into three phases: drawing the bow,
releasing the arrow, and hitting the target. In the accomplished archer these
three are one seamless whole, but while learning archery one progresses
successively through these stages. The three stages have their counterpart
in the practice of Rinzai Zen: drawing the bow corresponds to "arousing the doubt sensation"; releasing the bow corresponds to *kensho*, which
is the initial "seeing into" or *satori*; and hitting the target corresponds to
full awakening or Buddhahood. Using the language developed in this

book, drawing the bow is entering fully into ambiguity and releasing the arrow is being released from the tension of the ambiguity. This leaves hitting the target, and a Zen master says of this:

> The moon's the same old moon,
> The flowers exactly as they were,
> Yet I have become the thingness
> Of all things I see![1]

First let us "draw the bow." To do so we must truly enter the labyrinthine ways of ambiguity. Once this stage is discussed, I will give some indication of what is meant by kensho, and finally we can deal with the question: What does it mean to hit the target?

The Koan and the Basic Ambiguity

Zen Buddhism has two main schools: Rinzai and Soto. They differ from each other more in emphasis than in substance in the way they seek to come to full awakening or Buddhahood. The Soto school enters ambiguity by way of the face that says there is no ambiguity. It emphasizes the truth we are all already whole and complete; we are all already one. By reason of this we can sit in the midst of ambiguity with full faith in our intrinsic wholeness, the face that says there is no ambiguity. Although entry into ambiguity is through wholeness, subsequent practice is to remain steadfastly within the full ambiguity. This practice is called *shikantaza* or "just sitting."

In contrast, Rinzai Zen enters by way of ambiguity itself, through the doubt, or ambiguity, or double bind sensation, and this sensation—a kind of tension or yearning for a resolution—is enhanced by means of koans. For example, as noted in Chapter 1, a master might say, "If you say this is a stick I will punish you; if you say it is not a stick I will punish you! What is it?" Rinzai Zen also emphasizes the importance of kensho, which in Soto is played down because it can so easily be mistaken for hitting the target rather than as an essential step toward that end. However, Rinzai Zen considers the risk worth taking, because just as the correct release of the arrow is essential in archery, so kensho is essential during Zen practice. Furthermore, although koans are used to enhance the doubt sensation, it must be emphasized they are, nonetheless, responses to the question, "What does it mean to hit the target?" This unity in Zen of the means and the end, of the question and the response, is brought out in a dialogue in which a monk asked a master "Where is my treasure?" The master replied, "Your question is your treasure."

There are about 1,700 koans, and although some of them are more or less the same but use slightly different language, usually most are saying something quite specific. For example, someone asked Zen Master Joshu, "What is Buddha?" Joshu answered, "The oak tree in the garden." Another monk asked Zen Master Tozan "What is Buddha?" and Tozan replied "Three pounds of flax." These are two quite different responses to the same question, yet both hit the target, *and both are saying what it means to hit the target.* This multiplicity in unity is a delicate point, and a useful metaphor for gaining an appreciation of it is the diamond. Although each facet of the diamond is different, yet each is still one aspect of an indivisible whole. I shall come back to this again at the end of the last chapter.

Drawing the Bow

Zen koans have been misunderstood, not only in the West but in China, their country of origin. To understand koans one must be able to hit the target; koans come out of the awakened mind of a master and to be able to see into what this means one must work from one's own awakened mind. What, then, is this awakened mind; what is Buddhahood and how does one realize it? I have been using the word One, and it would be as well to translate Buddha as Oneness, or One mind. This question was asked of Nansen, one of the most famous of all Zen masters, and by considering his reply we shall be able to take the first step toward drawing the bow. The question asked was, "What is the Way," meaning both what is the end or awakened state (that is one mind), and how do we realize the awakened state. "What is the way to realize the Way?"

In the first "way" there is a further ambiguity. One might ask, "What is the way to Montreal?" and receive as an answer, "The 401 highway." Then one could legitimately ask, "What is the best way to go, by car or by bus?" What is the way to travel the way to the Way?"

"What is the Way?" The master replied, "Every day mind is the Way." Let's try to see into the implications of this.

I have said that consciousness, experience, or what Nansen calls "every day mind," comes out of the human response to ambiguity, or more precisely, out of the ambiguity in human form. I suggested that at some moment in the evolution of life the stress of ambiguity became so great (through the activity of mind) that language erupted and stabilized, or *fixed*, the ambiguity. This fixation provided a stage upon which the drama of humanity could be enacted, a drama based upon a constant flirtation with ambiguity, which sometimes is consummated in a creative love affair, but at other times collapses in warfare and violence. Put into other words, the stage is dependent upon a stable center which, through I-It, is constantly promised, although the promise is never fulfilled. This means that profound insecurity underlies consciousness, which we experience as angst or anguish.

Although stabilized to some degree, ambiguity is not resolved. It can be likened to a bubble on a stream which, although the pressures and surface tension inherent in the water are stabilized, nevertheless it is borne along by the water itself. As the Lankavatara Sutra says, "[There] is a constant transmigration . . . [things] never remain for a moment as they are, they flow like a stream."[2] Consciousness is a bubble carried by the stream of dynamic unity, which, as discussed earlier, in its very dynamism generates new kinds of instability. These in turn, call for new creativity to arrive at stability again and again. We see the same thing nowadays in the development of science: each new scientific discovery generates its own new set of problems calling for more scientific discovery. The adherents to the view that physics will shortly have all the answers in a magnificent Theory of Everything are like the old physicists who sought a perpetual motion machine. The only possible perpetual motion machine is ambiguity itself.

Zen Master Nansen says, "*every day mind* is the target and the way to hit the target." It is in its very lack of stability that every day mind gives us so much trouble. Every day mind is the mind of ambiguity, dilemma, conflict and pain; where is the person who does not carry conflict and division in his or her heart? Some conclude that Nansen does not mean what he says and explain this koan by saying that he really means a mind purified of its contradictions and judgments. But, then the next question would have to be, "What is the Way to clear the mind of contradictions," or "What is the Way?"

This, inevitably would lead us into a vicious circle. On the other hand, others would say Nansen is mistaken and that the way must lead to heaven,

away from the dust and grime of every day mind. Some Christian critics of Buddhism look upon Zen as kind of primitive pantheism and would
probably see Nansen's response as evidence of this.

Another koan helps clarify this point. A Zen Master was asked, "Is
an awakened person subject to the law of Karma or not?" He answered,
"He is not!" And for this he had to live for 500 lives as a fox.

Translated into more understandable terms, he was asked whether one
could escape from the rat race, to get out of the grip of ambiguity, to leave
behind the clutch of every day mind, and he replied, "Yes, it is possible."
For this he was punished for 500 lives.

On the face of it, Nansen's reply "everyday mind is teh Way" is pessimistic stoicism and the fate of this master, who has to live out 500 lives
as a fox, seems to confirm this pessimism. Indeed, Buddhism has long had
the reputation of being a "pessimistic religion." Nirvana was said to be
simply extinction, and the longing for nirvana, for annihilation, was the
outcome of a world-weary religion, a pessimism apparently inherent in
Nansen's reply. Optimism, however, comes from the belief, held by the
fox-master, that one can escape from ambiguity. The optimist exhorts us
to hold to the face that says there is no ambiguity, by seeking the one.
Pessimism on the other hand says we cannot ignore ambiguity, one cannot escape it and therefore holds to the face that says there is ambiguity.
Each of these, optimism and pessimism, is a whole way of life, like the face
of the young or old woman is a whole picture, although each is but half
the story. Nansen is neither optimistic nor pessimistic.

The koan of the fox-master continues with his seeking help from
another Zen master, Hyakujo, who says, "Ask me the question." The fox-
master asks, "Is an awakened person subject to the law of karma or not?"
and Hyakujo answers, "He does not ignore the law karma." Because of
this, the fox-master was released from his karma of living in the body of
the fox. Karma comes from the fact we can only ever, at one particular
time, live out half the ambiguity, and much of the burden of life comes
from unrealized possibilities—unrealized because we realized "the other
face" instead. [3] But we must not think Hyakujo gave the "right" answer
while the fox-master gave the "wrong" one. Nor must we think his answer cancels out the first in the way a plus will cancel out a minus.
Hyakujo's answer pushed the fox-master completely into the ambiguity
and this was his release! This is precisely what Nansen is doing with his

reply. Every day mind *is* the Way. But let us remember the complete ambiguity includes the face that says there is no ambiguity! In Nansen's koan, no-ambiguity is brought out when later in the koan he says, "It is like vast space. Where is a place for good and bad?"

A friend of mine, Dr. William Byers, a professor of mathematics, was intrigued by what I have said about ambiguity. One day, after we had talked about it over lunch, he wrote the following which, perhaps unwittingly, is also an interesting comment upon the koan about the fox. Dr. Byers' reflections help to show in what way Hyakujo's answer pushed the fox-master completely into the ambiguity and so released him from his karma. With Dr. Byers' permission, I am using what he wrote with some slight alterations because it puts the situation so well.

Byers begins by saying that as one example among a multitude of others of what is meant by the fundamental ambiguity, we should look at the statement itself: *Fundamentally there is an ambiguity, one face of which says there is an ambiguity while the other says there is no ambiguity, but this face itself is not unambiguous.* He then asks whether the content of this statement is clear or ambiguous? On the one hand the statement is clear, it has a precise meaning in terms of the English language, the logic is straightforward. This is the nonambiguous face; the face that presents a kind of theoretical hypothesis, which can be tested against empirical standards. However, if its objective meaning is thus unambiguous, then it contradicts itself when it says that only one face says there is no ambiguity. That is, the clarity of the statement is not unambiguous.

He then asks that one look at the statement of the fundamental ambiguity again and ask: "What does it mean?" When applied to itself it says that its own meaning is ambiguous, i.e., any attempt to understand it completely is *a priori* doomed to failure. It appears to have a built in self-destructive mechanism. Thus, the meaning of the statement is obscure, difficult to grasp conceptually, and in a word, ambiguous in the popular sense of the term. At this level the face which avers there is no ambiguity is denied.

Now all that has been said above about the complex nature of the statement of the fundamental ambiguity agrees with the original statement. Thus, we are back to thinking that the statement is generally true and clear, that the face that says there is no ambiguity is the right one. (As is pointed out elsewhere in this book, in normal speech and especially in scientific discourse only clear statements can be true, ambiguous statements are by definition false.) This puts us back where we began, in an endless spiral of ambiguity and clarity. Therefore (at a deeper level this time) the statement is ambiguous since we cannot determine whether it itself is true or false, clear or unclear. On one level it is clear but on another this clarity is ambiguous. Thus, the statement is an accurate evocation of the situation that it describes. It itself contains this ambiguity within ambiguity.

Basing his comments on reading *Creating Consciousness* in manuscript form, Dr. Byers went on further to say that this situation of interpenetrating ambiguity and clarity is generally an accurate reflection of the way things are. This is the dilemma that the rational mind confronts when it searches for certainty. This is the dilemma that Nansen and Hyakujo push us into, it is also the dilemma that the conscientious reader will have faced if they read this book with the idea that it contains a basic clarification of life's complexities. Such a reader should reflect back on the fundamental ambiguity and what it implies for their own drive towards oneness, which is what motivates the need for clarity. It points to the need for a larger context in which to discuss these questions. A context in which the clarity will be one dimension *but not the ultimate arbiter of truth.*

Byers further noted that not only this book but any book or theory, indeed consciousness and every day mind itself, must be looked at from this point of view. It is an inevitable consequence of the search to contain ambiguity through the word, which means through consciousness. Books and theories above all are written from the unambiguous point of view, which, according to the above principle, is incomplete and one-sided. The clarity which the best scientific theory can provide always contains, if we can but see it, its own ambiguity. This is the meaning of Godel's incompleteness theorem in the foundations of mathematics, the Heisenberg Uncertainty Principle in physics, or even the modern theories, which describe the chaotic behavior of complex systems. Thus, we might say that determinism implies complexity, which inevitably contains ambiguity.[4]

Kensho: Releasing the arrow.

Koan number 32 of the *Blue Cliff Record*, a famous collection of koans, reads as follows:

A monk asked Rinzai, "What is the essence of Buddhism?"
Rinzai, getting up from his seat, seized him, slapped him, and pushed him
away.
The monk stood still.
A monk standing by said, "Why don't you bow?"
When the monk bowed, he suddenly became awakened.

In the koan, "Hyakujo's Fox," it is said, "No sooner had the old man
heard these words [an awakened man does not ignore the law of causa-
tion] than he was awakened." What is this awakening, this *kensho*, what is
the connection between these two incidents, and what is the value of
awakening in the ecology of the spirit?

The Lankavatara Sutra is an important text for Zen Buddhism. This
sutra emphasizes the need for kensho and gives an elaborate structure of
the human mind to explain why kensho is necessary and how it is possible. The technical term for kensho is *paravritti* and D. T. Suzuki, who
translated the sutra, uses the rather unfortunate expression "catastrophe"
to translate the term into English. Let us first quote from the sutra and
then we shall spend a little time making it accessible in terms we have
been developing in this book. For the moment, *manas* can be translated
as mind and *manovijnana* as intellect. *Vijnana* can be said to be the senses
and *Alaya*, true self.

> It is due to the Alaya's self-purifying nature that there takes place a great
> catastrophe known as "turning back." With this turning back in the Alaya,
> Manas so intimately in relation with it, also experiences a transforma-
> tion in its fundamental attitude towards the Vijnanas. The latter are no
> more regarded as reporters of an external world, which is characterized
> with individuality and manifoldness. This position is now abandoned, the
> external world is no more adhered to as such, that is as reality; for it is
> no more than a mere reflection of the Alaya. The Alaya has been look-
> ing at itself in the Manas mirror. There has been from the very first
> nothing other than itself.[6]

Alaya is what I have called one/knowing/being. It is self-purifying
because it is *one*. One is always one. However as we have also seen it is
two: unity and null point, as well as me-as-center/me-as-periphery. Me-
as-center/me-as-periphery corresponds to manas, and as I have said manas

can also be called mind. As such it is Janus-faced. A turn about or paravritti occurs in the Alaya, which also affects the manas. Before the turnabout the vijnanas, or senses, were looked upon as providing information about an external world, they were reporters. The external world had the characteristics of "individuality and manifoldness." In other words, the external world contained a host of individual, discrete things. With the turnabout, this view is abandoned; the world is no longer regarded as being real in itself, but is now seen as a reflection of Alaya. From the very beginning there has been nothing other than Alaya, One/knowing/being.

In addition to perceiving the outside world as independent and separate, an *I* is born. The conception and the birth of I is the function of *manovijnana*. Manovijnana seeks to crystallize out the individual will-to-be of manas, in the same way I wants to make 'me' into *something*. It is the opposition of these two creations, me and world that creates the illusion of inner and outer, subjective and objective, and ultimately notion of the ghost in the machine.

However the human problem comes not from ambiguity as such, but from the ambiguity being contained by words. The Word is a blessing and a curse; with containment of ambiguity "the world" comes into being. But this world is a "contained" world and therefore finite and so lacking the freedom and spontaneity of pure awareness. This lack pervades all conscious existence. Words freeze ambiguity into "no-ambiguity," "outside" and "inside", into I and It. Frozen ambiguity we call consciousness: experience and existence. It is the stage of life. "Citta [as consciousness] dances like a dancer; the manas resembles a jester; the manovijnana together with the five vijnanas creates an objective world which is like a stage."[7]

The Lankavatara Sutra says the "Buddha's Nirvana has nothing to do with Substance, nor with Action, nor with appearance. With the cessation of the vijnana which is caused by discrimination, there is my cessation."[8] In other words, the world does not vanish, nor does action stop or even the appearance of things change, *what stops is discrimination, the search to make the null point finally articulate.* This is the turnabout, the kensho. Manovijnana, often translated as intellect, is that aspect of the mind obsessively concerned with 'grasping the point' One wakes up to the mistake. "As when the great flood runs its course there are no more waves, so with the extinction of [Manovijnana] all the Vijnanas cease." This is entering fully into ambiguity. The search to make the null point finally articulate is said, in Zen, to be the search for the last word. A Zen master's kensho poem says:

> Magnificent! Magnificent!
> No one knows the last word.
> The ocean bed's aflame
> Out of the void leap wooden lambs.[10]

The work of Manas and Manovijana causes an external world to become "recognized as external," which we have said is stabilizing the external world around "It" in the same way the internal world is stabilized around "I." The sutra goes on to say it must be the work of manas and manovijnana, again, properly executed this time, "to enable us to look at the world as having evolved *out of our own being.* . . . There must be a turning of the waves, the course of Manas and Manovijnana must be altered towards another direction than that which has been pursued hitherto."[11] To say the world evolves *out of our own being* is to say the world is knowing/being. This does not mean knowing *something* nor does it mean that *something* knows. The turning of the waves is no longer "downstream" to the null point but "upstream" to one/knowing/being, the primordial subjectivity.

In his book *Intuition,* Jacques Maritain declares that "All that [the artist] discerns and divines in things, he discerns and divines not as something other than himself, according to the law of speculative knowledge, but, on the contrary, as inseparable from himself and his emotion, and in truth as identified with himself." The Sufi says, "God creates because He wishes to know himself in beings who know him." Maritain says,

> the artist too creates because he wishes to know *himself* in his work of art. The subjectivity of the poet, therefore, is essential to poetry, subjectivity that is, "in its deepest ontological sense . . . a universe unto itself . . . which at the center of all the subjects that it knows as objects, grasps only itself as subject."[12]

The Lankavatara Sutra describes how "the whole system of mentation" depends upon the manovijnana as cause and support, and manovijnana in turn is dependent upon the whole system of mentation. By creating the Word, manovijnana brings the whole mentation into being. In turn the manovijnana is dependent upon the whole system of mentation and language in order to create more language. More language is needed to shore up the structure which threatens to collapse under the pressure of the inherent ambiguity. This gives rise to a situation with which we are already familiar: the *idea*, (that is "the whole system of mentation") gives rise to the *situation* while, at the same time, the situation modifies the *idea*. This constant creation and recreation is called the "wheel of Samsara," a Buddhist expression often thought of as the treadmill of life and which I have referred to as perpetual motion.

The direction toward which this whole complex has been going hitherto is in the direction of making the null point articulate. This is the function of manovijnana. One has the impression that something can be attained, something can be achieved, and that one can know the last word of Zen. This gives rise to the feeling that success, perfection, peace, and happiness can be attained. But just as a little child running down hill has to run faster and faster to stay upright, so we have to strive harder and harder to attain to this ever receding goal. Thus, ultimately, the need to attain comes out of ambiguity, the work of manas or awareness-of awareness, because, as the Lankavatara Sutra says, "Willing and thinking are inextricably woven in the texture of manas." However as we know this ambiguity is a harmonic of the more fundamental ambiguity, the schism in our very heart which gives rise to a separation, a separation that is expressed grammatically as subject and object, or I-It. The drive to overcome this separation, is uppermost in the mind; all the other levels of awareness that we have encountered such as pure awareness, knowing and being, awareness as awareness and awareness as being, are all in the background of the mind, present but ignored.

Let's now return to the monk shaken and beaten by Rinzai and ask what is his state of mind before the monk asks him to bow? A modern Zen Master, Shibayama roshi, talking about the role of the koan says,

> Suppose there is a completely blind man who trudges along leaning on his stick and depending on his intuition. The role of the koan is to mercilessly take the stick away from him and to push him down after turning him around. Now the blind man has lost his sole support and

intuition and will not know where to go or how to proceed. He will be thrown into the abyss of despair. In the same way, the koan will mercilessly take away all our intellect and knowledge. In short, the role of the koan is not to lead us to satori easily, but on the contrary to make us lose our way and drive us to despair.[14]

Rinzai is doing physically what the koan is doing spiritually; they both thrust the student into despair beyond hope of redemption by words. Both exhaust all the resources of his being. Words are a great release, but they are, at the same time, a great bondage. A Zen master expressed this by saying, "The thief, my child." In his interviews with the teacher the student will be told repeatedly, "Go beyond words, do not use words, let go your belief in 'something.'" It is by being pushed constantly in this way that the student "exhausts all the resources of his or her being." All the resources of the intellect means the verbal escapes and conceptual detours, and, when these are exhausted, the student ceases to run after the last word of Zen.

The fox monk, too, is pushed: "Is there a way out?"

"Yes," and one is punished.

"Is there a way out?"

"No," and one is released from punishment.

In being released from punishment a way out is seen to be possible and so one is punished. This spiritual double bind lies at the very heart of consciousness.

On Spiritual Irony

Zen is part of the Mahayana tradition of Buddhism, of which one of the more important schools is the *Prajna Paramita* school. *Paramita* means crossing to the other shore, beyond ambiguity. Prajna means to arouse the mind without resting it on anything, to release the mind from its obsession with the last word. Prajna Paramita thus means to reach the other shore beyond ambiguity by arousing the mind without resting upon anything.

To help us understand arousal of the mind, or what in Zen is called the "leap," let's consider irony, in which there is a leap not too dissimilar to the leap of prajna. This can give us a very clear hint of what is called for. Koans, with some latitude, can be regarded as forms of spiritual irony. Edward Conze, a well-known Buddhist scholar, called Zen "the Prajna

Paramita tradition with jokes." Mumon, the compiler of the collection of koans called the *Mumonkan*, uses irony constantly in the commentaries he appends to each koan.

A celebrated use of irony occurs in Shakespeare's play *Julius Caesar* during Mark Antony's address to the crowd just after Caesar has been assassinated by conspirators. When Mark Antony begins his speech "Friends, Romans, countrymen, lend me your ears. . . ." the crowd is very much on the side of the conspirators, thinking they had freed Rome from a tyrant. Early in the speech Mark Antony refers to Brutus, one of the conspirators, as an "honorable man." The crowd naturally interprets the designation as a compliment to Brutus. As the speech progresses, however, the expression "honorable men" is repeated no less than six times and at each repetition there is a heightened tension in the words until, at the end of the speech, Mark Anthony says,

> I fear I wrong the honorable men
> whose daggers have stabbed Caesar; I do fear it.

With this none but the dullest could be left in any doubt that what is really meant is "I fear I wrong these *thoroughly disreputable and dishonorable men'*." But Mark Antony does not castigate them in this way. Not because he is afraid of the crowd—by this time he has them thoroughly on his side—but because to castigate like this lacks the power of irony.

The strength of irony lies in the leap that must be made to appreciate the irony. This leap is to a new viewpoint, which gives a sudden change of context. It is similar to the sudden change of viewpoint that occurs when one sees the other aspect of the ambiguous picture of the young and old woman. However, whereas this latter change of viewpoint could be seen as a horizontal leap, in irony it is as though the leap is to a higher viewpoint. In his book *The Rhetoric of Irony*, Wayne Booth says, "The process of reading irony is like a leap or a climb to a higher level."[15] In the example from Shakespeare, it is as though the leap is made from "Brutus is an honorable man" to "Brutus is a thoroughly disreputable character." I say "it is as though" there is a leap to a higher viewpoint because in this "it is as though" lies the power of irony.

Let me explain. When encountering Mark Antony's irony, one is first led to infer he is saying that Brutus and the conspirators are honorable. He says,

If I were disposed to stir
Your hearts and minds to mutiny and rage,
I should do Brutus wrong, and Cassius wrong,
Who, you all know, are honorable men.

But by the end of his speech when he says,

I fear I wrong the honorable men
Whose daggers have stabbed Caesar.

The crowd roars out, "They were traitors!"

"They were traitors" is the higher viewpoint. Through the power of
Mark Antony's rhetoric everyone knows the conspirators have done a
dreadful and dishonorable thing. Because of this rhetoric all wish to leap
to this higher viewpoint, "They are not honorable at all!" But irony has
power because *one does not in fact make the leap* but stays instead with the
old viewpoint even though the leap calls out to be made. Indeed the
louder and more clamorous the call, and therefore the greater the restraint
called for, the greater the power of the irony. It is the restraint of not
leaping that makes the difference between irony and sarcasm, because with
sarcasm one simply has to make the leap; and the pain of sarcasm lies
precisely in being bullied into making a leap in this way.

With this understanding of irony—a leap that is not a leap—let's
return now to the koan in which a monk, Joshu, asks Master Nansen
"What is the way?" Nansen replies, "Everyday mind is the way."

This response contains great irony because it is from this everyday
mind with its anxieties, problems, and torment that Joshu is trying to find
a way out. If a member of the crowd in Shakespeare's play did not understand that Mark Antony's speech was ironical he would be at a loss to
understand the savagery that develops in the crowd toward Brutus and the
other conspirators. In other words he would hear "Brutus is an honorable man" in a literal way, he would be taken in by it. In the same way
if one were taken in by Nansen's irony, one would wonder why Zen
Buddhists spend so many hours in meditation, why the long and painful
struggle? Indeed, it took sometime for Joshu to appreciate the irony and
even then Nansen had to say, "It [everyday mind] is like vast space." This

vast space is the higher viewpoint. However, to appreciate the koan one does not take the leap to the higher viewpoint but stays firmly in "every day mind is the way." When Joshu became a great teacher in his own right and someone asked him, "What is the highest teaching?" he replied, "When I am hungry I eat, when I am tired I sleep." The only way really to see the aptness of the koan and to experience its power is to resist the leap and stay with the response just as it is; in the same way, to experience the power of irony one resists the leap to a new level. There is an enormous leap without any movement, without any change. This is seeing into a koan and it is the nature of awakening.

In a similar way we can look at the koan about the fox-master "Is an awakened person free from karma" as ironical.

The master said, "Yes!," and he was inviting the monk to make a leap—a leap to unity, to no ambiguity. In this there is no irony. Then, because karma comes in part from the unrealized parts of the ambiguity, and because the master chose one face and ignored the other, he left the other face unrealized. This means that as a fox, he had to live out this unrealized part of the ambiguity, the part that says there is ambiguity. The irony of the koan comes when Hyakujo said that an awakened person does not ignore the law of karma. He was pushing the fox-master fully into the ambiguity. He was calling for a leap of no leap. How does one "not ignore karma" other than by living it completely?

To appreciate fully this leap of no leap we must refer back to Mark Antony's irony. If you were to leap from "I fear I wrong these honorable men," you would leap to a higher viewpoint. This higher viewpoint is already embedded in the irony. The essence of the irony lies in the recognition that within the affirmation (Brutus is an honorable man) is embedded the negation (Brutus is a thoroughly dishonorable man). It is this negation that alone can make sense of the affirmative statement. With irony the viewpoint "Yes" requires and includes the viewpoint "No." In words with which we are now familiar, *this is that/this is not that*. However, the difference between irony and spiritual irony is that with the koan the leap is not to another alternative and opposing viewpoint, but a leap to *no viewpoint at all*. Indeed, many koans explicitly exclude the leap to a new and opposing view. For example, "If you say this is a stick I will punish you; if you say it is not a stick I will punish you! What is it?" You are damned if you do and you are damned if you don't. Zen Master

Hakuin likened it to a rat caught in a bamboo tube, unable to go forward, unable to go back, and cannot stay where it is. This is the fundamental double bind.

What does "leap to no view point at all" mean?

Recall that prajna means to arouse the mind without resting it upon anything. Suppose someone named George is absorbed in reading a book and a friend calls "George!" The mind of George is now thoroughly aroused but aroused to "What do you want, why do you call?" This is arousing the mind, but resting it upon something.

Now, if this "resting" is eliminated that is prajna. There is a leap, but to no new point of rest: a flash of pure knowing without content, a knowing that is its own being and which is not dependent upon knowing by reflection, knowing by concepts; that is knowing *something*. Knowing, which is its own being, is made possible by the awakening to unity upstream entirely of the search to reabsorb the null point. In terms of the Lankavatara Sutra, it is a turnabout in manas, a turnabout in "me" of me-as-center /me-as-periphery. It is a turnabout within subjectivity; a going beyond the person and so is not a psychological fact.

It is here that koans part company from irony and creativity. The leap of irony is really a leap of recognition, a leap from one form to another form, from one concept to another concept. "Brutus is an honorable man," is said in a context that can only mean Brutus is a dishonorable man. Everything cries out for the leap "Brutus is a traitor." Then recognition dawns. "Ah! Antony is being ironical." This recognition, a moment of creativity coming from dynamic unity, enables "yes" and "no" to maintain their opposition while becoming complements. "This" is "that" while all the while "this" is not "that." This means that irony requires words and concepts: yes and no, Brutus is honorable and Brutus is dishonorable. Thus irony, coming out of the basic ambiguity, is "a kind of exorcism," to use T. S. Eliot's phrase, which gives stability to consciousness.

On the other hand, the moment of truth in kensho is a moment not about the relation of concepts nor about the stability of consciousness. The yes/no of spiritual irony is not a yes/no of form but a yes of form and a no of beyond form. The yes/no of spiritual irony is (knowing/being)/ unity; it is not an exorcism but a fulfillment.

Let us consider another koan.

A monk asked Joshu, "Everything returns to the One. Where does the One return to?"

Joshu said, "When I was in Seishu I made a hempen shirt. It was a red one."

"Arouse the mind without resting it upon anything" is the same as saying, "All returns to the one." The monk is asking, "After the mind is aroused without its being rested upon anything, what then?" The monk interpreted "All returns to the one in a literal, that is non-ironical way." He saw it as a leap to emptiness, an absence. We cannot, however, stay there; to try to do so would be to make *something* of oneness. It is just on this shoal that most religions are shipwrecked. What is oneness, it is not an empty nothing nor a dark confusion; nor, at a more sophisticated level, is it the emptiness of the apophatic tradition nor even the emptiness of Samadhi taught by the Vedic tradition. To avoid these errors we must go on. But go on to where? If everything returns to the One what does the One return to?

Joshu says, "This shirt is red." This is the leap of no leap. In the Prajna Paramita school of Buddhism it is said "Form is only emptiness; emptiness only form."

Buddhism teaches that A is not A, that is why it is called A. Joshu's shirt is what it is. Joshu does not see it however as the unawakened person sees it: "something" out there, as a shirt; to see the shirt as Joshu would have seen it, one must go beyond ambiguity. To see it in this way we must leap to the one that goes beyond all duality. (A is not A). But we cannot stay there because. . . there is nowhere to stay. Everything returns to the one, including the one. "Where," asks the monk, "does the one return to?" This red shirt is one, this black pen is one, this flower is one. . . (that is why it is called A) but let us not be taken in by this.

> The moon's the same old moon,
> The flowers exactly as they were,
> Yet I have become the thingness
> Of all things I see![15]

A Hindu song sings, "The lord is in my eye, that's why I see him everywhere.

Everyday mind is the way.

Notes

1. Lucien Stryk and Takashi Ikemoto, *Zen: Poems Prayers, Sermons, Anecdotes* (New York: Doubleday Anchor, 1963) p.15.
2. D.T. Suzuki, *Studies in the Lankavatara Sutra* (Boulder: Prajna Press, 1981), p.167.
3. See more on this in Albert Low, *The Butterfly's Dream*, pp. 35-56.
4. Author's correspondence with Dr. William Byers, Professor of Mathematics, Concordia University, Montreal.
5. Katsuki Sekida, *Two Zen Classics* (New York: Weatherhill, 1977).
6. D.T. Suzuki (trans.), *The Lankavatara Sutra* (Boulder: Prajna Press, 1978), p. xxv.
7. Suzuki (1978, p 193).
8. Suzuki (1978, p 193).
9. Suzuki (1978, p 193).
10. Stryk and Takashi (1963, p. 7).
11. Suzuki (1981, pp. 200-201).
12. Maritain op. cit. p. 82.
13. Suzuki (1981, p.191)
14. Zenkei Shibayama, *Commentaries on the Mumonkan* (New York: Harper and Row, 1974).
15. Wayne C. Booth, *A Rhetoric of Irony* (Chicago: University of Chicago Press, 1974).
16. Martin Heidegger, *Essays in Metaphysics*, (New York: PhilosophicaL Library,1960), p. 30.

Chapter 23

Music:
A Window Upon Consciousness

We experience music by listening to it, and at the same
time we experience ourselves as listeners to music.[1]
VICTOR ZUCKERKANDL

The Word and the Evolution of Consciousness

OUR INQUIRY INTO EVOLUTION, creativity, and spirituality has brought us to the conclusion that they all come to a head with the creation of the *word*. Preceded by tension, distress, and conflict, the word emerges suddenly. This creation, the latest leap in evolution, is the original religious ceremony upon which all other ceremonies are modeled; it is also the paradigm for all human creativity. The emergence of the word is also the emergence of consciousness, an emergence that goes on ceaselessly, wandering up blind alleys, faltering and stumbling but always going forward. The cost of meandering, faltering, and failing is pain and violence; the benefit of the forward thrust is ever-greater security and flexibility.

The word (or, if one prefers, language), that fragile bridge across the abyss of ambiguity inhabited by the monsters of dread and violence, makes possible *stable reflection*. Stable reflection is more commonly called self-awareness, but stable reflection is a more descriptive phrase and does not reinforce the illusory notion of a self. Whereas animals and humans have the capacity to reflect, this reflection is not stable in animals, because, although capable of highly sophisticated communication, animals do not have language. Stable reflection is awareness-of awareness that endures because the danger of awareness collapsing in on itself in a vortex of anguish, pain, panic, and antagonism is, for a time, held at bay by language.

Élan vital?

The dynamism of evolution comes from oneness/(knowing/being), that is from the ambiguity this represents and from which the null point emerges. The dynamism is a drive towards reabsorbing the null point and so rediscovering unity. This drive, therefore, goes in one direction only and gives rise to *time's arrow*. This drive makes evolution necessary and all that evolves is a manifestation of it. The orthodox interpretation of evolution would say that evolution is an entirely purposeless affair that just happens by accident and so requires no underlying impetus. This point of view has been under attack, one way or another. Henri Bergson, for example, suggested an *élan vital* that provides the dynamism for evolution. However, what we are saying precludes the need for any special force or élan vital to provide the impetus for evolution. Evolution is the fulfillment of the imperative "Let there be one!" in the face of the basic ambiguity.

Orthodoxy says the reason for evolution is the struggle for survival in which only the fit survive, but no agreement has been reached on what those who survive are most fitted for, other than survival. But, now we can see that fitness to survive is a function of the ability to contain the ambiguity that underlies a given set of circumstances. The more stable but flexible the container, the greater the range of circumstances with which the container can contend. Ambiguity, not the jungle, therefore is the arena in which fitness is proven. The creation of the Word is a quantum leap in stability and flexibility, and has thus increased immeasurably the fitness of the human being to survive.

Telling the Word

The original word was *told* not spoken: the spoken word being a secularized version of the original word that was told. In keeping with this, the word would have been a *poetic* word, not bald prose which can only come into being when words are written down and so conventionalized and defined. With the arrival of prose, words would come to *refer* to a situation by *standing for it* and so would no longer be an essential part of it.

The example of a conversation will help illustrate the implications of what I mean by telling. To be engaged in a conversation is quite different from making a written report about it. Conversations contain the ambiguity, both in structure and content.[2] Most conversations follow a zigzag course, weaving in and out of contradiction and ambiguity. Not infrequently a person will stop halfway through a sentence and begin another, only to stop once more and start again, the whole weight and density of what he or she wants to say is so great a single sentence cannot contain it. The weight and density come from the contradictions and ambiguities. Conversation therefore falls more into the class of what I have called "telling." One tells another what happened. A conversation contains the ambiguity while the written report, at best, refers to it or, more frequently, ignores it, by selecting certain aspects and rejecting the rest. Indeed, the greatest difficulty in writing this book lies just in the fact that I have had to "refer," or point, to the ambiguity thus making the reader hold it at arm's length. But, as soon as it becomes objective in this way, the ambiguity loses its bite; that living, dynamic quality I want so much to bring to the reader's notice, is lost.

This ability to abstract certain aspects while ignoring the rest is greatly facilitated by logic, which says, in effect, ambiguity is unacceptable and all statements must be clear and distinct. The poetic word, which is at the opposite end of the spectrum to logic, contains fully the ambiguity and this is why the original word would have been a poetic word. The word *poetry* comes from the Greek *poiesis,* which means "creation." The beauty of words is they are self-generating, or autopoietic. In a manner reminiscent of evolution itself, languages evolve and proliferate, creating new species in the process.[3]

"Telling" is used in the same way that tell in "tell a story" is used. Young children love to hear a story told and insist upon the story being told exactly the same way each time. Thus telling is not communicating, but something quite different. It is a way by which stable awareness is maintained through ambiguity being securely contained. Originally, the bards would "tell" the myths of the tribe, chanting or singing them often to the accompaniment of stringed instruments. The storyteller or bard was highly revered because telling the story of the tribe gave stability. The storyteller held consciousness in place because, without the story, the dark powers could erupt bringing havoc and destruction. Later these myths were enacted in mystery plays, then in theater and so to the films, plays and novels of today. In this way it could be said the sit-com is heir to the mystery plays.

The Word and Song

In the original telling, because of the intensity of the forces being held together and contained, besides being poetic, the word was sung and danced; and only later, when the word was fused with communication, would slower speech have evolved wherein words became things. Victor Zuckerkandl, an authority on music, said, "Many investigators assume that speech was originally a sort of chant, and that it was only during evolution that the two branches separated into the language of words and the language of tones."[4] Leonard Bernstein said, "I have often thought that, if it is literally true that "In The Beginning Was The Word," then it must have been a *sung* word, and that God would have sung *Y'hi Or* [Let there be light] rather than simply have said it."[5]

It should not escape our attention that singing, chanting and dancing have always played an important part in religious ceremonies because, as emphasized above, an important function of religion has been to hold the creative word in place. As the original word was likely sung and danced, we could expect that an analysis of music will give us another way of looking at the basic ambiguity and at what is meant by "stable reflection." We have come to see music as a form of entertainment, and, just as the word has degenerated into chatter, so music has degenerated into *muzak*. Yet at its height, music can be looked upon as a window into consciousness itself, and it is from this perspective that I am considering the role of music.

The rituals of the Navajo Indians beautifully illustrate the connection between music, words and religion. In the Navajo's life, song is everywhere: in ceremony, dance, herbal medicines, poetic texts, mythic background, body painting, the making of prayer offerings, and the great sand paintings. Furthermore religion, like music, is all-pervasive. "The

Navajo's world is inclusive: the sacred is not compartmentalized in any one time or space but is everywhere. Art is appreciated for its own sake, but also for its essential functions in exorcising malign powers and invoking benign powers to heal disharmony in one's relation with the cosmos."[6] Art, therefore, is appreciated for its essential function of containing the ambiguity.

One particularly interesting ceremony is the ceremony of the pollen. A pinch of pollen is taken, a small amount is deposited on the tongue, another on top of the head and the rest scattered in front of the celebrant, or up toward the sun, blessing the place where the ceremony is taking place. The pollen on the tongue is a blessing of the breath of life and that breath made articulate in speech. "The most potent force in the Navajo Universe is wind given form in speech or song. To the Navajo the word is not the symbol of the object but . . . quite the other way around. Any given object is only one, transitory, imperfect manifestation of the word." Something of the force of the song for the Navajo can be understood from the following:

> The directions of the world, the deities who live there, the powers of the wind, and the articulation of the wind in speech and more powerfully yet, in the sacred phrases of ritual song are all implied, [in the song]. When the singer lifts his voice [in song] *the identification of humankind with all the forces takes place.*[7]

This echoes what we have said about the uttering or chanting of the first word: at that moment all was at One with all.

Music and Dynamic Unity

Music, the word, and religion at their inception were not isolated, separate phenomena. Evolution, however, proceeds through an emphasis upon one or other aspect of the ambiguity and this in turn brings about a steady differentiation. The word stabilized the ambiguity by fixing experience and so made things, entities, qualities, and so on possible. Music on the other hand favors the dynamic aspect and makes dynamic unity audible. Obviously, insofar as "the most potent force in the Navajo Universe is wind," the Navajo looked upon unity as dynamic in much the same way as we are doing. When I talk of oneness, I too am referring to the dynamic source of all energy and movement. Furthermore, ambiguity and dynamic unity are not something abstract and remote from us. The effect of ambiguity is ever present in us as tension, anger, anxiety, depression, joy, and enthusiasm. It gives rise to the dualities of the structure within the organism: the biceps and triceps, the systolic and the diastolic blood pressure, the left and right brain, the sympathetic and the parasympathetic nervous systems, the thyroid and the parathyroid, and so on. Ambiguity, too, is contained by all the structures we see around us: in some it is held rigidly in what we call matter; in others a range of flexibility is found and this we call life. Most flexible of all is the container we call consciousness, with the word as its original structure. All these structures come out of the intention, or *drive* forward, a *drive* toward the null point. This same drive has created music; nothing so far has been able to excel in flexibility that dimension of the word we call music, particularly music as it has been developed in the West. Music is a perfect, flexible container for ambiguity and in it we find a concrete expression of what we have been saying about dynamic unity, ambiguity, the search for the center, and so on. Music allows dynamic unity, to be *heard*. In the same way that some words are stains, which make accessible insights too fine to be directly known by the conscious mind, so we shall see music too, in its way, is a stain making dynamic unity audible.

The Meaning of Music

Zuckerkandl says that when we think of music, "We instinctively think of a language." What the two have mostly in common, he says, is both *mean* something. However, whereas music and its meaning are one, the meaning of a word is *external* to it. *Here* is the word, a complex of sounds or signs; that object over *there* is what the word means. By referring to what the word means, we can translate from one language to another, but we cannot translate from the music of one culture to that of another. Whereas words mean what they point to, with music *the pointing is the meaning*. This means that they are static while music, because the meaning is in the pointing, is essentially dynamic.

What Zuckerkandl suggests is one way the connection between words and their meaning can be understood. A good example of the words to which he refers are words that one might meet with in a set of written instructions on how to assemble an appliance. In *Science and Sanity*, Alfred

Korzybski proclaimed with great joy that words are not the thing, the map is not the territory. Implicit in this is just what Zuckerkandl is saying: words point to things. Korzybski said, "All language can be considered as names either for unspeakable entities on the objective level, be it things or feelings, or as names for relations."[8] Although this may be true in sophisticated communication using words, it is not true for the more original use of words, nor is it true of poetic words. Zuckerkandl comes nearer to what we mean by "word" when he talks about religious symbols. These, he says, are not mere signs indicating or pointing to the divine being. Rather, he says, the "Deity is directly present in the symbol, is one with it. Here, the symbol is that to which it points, it is God."[9] This is true of the Word, as well as words used in a poetic, creative way. Here both music and the word point, but music just points whereas the word points to itself. When one sings poetic words, therefore, the effect is to give words enormous power. The very singing itself is a full expression of the ambiguity and the dynamism or pointing that comes out of it.

Music: Knowing or Being?

A basic question has recurred repeatedly throughout this book: what relation do knowing and being have to one another? Is the one a function of the other or are they independent of each other? This same question arises if one thinks about music. Is it simply a physical phenomenon, or is it a purely mental one, pure subjectivity? Or is a third alternative possible, one that can include both knowing and being, yet is neither? Zuckerkandl says,

> We must not forget that our language, which conforms to our mode of thought, provides a vocabulary for physical phenomena and for psychic phenomena, *but none for phenomena that belongs to neither class:* (my italics) a source of frequently insuperable difficulties in all investigations that do not readily fit into the traditional pattern of thought.[10]

This difficulty of talking about that which belongs exclusively "to neither the physical nor the mental," neither being nor knowing, has plagued us throughout this book, forcing me to talk in circuitous and obscure ways about things which are in themselves very clear and direct.

Zuckerkandl says music does not come out of the physical nor out of the psychic component but out of *a third, a purely dynamic, component.* I want to pursue this intriguing idea as it is so close to the very basis of what I have been saying about dynamic unity that underlies creativity and evolution. Is it possible this third, *a purely dynamic* component of which Zuckerkandl speaks is in some way related to dynamic unity?

Because of dynamic unity, the world/life/consciousness is always going *somewhere,* and that somewhere is always *toward* the center. *Going to* the center is the purpose and goal of existence. Now this same going *toward* the center underlies music also. "Listening to music," says Zuckerkandl, "we are *between tones* [my italics] from tone to tone."[11] What he calls, *external-psychic,* and what we have called one/knowing/being, "would then prove to be something purely dynamic, not feeling but force—a force for which the physical would be as it were transparent."[12]

Let me again quote Zuckerkandl to help us make this point clear.

> To hear a tone as dynamic quality, as a direction, a pointing, means hearing at the same time beyond it, beyond it in the direction of its will, and going toward the expected next tone. Listening to music, then, we are not first in one tone, then in the next, and so forth. We are rather always between tones, on the way from tone to tone; our hearing does not remain with the tone, it reaches through it and beyond it."[13]

The essential point is this: that with music we *hear dynamic unity.* In order for you to see how this relates to the main themes of the book, let me recapitulate the presentation we gave earlier of how dynamic unity emerges.

Recapitulation

At the origin is unity, unity as intelligence, unity that is reality itself. Oneness/ knowing /being. At this original level, knowing and being are not two: knowing *or* being; but they are not one: knowing is knowing; being is being. Then knowing separates *as* being, what we have called "awareness-as being." At this stage an incipient dualism appears. The mirror reflects itself. This is called samadhi in Sanskrit. I wrote about this progressive separation of knowing/being in experiential terms in *The Butterfly's Dream.*

Knowing as being prepares the way for the next step: knowing *or* being. A further ambiguity emerges with the emergence of knowing as being and knowing *or* being. One of the difficulties that our later explanation of music will help us to overcome is that knowing and being, as words, are abstract terms *although what they refer to is the very opposite of abstraction.* By *being* I mean *reality*; by *knowing* I mean *that which makes everything possible as an experience.* Look around the room: that is knowing/being; you know the room, you see the chair, you hear the sounds, you feel the warmth. Seeing, hearing, feeling: these are modifications of knowing. The chair, the sounds. the temperature, these *are*. We use the word being for all that is. Feel whatever it is that you are presently feeling: interest, boredom, anxiety, frustration: that too is knowing/being. Furthermore, the ambiguities that emerge come out of the very nature of knowing/being. Knowing/being is itself ambiguity and is the source of all ambiguities. Ambiguities are not the result of some external influence.

An example at the human level of an ambiguity that emerges out of knowing/being is the very inability to determine the relation of knowing and being This inability has been a main theme of this book with the ever present need, nevertheless, to try to do so. A multitude of myths, philosophies, and variations on this question of the relation of knowing and being have proliferated over the years and in all parts of the world. The inability of philosophers to find a resolution to this question is not only because of the limitation of the human mind but also because the human mind itself comes from ambiguity and life's endeavor to find a resolution.

Another ambiguity is seen once one tries to answer the question "What am I?" I am, but *what* am I?"

Oneness is an imperative: "Let there be one!" Faced by the ambiguity of "knowing or being" and, unable to resolve it in favor of one or the other, an oscillation of knowing and being begins. The oscillation increases in speed because oneness is oneness, an absolute, and cannot be denied. You cannot have relative degrees of oneness, of either knowing or being. I am well aware that some people may object to what I am saying and will argue that the opposition of knowing and being is not cosmic but human, coming from the way the human mind operates. Such an objection comes from a belief that the human mind is an arbitrary appearance that just happened to arise in nature. I am saying, on the contrary, that no distinction can be made between the cosmic and the human except the distinction of scale. This is implicit in the ancient idea of the microcosmos, or monad. Far from being an accident, consciousness is essential and inevitable; it has arisen out of the very nature of existence.

Oneness is absolute, and yet the oscillations cannot reach an infinitely fast speed; they cannot go above a certain ceiling and so another hiatus occurs. The limitation comes from the null interval, the interval that is neither knowing nor being. I illustrated the null interval by asking you to consider the transition from observer to participant, or to see the old woman and then see the young woman of the Gestalt picture. When going from one to the other, a null interval arises that is neither one nor the other. We also referred to Escher's Man at a Picture Gallery to help illustrate this point, and said the white circle in the picture hides the null interval, which is neither observer nor participant.

When the duration of knowing or being is as short as the null interval, freezing occurs. If the oscillations were to exceed this limit, both knowing and being would swallow each other in a vortex of annihilation, a vortex of knowing/swallowing/being, being/swallowing/knowing, neither of which can occur, as each is equally valid. This freezing gives rise to what I have called the null point, which can neither be known nor said to be, but is not imaginary nor nothing; the null point is a unity, but a polar opposite to Unity, because Unity is totally inclusive, the null point totally exclusive. One of the things that I have pointed out earlier is the enormous unlimited power of unity, a power I have tried to convey by saying it is absolute. The null point has all the power of unity but in an inverse way. It would be as though an infinite implosion and an explosion were occurring constantly and simultaneously. The old physics question of what happens when an irresistible force meets an immovable object is perhaps also trying to convey what we are trying to describe.

With the emergence of the null point, and the implacable opposition of the inclusive and the exclusive that this generates, a completely new kind of creativity or energy arises. Because the word *creativity* suggests "knowing," and *energy* suggests something physical, I have opted for the expression *dynamic unity*, which is both knowing as creativity and being as energy. Dynamic unity can be considered to be a field centered upon a point, which is both source and destination, and we have symbolized this as:

Knowing/being have no dynamism of their own. It is only in the presence of the categorical imperative, "Let there be one!" that dynamism arises, an irresistible dynamism in the face of an implacable barrier set up by the null area. On the other hand, although knowing/being is without power, without knowing/being the dynamism of unity would be without form. All forms, from the photon to the human being, from the first word to the world's civilizations are media for the expression of the one.

Stephen Hawkins said that if we attain a true understanding of life and the world then,

> It should be understandable in broad principle by everyone, not just a few scientists. Then we shall all, philosophers, scientists, and just ordinary people, be able to take part in the discussion of the question of why it is that we and the universe exist. If we find an answer to that, it would be the ultimate triumph of human reason — for then we would know the mind of God.[14]

I am suggesting that by listening to music we do not come to know the mind of God but we do hear the voice of God. This idea becomes all the more compelling when we realize the Hebrew word for the voice of God is *dabhar*, the basic meaning of which is "to be behind and drive forward"; dabhar "is dynamic both objectively and linguistically."[15]

Thus, I concur with Zuckerkandl that when we hear music we hear force, dynamic unity, dabhar; what is behind and drives forward. This force does not have its origin in either the objective or the subjective, in the mind or in the physical world. This is why Zuckerkandl says the dynamism of music "works through the physical without touching it." If music is the voice of dynamic unity, by studying this voice we shall learn more about dynamic unity itself.

Music as a Force

To acquire status in the world, Zuckerkandl says, a thing has to make good its claim by being tangible and visible. "If I see something that I cannot touch, if I touch something that I cannot see, if I hear something without discovering a tangible-visible source for it, I know that I am deluded."[16] We have invented instruments of many kinds to enable us to extend the range of the tangible-visible. Even so, all that instruments reveal to us is still ultimately tangible and visible. Sense perceptions, which are not simply delusions, are then perceptions of phenomena in the objective world. Nevertheless, a class of phenomena exists that are not subject to the tangible visible test, and not necessarily delusory. These are subjective phenomena: dreams, thoughts, emotions, pain, and so on. Thus, we arrive at two quite distinct real worlds, the outer and the inner, the objective and the subjective.

A real sound and an imagined sound are quite different; a note, played on a violin, is obviously a phenomenon of the external world. It comes from the vibration of air; a vibration put into motion by the violin string being scraped by the bow. The care with which violins are made, tuned, and cared for testifies to the fact that these sounds are phenomena of the external world. If something changes in the sound, something must have changed in the physical process, either in the violin or in the way the violin is played.

This, however, is only true of the sound on its own, or of a set of sounds played randomly, not to the sound as a *musical event*. In the musical event a dynamic quality in sounds emerges. The important thing about this musical event is that nothing corresponds to it in the physical event. To quote Zuckerkandl, "We say we hear, that is perceive in the external world through the sense of hearing, something in the tones of a melody to which nothing in the physical world corresponds."[17]

Before continuing I must make a preliminary distinction between sounds and *tones*. We shall be elaborating upon this distinction as we progress through this chapter. For the moment, let it be noted that tones are sounds within a musical structure. By musical I mean Western Classical music. What this definition means in detail will emerge as we go on.

If it is true that, as Zuckerkandl says, nothing in the physical world corresponds to the play of forces in tones, is it because these forces cannot be found in the tones themselves but, instead, must be sought in the mind of the hearers? If the force is not in the objective world and is not delusory, then it would have to be a subjective phenomenon.[18] William Van Dyke Bingham says, "The unity which marks the difference between a mere succession of discrete tonal stimuli and a melody, arises not from the tones themselves: it is distributed by act of the listener."[19] One way that psychologists have tried to explain the phenomenon of melody is by saying we are conditioned to expect certain sequences in music and by working with these expectations, by working with what are more popularly called the "association of ideas," a composer can produce musical tensions and effects. This theory, however, will not work because, according to Zuckerkandl, an analysis of musical compositions will show "in general the probability of tone y being followed by tone x is just as great as the probability that tone x will be followed by tone y." This destroys the credibility of the theory.

Zuckerkandl gives further reasons for rejecting the association and behaviorist theories of tonal meaning and says in conclusion:

> any theory which attempts to refer the possibility of the artistic experience back to conditioning, repetition, habit, learning, to sequences that have become mechanical, cannot but leave the element of creativeness out of account. Since every work of art is essentially creation (more accurately, creative discovery) no association or behaviorist theory can ever give an adequate interpretation of artistic phenomenon.[20]

So the question remains: we hear force in music; what is meant by this word force? Gravity is a force and so is electro magnetism. Is this the kind of force we are referring to? Gravity and electro magnetism are forces holding the world together as well as monitoring the nervous systems of human beings. However, while we do not directly perceive the force itself because it is not physical, it is still dependent upon the physical. Indeed, paradoxically, the only way we can know about it is through the action it has on material objects. However, we are not referring to this kind of force when we say one hears force. Nor are we talking about an immaterial force. "The talk of immaterial or super material forces, that is, of forces whose action is not manifested in a continuous material trace, we can now dismiss as fantasy or poetic metaphor."[21] "What," Zuckerkandl asks "would a force be that does not act in some body or other?"

We seem to be in the presence of a mystery, we hear force, but what we hear does not come from the external, objective, world, nor from the internal subjective world nor even from the kind of force dependent upon objects with which we have become familiar through physics. We must bear in mind that the word *force* is to be understood literally and not metaphorically. The phrase, Zuckerkandl maintains, means exactly what it says:

> We have encountered an action of forces which not only does not co-incide with its material consequences, but with which *no material phe-nomenon can be correlated at all.* Musical tones are created by a force, a dynamism, which does not leave any trace whatever in the material world. This force moreover is not a mental phenomenon, not purely subjective.[22]

Now this is precisely the kind of force that I call dynamic unity. It is not physical nor is it mental; not being nor knowing.

Awareness-of tone as Opposed to Awareness-as sound

If you are present at a parade in which soldiers are marching to a band, and there are many people around, you are aware-of noise: the shuffle of feet, people cheering, dogs barking, the noise of the band, and so on. But, we also hear more than just noise. In hearing noise *we reach through the sensation* to an object, to the marching feet, the barking dog, etc. With noise we can ask what makes the noise, in the same way that of the color, hardness, odor, we can ask, "What possesses the color, the hardness, the odor?" We cannot however ask this of tone because tone, as Zuckerkandl points out, is not the sensation of a thing. The conclusion Zuckerkandl draws is, because music exists, *the tangible and visible cannot be the whole of the given world.* "The intangible and invisible is itself part of the world, something we encounter, something to which we re-spond."[23] Now this is just the same conclusion that I reached when in Chapter 11 I discussed me and you.

To connect what Zuckerkandl is saying and what I said about me and you, let me be more precise and, instead of saying one is "aware-of noise," say one is "aware-*of* awareness-as noise," aware-*of* awareness-as the sound of marching feet, awareness-as the bark of the dog, awareness-as the cheer-ing. Similarly, to ask about color is to ask about awareness-as color, to ask about hardness, odor, and so on is to ask about awareness-as hardness, as odor and so on. In other words, we do not reach through the sensation to an object; we are awareness of awareness-as the object. But, this is not so with tones. Although we are aware-as sounds and aware-as noise, *we are not aware-as music.* We are aware-of music, directly aware-of tones. The force that Zuckerkandl speaks of, and what I have called dynamic unity, is what gives rise to 'focussed awareness.'

Focussed awareness is pure awareness (pure meaning without object.) It is true that when we hear music we hear sounds in succession that we call melody, or simultaneously which we call harmony. But these sounds in themselves are not music. The essence of music is what Zuckerkandl is calling force. To listen to music requires a kind of concentration — just start rustling paper at a public concert when the orchestra is playing the slow movement of Beethoven's 9th! I have even heard a conductor admonish the audience not to cough so much. We do not need a concentrated mind so that we can hear the *sound* of the music. A concentrated mind is 'awareness-of.' Music, which is the voice of dynamic unity is also the voice of 'awareness-of,' concentration, or attention. So the concentrated mind does not go out *towards* music. 'Going towards' is already the concentrated mind, and this means that it is also, already, music.

Intention and Focussed Awareness

Throughout this book I have been saying focussed awareness can be found only in association with awareness-as. It is like the sea and the waves; to have waves one must have the sea; to have focussed awareness, one must have awareness-as. Now we are speaking of *pure* focussed awareness. This is like talking about waves without the sea. What do we mean by "pure awareness." Upstream of focussed awareness a more fundamental force is active. This is called intention, drive, motivation, urge, and so on. Intention is intensely acitve as it is the emissary of dynamic unity. When it is expressed through awareness, intention becomes focused awareness, concentration, attention, or interest.

However, we must not think of intention as simply a mental event. We can see this is so if we think about the effect that music has on us. It is not simply the *mind* that is affected by the presence of music. The body is affected also, and this is evident in dancing, marching, or working in time with music. These activities we also associate with *intention,* which therefore is not simply expressed through awareness, but also directly through physical activity. When I stand up, walk, talk, eat and so on, this requires intention, which, I suggest is *idea in action*. But, as we were at pains to point out, idea is not something either mental or physical. It is a field. When this field is given a direction it becomes intention.

A reader might object and ask where the focused, dynamic unity is in walking or talking. But, it is a matter of degree. I remember seeing a woman on TV who won the women's marathon walking event in the Olympics. She was filmed making the last circuit of the event. She was quite evidently completely exhausted and in agony, but she did not stop. She just kept going. What was it that enabled her to keep going? Milt Erikson tells of his experience as a youth learning to walk again after having been smitten by polio and it is quite evident that it required immense commitment, or intention. If one sees a baby learning to walk one realizes how much intention is involved.

The Sufis use the word *himma* for what we are calling the emisary of dynamic Unity. Himma means, "the act of meditating, conceiving, projecting, ardently desiring—in other words having (something) in the *thymos* which is vital force, soul, heart, intention, thought, desire."[24] With himma dynamic unity is brought to bear directly, it is focused upstream of consciousness.

Music gives the field a direction. When we dance, march, or work to music we experience a certain freedom. This freedom is pure intention; intention freed by music. Thus, just as we could say music is hearing dynamic unity, we could also say music is hearing *intention*. When we move, dance, march, indeed even do something as simple as turn a page, intention is involved and intention, as such, is neither physical nor mental. Music, by using and transcending ambiguity, releases us from the burden of ambiguity and gives intention a freedom, a spontaneity. Everyone marches, dances, even works, with more freedom and spontaneity when these activities are accompanied by music. We can see from this how the ancients saw music as being an inspiration from the gods. Composing, playing, listening, and physically responding to music is the play of pure dynamic unity; it is dabhar, the voice of God. The question of psychic energy, mental energy, libido, *élan vital*, or whatever one might call it, is a crucial issue and one that has been hotly debated. It is our contention that dynamic unity fills the role that many of these energies have been called upon to fill although *it is not a specific kind of energy*. We cannot be aware as dynamic unity. This means that it is not accessible to any of our senses, nor can it be imagined or conceived, which is why many would reject it as fantasy.

An example of the difference between sound and music

How can we arrive at an understanding of the difference between sound and music in a more concrete way? If it is true that music is the voice of God, we should be able to use any piece of music to demonstrate what this means. Zuckerkandl uses as an example a melody from Beethoven's 9th symphony. I will use a piece that is better known: *Twinkle, Twinkle, Little Star*. If you are not familiar with music please do not despair and turn the page. The point that will be made is extremely simple but none the less vital for our whole thesis.[25]

If the last note of this melody were to be 're' instead of 'do', you would feel something was wrong, something is left unfinished, something is lacking about the whole thing. You would feel this regardless whether you are a musician or not, provided you are not tone-deaf. You might like to sing it to yourself to see the difference between having 're' as the final note and having 'do'. We accept 're' 're' 'do' but reject 're' 're' 're'. Why is this? What makes the difference? The difference obviously has something to do with the last note: 're' is wrong, 'do' is right. If we were to take the note 're' and play it completely on its own, then ask whether it is usable as a concluding tone, the question would not make sense, we could not get an answer. On its own the sound made by a violin, or a bird, or the horn of a truck, is not a tone. When I listen to sound, I am simply aware- of awareness-as the sound. However within the context of this melody, *Twinkle, twinkle little star*, the question *does* make sense. Within this context the note 're' lacks something. But what is wrong about it cannot be discovered through either an examination of the note on its own, or through an investigation of the associations and experiences we have had with it in its relation to other notes.

Zuckerkandl says we can best designate the quality in the note $\sharp$ 're'
in *Twinkle, Twinkle, Little Star*, as:

> a state of disturbed equilibrium, as a tension, a tendency, almost a will.
> The tone [is] active and seems to point beyond itself seeking, one might
> say, a release from tension and restoration of equilibrium. Furthermore,
> it seems to look in a definite direction for the event that will bring about
> this change; it even seems to demand the event.[26]

If we ask whether we can use the other note 'do' as a concluding
tone, this question too will not make sense, because it, too, by itself is
simply a sound. But when it is played at the end of the piece of music
it acquires a property that it does not have when played by itself. In the
context of *Twinkle, Twinkle, Little Star*, instead of having a disturbed equilibrium, of having tension and dissatisfaction, it has the opposite quality
that of satisfaction and relaxation of tension, and one might even say self-
affirmation.[27]

What takes place between the two tones is a sort of play of forces
comparable to those between a compass needle and a magnet. With one
of the tones, 're', the compass needle goes in a direction, points toward
and strives after a goal; with the other tone, 'do', the magnet dictates the
direction and draws or attracts to itself. The first wants to go beyond itself; the other to be itself.[28] In a keynote this tension is at its maximum
because, as we shall see in a moment, the keynote is both at the center
and at the periphery, magnet and compass, simultaneously.

"It is this dynamic quality that permits tones to become conveyors
of meaning," says Zuckerkandl.[29] To understand better how the dynamic
quality does this, we shall use a simple notation devised by Zuckerkandl.
It is quite elementary and should present no problem to anyone, even
those who say they know nothing about music.

A number of different keys are available to a composer when composing music. For example keys C, D, F, and so on. Each key or tonal
system has seven tones. To be able to designate the sequence of tones true
for all keys one can use the notation: $\hat{1}$ $\hat{2}$ $\hat{3}$ $\hat{4}$ $\hat{5}$ $\hat{6}$ $\hat{7}$. This
notation will help us see that any particular tone has a different dynamic
quality depending on the key in which it appears. Using these symbols,
Zucker-kandl points out that what we heard at the end of the melody

is not simply two sounds of definite pitch, 'd' and 'c,' but two tones having definite places in a seven-tone system. What this means is that tone 'd' in Key D, will be $\hat{1}$, but in key C it will be $\hat{2}$. We illustrated what is meant by "having a direction," "pointing beyond itself," and "one tone gravitating toward the other" by using re, the last tone but one of the melody Twinkle, Twinkle Little Star. This, in the notation that we are now using, is Tone $\hat{2}$ gravitating to a tone $\hat{1}$ of the same seven tone system. On the other hand, the other tone, tone $\hat{1}$ of that system, is the attraction, it gives direction, it points to itself.

The disturbed equilibrium, this striving after, this yearning, is not only a quality of 2. *All* the tones in a tonal system can be said to reach for, yearn for, the tonal center, tone $\hat{1}$. However, because each tone has a different position in the tonal system, each tone reaches for, or points to, the tonal center $\hat{1}$ in its own unique way. So although each tone is always One, always dynamic unity, this dynamic unity is always different in different tones. Thus, we could say that we do not hear individual tones but rather we hear *the multiplicity of unity.* Multiplicity of unity *is what we could call meaning* and it is this meaning that we respond to in music.

Each tone has a unique quality that comes from its relation to the keynote as source and center. The tone carries this relation within itself, and it gets its meaning from that relation. We can hear even the very first tone of a composition as meaningful and dynamically active as a musical tone because of the relation that it has with the key tone. This is so even though the opening tone may stand on its own for a while. However, and this is even more important, it is this relation that a tone has to its tonal center which evokes emotional response.

Music and Emotions

Music and emotions are undoubtedly connected, and many people have wondered about this connection, but so far no adequate explanation has been given. We all know martial music arouses pride, love songs arouse the feelings of love, funereal music makes us sad, dance music makes us feel lively, and so on. That music does this universally can be no accident. But no one has really been able to fathom what can be the connection between the meaning of music and the arousal of feelings. I am suggesting that the connection is to be found in the deep structure of ambiguity that is common to both emotions and music. Feelings and emotions arise out of this ambiguity, while music contains it. Feelings vary according to how and to what degree the ambiguity is contained. This gives support to the old platitude, "Music [which helps contain the ambiguity] soothes the savage breast."

Leonard Bernstein maintained that a universal musical competence, similar to Chomsky's universal linguistic competence, is present in us all. This belief was encouraged by a discovery he made that the same four notes were used by a variety of different composers as basic themes for their music. He noticed that the first four notes of the Copland variations, which are the germ of the whole composition, are the same four notes used as the subject, or motto, in Bach's C-sharp Minor Fugue, the variation to Stravinsky's Octet, Ravel's Spanish Rhapsody, *and* some Hindu music that he recalled. "From that time to this," he said, "the notion of an inborn musical grammar has haunted me."[30]

One of the more striking examples of this inborn grammar is that children tease one another using two very special notes. The same notes are used when calling to one another and are used in singing games and in games of tag. Bernstein notes that,

> Research seems to indicate that this exact constellation of two notes (and its three note variation) is the same all over the world, wherever children tease one another, on every continent and in every culture. In short, we may have a clear case of a musico-linguistic universal.[31]

Anyone who saw the film *Death in Venice* must surely remember the theme music. It was the Adagietto from Mahler's Symphony Number 5, a haunting, swooning piece of music with an aching yearning, of something unresolved, unattained. The yearning quality comes, as one might now begin to expect, from ambiguity. Musically, it is *the same ambiguity that underlies the teasing song of children*. Let us clarify this. In the opening bars of the Adagietto, Bernstein pointed out, is some preliminary vamping on a harp, vamping which is *syntactically* ambiguous regarding the beat and meter and regarding the key. The key of the Adagietto is F, but this key is only *suggested* by the harp because in the tonic triad it plays only the tones A and C, leaving out the very *center* of the triad, the fundamental note F. This arouses ambiguity because the two notes we hear could turn out to be two -thirds of an entirely different triad, namely, A minor; one is therefore not sure which key one is really in. The importance of this is brought out if we recall what we have just been saying about the importance of the tonal center in giving meaning to the tonal structure.

Bernstein however goes on further and points out that, "It is exactly like that children's teasing chant . . . Those two same notes . . . the tonic fundamental of those two overtones is not sung because it is present by implication only."[32] We must bear in mind that the tonal center serves the same function in music as the dynamic center serves in consciousness, indeed they are one and the same, or rather the one is giving voice to the other. If the center is ambiguous, then either a yearning for its appearance or pain because of its absence arises.

It could be said in the Adagietto a musical structure has been established that has *two centers*, when in the nature of things there *can only be one* center. Or, to use terms with which we are more familiar, *the music has a structure which has F as center and simultaneously F as periphery: [me-as-center/me-as-periphery.]* This means that this piece of music takes us to the very source of experience. Not only this but, depending on the context, the tension generated by violating the expectation of a firm tonal center can give one of two results: a yearning, loving, wanting-to-come-together, as in Mahler, or an irritating, hurtful, separating, wanting to reject as in the teasing of the children. For the Sufi, God was yearning, the yearning that is a basic impulse in the universe, the whole yearning to be united with the center, to reabsorb the center. This Adagietto of Mahler gives this yearning musical form. On the other hand, the teasing notes of the children give musical form to the absence of the center giving pain and anguish leading to violence and, in the case of the Aztecs, for the need for perpetual human sacrifice. The same two notes point to the same ambiguous but absent center: the center that is also at the periphery.

Music, therefore, does not *express* emotions. Emotion is the response to ambiguity, the multiplicity of unity. A deeper understanding of what this means can be gained by referring to the idea of *tonal motion*. Tonal motion, according to Hegel, "echoes the motion of the innermost self." "[Music] penetrates with its motion directly into the inmost seat of all motion of the soul." This motion of the soul includes what we call feeling and emotion. Zuckerkandl says, "The unity of music and motion is primordial, not something artificial, it is not contrived nor is it learned."[33] So what is tonal motion?

Tonal motion

I have said that dynamic unity means unity going toward unity. This implies two unities, and indeed I have said that dynamic unity comes out of exclusive and inclusive unity. Nevertheless, I have insisted upon unity as *one,* indeed I have emphasized that a universal imperative insists, "Let there be one!" Let us therefore, using music as a metaphor, see how this contradiction can be understood. To do this let me discuss in more depth what I mean by unity is *going toward* unity.

Going toward implies motion, and motion implies both *something that moves,* and something that endures; something that is the same from one moment to the next. This implies *something that does not move* as a background, or frame of reference. "The only motion in the physical universe is motion relative to something else."[34] However, as I have emphasized, tones do not move; tones *are* movement. They are dynamic unity. Moreover, to hear tones is to hear nothing but tones; beside the tones there is nothing else. So where does the movement come from?

One of the more acceptable ways to explain the strange phenomenon of music as motion is to say tones move through tonal space and the full range of pitch available defines tonal space. Therefore, it could be said that each tone has its particular pitch, which gives it its particular place in tonal space. Movement would then be the rise and fall of the pitch of tones in tonal space. (Figure 29). This would be comparable to an display sign in which an arrow of neon light flashes back and forth, an illusion achieved by switching on and off different lights in sequence.

Although this explanation has some merit, it does not fully explain the dynamic quality of music, the feeling of movement, of advancing and receding, of being held in suspense; the feeling of the relief and failure to gain relief, and all the rest that comes when one listens to music.

Pitch, we can say, is not the *cause of motion* in music but a property of the sound of music. Zuckerkandl rejects the tonal space theory

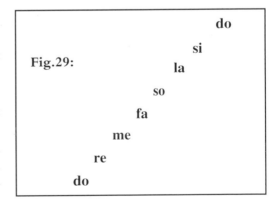

Fig.29:

do
si
la
so
fa
me
re
do

of movement and prepares the way for an alternative understanding by saying the atom of music is not the tone *but the interval between two tones.* [35]
This interval is not static, as it is in the above explanation, but dynamic,
and Zuckerkandl says that it is the difference in the dynamic quality which
makes the interval a musical phenomenon.[36]

This last statement is very important in gaining an understanding of
what the expression "going toward" implies. If we can understand what
is meant by "the difference in dynamic quality," we shall have no difficulty
with the statement: "The atom of music is *not the tone but the interval between two tones.*"

When we listen to a do-re-mi-fa scale being played, the last tone 'do'
is not simply a last tone of the series. What is more significant is that it
is also the *goal tone of the series.* Acoustically this goal tone is an octave
higher than the starting tone. But, *dynamically the goal tone is also the starting
tone,* because, as we know, do = do, C=C1 or, using the notation of
Zuckerkandl, $\hat{1} = \hat{8}$ This means we arrive at where we start.

do	re	mi	fa	sol	la	si	do
$\hat{1}$	$\hat{2}$	$\hat{3}$	$\hat{4}$	$\hat{5}$	$\hat{6}$	$\hat{7}$	$\hat{8}$

"The schema must be departure from . . . advance toward . . . arrival
at the point of departure as goal."[37] This means that at the beginning the
motion goes in one direction, and at the end it appears to go in the
opposite direction. The point at which the direction is reversed is $\hat{5}$. Let
us recall that all tones are striving towards $\hat{1}$ as the center. What I am now
saying is that all motion from $\hat{1}$ to $\hat{5}$ is motion against the forces in operation that is away from $\hat{1}$ while the motion is a force striving towards
$\hat{5}$. With the attainment of $\hat{5}$ the motion is now with the forces going
in the direction of $\hat{8}$. This is because as we have said $\hat{1} = \hat{8}$. In addition this means $\hat{5}$ points both ways and is therefore a complement of $\hat{1}$.

Let me elaborate upon that. We have said $\hat{1}$ is both source and goal,
which, in the terms that we have developed, is me-as-center/me-as-pe-
riphery, and could be visualized thus $\longleftarrow \hat{1} \longrightarrow$. $\hat{5}$ could also be visualized in this same way, but this time as a mirror image $\longrightarrow \hat{5} \longleftarrow$ Music, in its very basic structure, coincides with the basic structure under-

lying life, which we have shown to be the basic ambiguity.

Figure 31 will help illustrate these ideas:

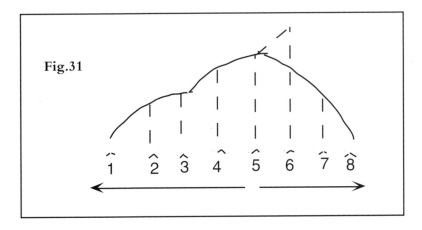

Figure 31 shows the organization of the dynamic field as it reveals itself when going up the scale.

At the beginning of the scale, tone $\hat{2}$ and $\hat{3}$ are going away from $\hat{1}$ — that is against the force coming from their attraction to $\hat{1}$. After a given point in the scale, although the pitch of the tones continues to rise, in other words *without changing tonal direction,* the tones go *toward* $\hat{1}$. The tonal center to which tones go in the descending segment of the curve on the way home *is exactly the same tone* they left behind in ascending segment. This means in effect they go toward a tone by going away from it.[38] Leaving is a returning; the start is the goal. "In the beginning is my end," as T. S. Eliot says in *The Four Quartets.*

Put in a slightly different way, we could say that in a given key, let's say C, the tone C is the dynamic center, the source and destiny of all tones. C and C1 are not the same. There are two C's: one that we could designate as starting C while the other is goal C1. To get from C to C1 one must climb through 7 pitch variations. And yet C and C1 are both, at the same time, C: *there is no difference. C and C1 are both the dynamic center.*

However, and this is the crux of the issue, only one dynamic center is possible within a dynamic tonal system. Zuckerkandl defines a dynamic system as one in which the "whole is present and operative in each individual locus, in which each individual locus knows, so to speak, its position in the whole, its relation to a center."[39] If one does away with the one tonal center, one does away with Western classical music. Because C is both source and destiny, C is therefore both center as source and periphery as destiny. This, as I have said a number of times, in a dynamic system is impossible. Out of this impossibility comes dynamism, the yearning, the promise of resolution on one hand, and discord and insufferable pain on the other.

Life itself has the same underlying motion. We have the expression "I'm getting somewhere at last," or "My life isn't going anywhere." We get the feeling of being carried along on a stream. That life is a journey, that we are travelers, that life has a purpose, a goal. This is part of our basic myth. If we can understand what Zuckerkandl is saying about hearing dynamic motion, we will realize music is hearing life going somewhere. We are going toward the null point. This is the Promised Land. In music, in a way, the Promised Land is reached. A piece of music by one of the great composers gives great satisfaction. This comes from passing with them through different kinds of musical trials and finally arriving at the goal. However, I emphasize "in a way" music reaches the Promised Land. That it does not do so in fact is confirmed when one realizes that the composer goes on to compose more music and listeners search out new compositions.

Music and the Monad

My interest in making this study is not limited simply to music but, rather I wish to use music to make deeper truths accessible. When thinking about a *tonal system*, we must have in mind at the same time the monad. The tonal system is a monad. Robert Fludd, a sixteenth-century philosopher, was famous for his use of the Pythagorean notion of the monochord and used it as a symbol of the cosmos, the macro- as well as the microcosmos. Just as all tones within a given key are derived from the one tone so all elements of the monad are derived from the one. The macrocosmos as well as the microcosmos emanate from the one tone.

Dynamic unity changes as it progresses through the scale of tones 1-7, but although dynamic unity changes in this way, it never changes because it is one, and is always one. It is interesting to note that numbers can also illustrated this. Poincaré, for example, says, "Every whole number is detached from the others, it possesses its own kind of individuality, so to speak; each of them forms a kind of exception."[40] Marie-Louise

Von Franz in her book *Number and Time* comments upon this by saying, "this individual aspect of number appears to contain the mysterious factor that enables it to organize psyche and matter jointly."[41] This mysterious factor is unity. Every number is one; every number is the monad. Yet again every number is also part of an unbroken continuum. As Von Franz goes on to say, "every individual numerical form or structure qualitatively represents an indivisible whole. This continuum should not only be conceived of as an indivisible whole, but as a continuum in which every individual number represents the continuum in its entirety."[42] Zuckerkandl said something very similar about tones: "Although tone is always unity, always one, it is always different in different tones. Thus we could say that we do not hear individual tones but hear multiplicity in unity."[43]

Von Franz also says, "all numbers are simply qualitatively different manifestations of the primal one (the monad) . . . the unus mundus."[44] All numbers are qualitatively different manifestations of dynamic unity. This in turn is strikingly similar to what we said earlier of Ibn 'Arabi's understanding. This great Sufi master said that the universe is the whole and no individualized being can be that whole. Yet, as Corbin comments,

> Here we have a kind of kathenotheism verified in the context of a mystic experience; the Divine Being is not fragmented, but wholly present in each instance, individualized in each theophany of His Names, and it is invested in each instance with one of these Names that He appears as Lord.[45]

As the Zen master Hakuin say, "All beings are Buddha."

Let us remember Zuckerkandl's definition of a dynamic system as one in which the "whole is present and operative in each individual locus, in which each individual locus knows, so to speak, its position in the whole, its relation to a center."[46] Von Franz, Ib'n Arabi, Zuckerkandl, Hakuin, are each in their way expressing a common understanding: one is one yet also a multiplicity, and this multiplicity is not simply a collection but a dynamic Unity.

All of this takes us back to Leibniz's New Monadology in which he says,

> each [monad] has relations which express all the others, and that consequently, is a perpetual living mirror of the universe. And just as the same

town, when looked at from different sides, appears quite different and is, as it were, multiplied in perspective, so also it happens that because of the infinite number of [monads], it is as if there were as many different universes, which are however but different perspective representations of a single universe from the different points of view of each monad.[47]

A well known, and exceedingly beautiful metaphor for unity as multiplicity is to be found in the Buddhist classic text the Avatamsaka Sutra.

Innumerable ornaments in the form of small crystal marbles . . . are interlaced in various patterns forming a great complex network. Because of the reflection of light, not only does each and every one of these marbles reflect the whole cosmos including the continents and oceans of the human world down below, but at the same time they reflect one another, including all the reflected images in each and every marble, without omission.

And so we have come full circle, back to our initial chapter. All is One. Out of the shimmering luminescence of this One arise matter, life and consciousness, you and me.

Notes

1. Victor Zuckerkandl, *Man the Musician* (Princeton: Princeton University Press, 1976).
2. For more on this see Albert Low, The Butterfly's Dream
3. See Ludwig Wittgenstein, *Language Games.*[Any bibliog. data?]
4. Victor Zuckerkandl, *Sound and Symbol Music and the External world,* Trans. Willard Trask (Princeton: Princeton University Press, 1969).
5. Leonard Bernstein, *Six Talks at Harvard* (Cambridge: Harvard University Press, 1976), pp.15-16. Bernstein also said music is heightened speech. That Bernstein felt language and music are one is made clear by the structure of his talks which are divided into subheadings of: Musical Phonology, Musical Syntax, and Musical Semantics, headings which he owes to linguistics. He said, furthermore, that his interest in the unity of music and language came from a study of linguistics, particularly linguistics of the kind taught by Chomsky. He felt, as did Chomsky, a study of linguistics could shed light on the nature, structure, and function of the human mind, and he was convinced music too could give this kind of insight.
6. David P. McAllester, "Coyote's Song," *Parabola,* vol. V, no. 2, (May 1986), p. 49.
7. McAllester (1986), p. 49

8. Alfred Korzybski, *Science and Sanity* (Lancaster Penn: The International Non-Aristotelian Library Publishing Company, 1933), p. 20.
9. Zuckerkandl (1969, p. 69).
10. Zuckerkandl (1969, p. 60).
11. Zuckerkandl (1969, p. 137).
12. Zuckerkandl (1969, p. 63).
13. Zuckerkandl (1969, p. 65).
14. Stephen Hawkins, *A Brief History of Time* (New York: Bantam Books, 1988).
15. Thorlief Borman, *Hebrew Thought Compared with Greek* (New York: W.W. Norton, 1970), p. 65.
16. Zuckerkandl (1969, p. 55).
17. Zuckerkandl (1969, p. 22).
18. Zuckerkandl (1969, p. 42).
19. Zuckerkandl (1969, p. 44), quoting William Van Dyke Bingham, *Studies in Melody* (Baltimore: Monographic Supplement No. 50 of the Psychological Review), 1910.
20. Zuckerkandl (1969, pp. 45, 52).
21. Zuckerkandl (1969, p. 55).
22. Zuckerkandl (1969, p. 56).
23. Zuckerkandl (1969, p. 71).
24. Corbin (1969, p. 222).
25. By and large we are paraphrasing Zuckerkandl's explanation. See *Sound and Symbol*
26. Zuckerkandl (1969, p. 19).
27. Zuckerkandl (1969, p. 20).
28. Zuckerkandl (1969, p. 20).
29. Zuckerkandl (1969, p. 21).
30. Bernstein (1976, p. 7).
31. Bernstein (1976, p. 16).
32. Bernstein (1976, p. 197).
33. Zuckerkandl (1969, pp. 78-79).
34. Gary Zukav, *Dancing Wu Li Masters* (New York: William Morrow and Co.,1979) p.180.
35. Zuckerkandl (1969, p. 90).
36. Zuckerkandl (1969, p. 24).
37. Zuckerkandl (1969, p. 97).
38. Zuckerkandl (1969, p. 36).
39. Zuckerkandl (1969, p. 102).
40. Marie-Louise von Franz, *Number and Time* (Evanston: Northwestern University Press, 1974), p. 60.
41. Von Franz (1974, p. 61).
42. Von Franz (1974, p. 59).
43. Zuckerkandl (1969).

44. Von Franz (1974, p. 59).
45. Corbin (1969, p.121).
46. Zuckerkandl (1969, p, 59).
47. Morris op.cit p.13.

Appendix 1

Quantum Reality

The following are eight different views on Quantum reality. Leading physicists hold one or other of them.‡

Quantum reality #1

The Copenhagen interpretation, which says there is no deep reality. "This far from being a crank or minority position [is] . . . the prevailing doctrine of establishment physics."

Quantum reality #2

Reality is created by observation. Although the numerous physicists of the Copenhagen school do not believe in deep reality, they do assert the existence of phenomenal reality. What we see is undoubtedly real they say, but these phenomena are not really there without observation. "No elementary phenomenon is a real phenomenon until it is an observed phenomenon," is the way one physicist put it.

---

‡ Taken from Nick Herbert, *Quantum Reality: Beyond the New Physics: An excursion into the metaphysics and the meaning of reality* (New York: Doubleday Anchor, 1987).

Quantum reality #3

Reality is an undivided wholeness. This is a point of view stressed by the well known physicist David Bohm who said, "One is led to a new notion of unbroken wholeness which denies the classical analyzability of the world into separate and independently existing parts . . . The inseparable quantum interconnectedness of the whole universe is the fundamental reality."

Quantum reality # 4

The many worlds interpretation. Reality consists of a steadily increasing number of parallel universes.

Quantum reality #5

The world obeys a non-human kind of reasoning. Some quantum logicians claim that the quantum revolution goes so deep that replacing new concepts with old will not suffice. To cope with the quantum facts we must scrap our very mode of reasoning in favor of a new quantum logic. "Einstein threw out the classical concepts of time; Bohr throws out the classical concepts of truth . . . Our next step is to think in the right way, to learn to think Quantum logically. "

Quantum reality #6

Neorealism. This is the view that the world is as one sees it and consists of ordinary objects. These ordinary objects consist of attributes of their own whether observed or not. With certain exceptions the world outside seems populated with ordinary entities. However, the unremarkable and common sense view that ordinary objects are themselves made of objects is actually the blackest heresy of establishment physics.

Quantum reality # 7

Consciousness creates reality. Among observation created realists, a small fraction asserts that only an apparatus endowed with consciousness (you and I) is privileged to create reality. The one observer who counts is the conscious observer. "It is not possible to formulate the laws of quantum mechanics in a fully consistent way without reference to the consciousness . . . It will remain remarkable in that whatever way. Our future concepts may develop that the very study of the external world led to the conclusion that the content of consciousness is the ultimate reality."

Quantum reality #8

The duplex world of Werner Heisenberg. The world is two fold consisting of potentials and actualities. If only phenomena are real and the world beneath phenomena is not, if observation creates reality, what does it create reality out of? Are phenomena created out of nothingness or out of more substantial stuff? The quantum world is not a world of actual events like our own but a world full of numerous unrealized tendencies for action. These tendencies for action are continually on the move growing merging and dying according to exact laws of motion discovered by Schrodinger and his colleagues. But despite this activity nothing ever actually happens there.

On the Idea of an Oscillating Universe

Buddhologist Theodore Stcherbatsky, commenting upon a dictum of the Buddhist philosopher Santaraksita says,

> The momentary thing represents its own annihilation . . . there is . . . never beginning and never stopping, infinitely graduated, constant change; a running, transcendental, ultimate reality . . . There is . . . in every next moment not the slightest bit left of what has been existent in the former moment. The moments are necessarily discrete; every moment, i.e., every momentary thing, is annihilated as soon as it appears, because it does not survive the next moment.[1]

Commenting upon this fundamental oscillation, Sherbatsky continues,

> This kind of annihilation, transcendental annihilation, is not produced by concurrent causes. Since existence itself is constant annihilation, it will go on existing, i.e. being annihilated and changing, without needing in every case any cause of annihilation.[2]

A similar account of oscillation is to be found in Sufi cosmology. The following comes from Henry Corbin in his discussion of the thought of Ibn 'Arabi:

We look upon existence, our own for example, as continuous, past-present-future, and yet at every moment the world puts on a "new creation," which veils our consciousness because we do not perceive the incessant renewal. At every breath of the "Sigh of Divine Compassion," being ceases and then is; we cease to be, then come into being. In reality, there is not "then," for there is no interval. The moment of passing away is the moment in which the like is exisentiated . . . For the "Effusion of being" that is the "Sigh of Compassion," flows through the things of the world like the waters of a river and is unceasingly renewed. An eternal hexeity takes on one existential determination after another, or changes place, yet remains what it is in the world of Mystery. And all this happens in the instant, a unit of time that is indivisible *in concreto* (though divisible in thought), the atom of temporality which we call the "present" though the senses perceive no interval.[3]

David Peat, a well-known writer on theoretical physics, says in his book *The Philosopher's Stone*:

> The world is in a constant state of transformation [and] within that transformation, the universe touches what could be called a ground of unconditioned creativity . . . the nonunitary universe is involved, at each moment, in a constant cycle of birth and death.[4]

He goes on to say, "Faced with the mystery of a universe in continuous process of creation and death, it is natural to ask, What happens within this magical instant in which the universe ceases to exist? Such an instant lies totally outside time; the universe dissolves and comes in contact with, for want of a better description . . . what we will call its creative source."[5]

In Scherbatsky's *Buddhist Logic* it also says,

> We are faced in India by two quite different theories of a Universal flux. The motion representing the world process is either a continuous motion, or it is discontinuous, although a compact one. The latter consists of an infinity of discrete moments following one another almost without intervals. In the first case the phenomena are nothing, but waves or fluctuations standing out upon a background of an eternal all pervad-

ing undifferentiated matter with which they are identical. The Universe represents a legato movement. In the second case there is no matter at all, flashes of energy follow one another and produce the illusion of stabilized phenomena. The universe is a staccato movement. The first is maintained in the Sankhya system of philosophy, the second prevails in Buddhism. We have here a case, not quite unfamiliar to the general historian of philosophy, of two contrary philosophical systems both apparently flowing from the same first principle.[6]

Here we see an anticipation of the wave particle ambiguity of modern physics.

Notes

1.   Theodore Stcherbatsky, *Buddhist Logic* vol.1 (New York: Dover Publications, 1962), p. 95.
2.   Stcherbatsky (1962, p. 95).
3.   Corbin (1969, p. 201).
4.   David Peat, *The Philosopher's Stone: Chaos, Synchronicity, and the Hidden Order of the World* (New York: Bantam Books, 1992), pp. 134-138.
5.   Peat (1992, pp. 134-138).
6..   Stcherbatsky (1962, p. 83).

The Ambiguity of Subjectivity

The word *subjective* is ambiguous, and we should clearly distinguish between two different uses of the word. In the first place, it means the *subject* as opposed to the *object* in the subject/object polarity. In the second place, it means *me* in the expression me-as-center/me-as-periphery, which is the concrete expression of One/knowing/being. In this case, what we usually think of as subjectivity and objectivity are transcended, and One Mind remains.

The expression one/knowing/being has a further inherent ambiguity that we can make use of to avoid the subject/object dualism and bring home the ambiguity of the experience of me which is otherwise extremely difficult to do. This ambiguity of me, as we know from our studies of me-as-center/me-as-periphery, is not simply a semantic ambiguity, but comes out of the very nature of subjectivity, out of the very nature of *me*. In order not to complicate a presentation that is already difficult enough, I will concentrate upon the ambiguity inherent in one/knowing leaving to one side the being dimension.

One/knowing has four possible interpretations: the first two come from the ambiguity of the word knowing, the second two from the ambiguity of the word one.

In the expression one/knowing, knowing is both a verb and a noun. When used as a verb, one/*knowing*' means the one who knows, one that is in the process of knowing. When used as a noun, *one*/knowing means a knowing which is one, a unity or gestalt. The second pair of ambiguities arises when the emphasis is put upon one as in *one*/knowing. The word one is ambiguous because it is being used both as subject and as object. It is subject because it is always some*one* who knows, even if this someone is the cat or dog or the flea on the cat. But, one is also an object because, as we have just said, everything we know is one,[1] it is known together in one grasp, one comprehension,[2] one/*knowing*. The Gestalt psychologists have pointed out we do not know a collection of separate things, except in exceptional circumstances, and even then they are known against the background of a Gestalt, or a totality of things. We always know a whole or one. In this case, the one that is known is object.

Let us now return for a moment to One/knowing where one is used as subject. I said just now that there is always "someone who knows," because this made it easier at the time to make the point we wanted to make. However, an incipient duality dwells in the expression "one who knows" which the expression one/knowing does not have.

All situations, at least as we know them in the West, are divided into subject and object. "I see the cat," "the dog bit the man," "the cow jumped over the moon," and so on. I, dog, and cow, are the subject; cat, man, and moon, are the object. However, although a situation may, with the help of language, be divided into subject and object in this way, it is still, nonetheless one/knowing - *one situation.* "One *who* knows" obscures this one situation. It contains a whole metaphysics, which we are trying to bypass, a metaphysics based upon the assumption of a knower (subject) and something known (an object.) One/*knowing*, although it means approximately the same thing, does not harbor this duality. Its very ambiguity allows us to speak without falling into the dualist trap. "Knowing" is therefore not the attribute of a person, soul, or other kind of thing, but it may be focused by a viewpoint. Each sentient being is one/knowing, one *view*point, without there being any entity that *has* this viewpoint. Furthermore, this view*point* is one world, without there being any *thing* or *object* which is the world. The *view*point as focus, and the view*point* as that focussed upon is one, one/knowing.

The use of the word viewpoint, just like the expression one/knowing, also brings home this ambiguity, and I have tried to indicate this with the use of italics. By ***view***point is meant a "seeing" (a knowing) point or center. The view***point*** refers to a center or point where the knowing occurs. As a center, or point, the viewpoint is one, undivided, but because this center is both subject and object, the process and the result of that process, it means that one is not unambiguous.

Notes

1. See Albert Low, *The Butterfly's Dream.*
2. Comprehension + com : together prehension : holding

The Dynamics of Space

It might be questioned how dynamism of the kind that can be used to heal, to induce religious ecstasy, to empower the ruler, and to bring the gods to earth, can be generated by a space.

On Sunday May 7, 1989, The Montreal Gazette carried large headlines WHERE SPORT GOES CRAZY, and in the text it says, "when it comes to soccer, the British wage something short of all-out war." The article then recounted a number of horrifying stories to support this view. For example, the British supporters of a soccer team attacked the supporters of a rival Italian team. In the following melee 39 people were trampled to death, and 450 were injured. Later 14 British fans were sentenced to three years in prison. Furthermore, this was only one of many such incidents.

To get some idea of the forces at work, let us try to look at a soccer game completely objectively. A visitor from another planet happening to come upon a game of soccer being played would, every now and then, see half of the crowd leaping up in the air, arms up-stretched, throwing caps, programs, and what have you up in the air, with faces beaming with smiles, clapping one another on the back nodding their heads and stamping their feet in a kind of dance of ecstasy. The other half of the crowd is bent over looking down to earth, cursing, throwing hats, programs and rattles onto the ground, looking around belligerently waiting for someone to say a word out of place. The cause of this was a goal has just been scored. What does this mean, in the terms we have been using?

Suppose a World Cup final game of soccer was to be played one day and for one reason or another you had to visit the stadium a day earlier and while there you looked down upon the field. You would have seen a serene, green field marked out in the following way without, of course, the two large circles.

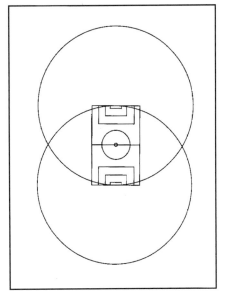

If someone were to ask you where is the center of the field, you would have no difficulty in pointing it out. Furthermore, there would be no tension in the air at all, except perhaps the slight tension of expectation.

Next day, the crowds would begin to arrive, and great tension would begin building up, and if left to itself, it would become unbearable having no focus. Very often music would be played to relieve this tension. When the players trot out onto the field, a roar of relief erupts and, after the formalities have been completed to determine which end each team will play from, a completely new kind of dynamic will appear regarding the playing field. Where is the center now? At the time of kick-off, one would probably settle for the same center as erstwhile. But the situation changes when the ball leaves the geographic center. The geographic center loses its place, and *three* new centers come into being, each one being *the* center. If you were a supporter of one team these three centers would have a particular dynamic arrangement. There would be *our* goal and *their* goal. Our goal is the center; their goal is at the periphery of our center. The person standing next to you may be a supporter of the other team. He will also say *our* goal is the center; *their* goal is at the periphery. This has no significance geographically because, at half time, the teams turn around and operate from the other ends.

However, everyone's attention is on the ball which is the *dynamic* center. This dynamism changes constantly depending on the location it has on the field, just as the dynamism changes in a tone depending on its position in the tonal field. If the ball goes out of the boundaries of this field it loses its dynamism completely and for the moment becomes simply another object. The playing field is a field of force generated by the goals at each end and both of which are at the center, and simultaneously at the periphery of the other. This field of force peaks at the point where the ball happens to be. This peaking induces the dynamism into the ball.

Consider now the following configuration. A World Cup final match is under way with five minutes left to play. The present scores are White -1, Black -1.

The ball is at point x, with White on the offensive. At this moment if you took the pulse rates and the blood pressures of the supporters there you would find most had racing pulses and elevated blood pressures. Many would be shouting out curses or encouragement, trying to give voice to the tension they are feeling. Others would be holding their breath, totally concentrated. Does all this tension occur because a ball of leather is at a particular place in a field? No,

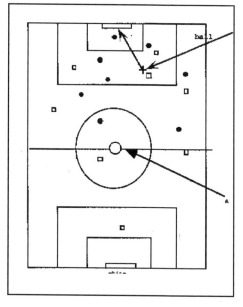

of course not. What is being enacted is the fundamental drama of existence, the drama of being and not being.[1] And then, the White team scores the goal, and everyone goes mad.

What does it mean, "White scores a goal." At that moment Black's goal, ceases to be a center. It is overpowered and becomes completely peripheral to White's goal. Not only this, the dynamism leaves the ball and is found to be located in the White goal. This is the same kind of thing I described earlier when two cats glared at each other until one broke down and ran away. This means that simultaneously the supporters of the Black team lose their centrality and become centered upon White in a condition of humiliation. Therefore, their whole force is directed downwards, down to earth (*humus* from which the word humiliation is derived.) This action is away from the center, to the periphery. They look down, throw things down, stamp their feet, and bow down. In the case of the cats they run away. The supporters of the White team rise up, jump up to heaven, to the center, their whole force is to the pinnacle the source of all power, to the center as up.

Notes

1. At Chichin Itsu in Mexico there is a Mayan temple site, which has a ball court that blends elements of a football and basketball court. On this temple field, a game was played. The members of the losing side were put to death.

Index ~ Subjects

Index ~ Names

ALBERT LOW is director of the Montreal Zen Center and is
a leading voice in contemporary Zen Buddhism. He became
a student of influential roshi Philip Kapleau in 1966 and completed
formal training in 1986. His publications include: *Zen and Creative
Management, The Iron Cow of Zen, Invitation To Practice Zen,
The Butterfly's Dream, The World A Gateway: Commentaries on
the Mumonkan,* and *To Know Yourself.*